WHITE POLITICAL WOMEN

WHITE POLITICAL WOMEN

Paths from Privilege to Empowerment

Diane L. Fowlkes

The University of Tennessee Press

Knoxville

The paper in this book meets the minimum requirements
of the American National Standard for Permanence
of Paper for Printed Library Materials.
∞
The binding materials have been chosen
for strength and durability.

Library of Congress Cataloging in Publication Data

Fowlkes, Diane L.
    White political women : paths from privilege
to empowerment / Diane L. Fowlkes. — 1st ed.
        p.   cm.
    Includes bibliographical references and index.
    ISBN 0-87049-717-0 (cloth : alk. paper)
    ISBN 0-87049-718-9 (pbk. : alk. paper)
    1. White women—United States—Political activity.
2. Feminism—United States.   3. Right and left (Political science).
I. Title.
HQ1236.5.U6F68   1992   91-10605
305.42'0975—dc20   CIP

Contents

Tables

Preface

During the writing of this book, I have come to understand that my
desire to learn about political women in general springs in part from
wanting to understand my own life as a woman who, over the years,
has been involved in politics in various arenas of conflict. The years
of my life have spanned a period that has included a world war followed by continual rounds of political movement for racial and
sexual and economic justice. My arenas of conflict, which have been
located in a region, the South, within a nation, the United States,
include—from the earliest years—first my childhood and then my
marriage families and—within academia—the discipline of political
science and interdisciplinary women's studies. But, whatever the
motivations for my search, the more I have sought to learn about
political women in general, the more I have come to doubt that such
general knowledge is possible.

The more I have sought to apply the scientific methods of theorizing that I learned during my formal education as a political scien-
tist, the more I have come to question the basic assumptions under-
girding such methods. In particular, as a self-educating student of
feminist theory, I have come to question not only whether there is
essential reality to be known but whether "man," much less the rest
of us, can develop universal knowledge of such reality. I have also
come to question the objectivity that political science, at least behavioral political science, claims and requires be used in the development of presumed universal knowledge of political "reality." Feminist epistemology has unmasked the purported essentialism of "re-

ality" and the purported universalism and objectivism of knowledge as presented by Western natural sciences and by those social sciences that model themselves on the natural sciences. Those sciences have been shown to be profoundly perspectival, that is, developed not from some neutral Archimedean standpoint suspended in space and time and looking down on nature but from a white masculinist standpoint grounded in the ongoing everyday lives of a dominant scientific elite.

But feminist studies themselves have not been immune from the viruses of racial, heterosexual, and economic privilege and, therefore, are also subject to critiques emerging out of those political movements that continue to struggle for racial and sexual and economic justice. Such critiques move some scholars/activists within academia to advocate that our studies avoid presuming *a priori* essentiality and universality and instead consider those qualities hypothetical and possibly socially constructed to serve the power interests of the privileged. Such critiques suggest that we should seek to learn as much as we can about the particulars of peoples' lives, especially of variously oppressed peoples' lives, so that such knowledge can be applied to liberatory ends. There is a strong suspicion that transforming oppressive structures in everyday life might result in demystifying the apparently unchangeable essentiality and universality that allows societal and institutional structures to be described and explained in universal statements.

Such scholars/activists further advocate that neutral objectivity be eschewed in favor of a different kind of objectivity realizable by demanding places and voices for all possible perspectives in the discursive search for significant questions and answers. The struggles against a presumed essentiality and universality are intimately linked to the struggles for inclusivity as the ground for objectivity. Thus, Black feminists and Lesbian feminists and Marxist feminists have been among those vehemently challenging one another as well as white liberal heterosexual feminists in the various disciplines and in feminist theory to recognize the necessity of using perspectival approaches. Such approaches will unmask the questionable essentiality and universality tacitly claimed by those speaking of "Woman" and even of "women" or of "white women" or of "Black women" or of any women identifying themselves as a group by the various marks of oppression and/or privilege according to race or ethnicity or sexuality or class, among others.

Even political science over the past twenty-five years has become more than ever a "political" science. The profession is populated by various groups who identify themselves not just as scholars but as particular sorts of scholars, such as Black, Chicano, feminist, Gay and Lesbian, or Marxist political scientists. In other words, they identify themselves as scholars in terms of perspectives associated with race, ethnicity, gender, sexual preference, or economic class. I believe the overt politicization of the discipline is a useful development in that it can help us to avoid being trapped in the straitjacket of a discipline—if "discipline" means a prescribed and unified set of questions and answers about a commonly defined phenomenon. Whaever the disciplinary character that some political scientists attribute to our endeavor, political science has been shown, in fact, to be interdisciplinary and to have always been borrowing ideas and ways of knowing from a variety of other so-called disciplines. Political science can now benefit from listening and responding more carefully to feminist theory, as feminist theory itself responds to demands for greater inclusivity of knowers and known.

One of the significant ideas that political scientists hear from feminist theorists is a reiteration of the challenge to the essentiality of social reality and the universality of social scientific knowledge. Though I in no way claim to have answered the questions about the validity or invalidity of the notions of essentiality and universality, what I have found in the process of writing this book certainly supports the proposition that those notions should be questioned. Since the twenty-seven white women I interviewed are not alike, it is obviously the case that white women—indeed, all women—are not alike. That is, there appears to be no quintessential Woman, or white Woman, about whom universal knowledge can be claimed. Even so, I find among these twenty-seven women some interesting and overlapping patterns of thoughts and actions. Similar overlapping patterns no doubt could be found within and among various groups of women of color and even among various groups of white women and women of color. We will not be able to seek, and possibly find, such overlapping patterns, however, until we conduct studies with many more groups voicing many different perspectives.

I find myself writing, then, out of a place of conflict in relation to other knowers. The conflict is manifested in such questions as: Am I writing to political scientists or to feminist theorists or to both? To scholars in academia or to general readers beyond the campus or to both? To women or to men or to both? To white people or to people of color or to all? And so on. The manifestations of the conflict are many, but they flow mainly from what I perceive to be the juxtaposition of three interrelated sets of ideas about knowers and known that have been shaping my project to understand political women. Three sets of ideas—about who I am as a knower, about where I stand in relation to the women I seek to understand, and about how I approach my project—vitally affect the form and content of what I learn and how my audience judges its significance. Each of the three sets of ideas contains two elements that exist, at least for me, at least for now, in opposition. The first set of elements consists of conflicting ideas about who can know, about the identity of the knower and the legitimacy of the knower under the terms of "the dominant culture." In my case, I as knower am someone experiencing a continually emerging identity as a middle-aged white middle-class heterosexual female academic who lives and works often in opposition to dominant cultural beliefs about and expectations of women like me in contrast to women and men not like me. In this set of oppositions, I, along with some others in varying degrees, share only partially the power of the dominant group in science and in academia—these continue to be older white upper middle-class heterosexual men—to define who can know and what is worthy of being known.

The second set of elements consists of two conflicting ideas about the best location for the knower seeking to learn about some specified "reality." One idea is that the knower should work from a neutral objective standpoint outside the "reality." The other idea is that the knower should work from an engaged standpoint inside the "reality."

The third set of elements consists of two conflicting ideas about ways of theorizing. One idea is that theory must be scientific, meaning that the set of propositions that constitute theory, that *explain* "reality," must be deductively arrived at and transformed into hypotheses, which then must be tested through the collection and analysis of quantifiable data. The other idea is that theory may be developed inductively, working qualitatively from the data of particular experiences to more general propositions that *provide understanding of* "reality."

But I understand the three sets of oppositional elements to intersect so that together the three sets share the potential for becoming multiple ways of knowing that accord respect to multiple sets of knowers. It will be through profoundly political acts of challenging received knowledge at its roots in the arenas of ontology, epistemology, and methodology that we as knowers may bring about a transformation in the creation of liberatory theoretical knowledge.

In acknowledging the sources of conflict that play across the space in which I write, I hope to draw proponents of the various oppositional elements into my audience. In this way, I answer my questions about those to whom I write. I write to women who, like me, identify as white, middle-class, and heterosexual, at the same time that I write to women and men in all the other social locations of our socially constructed world. I write to those in academia as well as to those in the community beyond the campus. Among those in academia, I write to political scientists both on and off the path of scientific method at the same time that I write to feminist theorists of all persuasions.

Just as feminist scholars in political science and in women's studies have been raising questions about how to approach research on women's lives, so feminist activists have been raising questions about political "reality" and about the most effective arenas and strategies for political action. The contemporary women's movement of the late 1960s and the 1970s directed women's energies to identifying and addressing a diverse range of practical problems in women's everyday lives. Women in the movement were concerned with the constraints of the law and of custom on their personal autonomy and creativity and on their abilities to exercise choice in

questions of sexuality, health, and reproduction, to defend themselves against physical violence in the household and on the streets,
to be economically self-sufficient, and to exercise political power.

Women outside the movement were also affected by the subtle
and not-so-subtle changes occurring in women's lives more generally. If these changes were not always material, they at least were
cultural, in that women began to think about new possibilities for
women's, and consequently men's, lives. These new possibilities
were welcomed by some and feared or castigated by others, thus
engaging the Democratic and Republican parties and others in a
great political debate that continued through the 1980s and into the
present, from the halls of national, state and local governments to
the most intimate personal settings.

Spurred by movements and countermovements, feminists and
antifeminists took their conflicts over legal reforms into conventional white-male–dominated electoral politics and public policy-
making. Some feminist women, however, rejected conventional institutionalized politics in favor of creating their own collective
means for addressing problems as they defined them. Such feminists
consider their actions to be profoundly political and to range from
consciousness-raising to providing services for women and their
children to establishing collective forms of economic enterprise to
creating a way of life—women's community and women's culture.

From this earlier debate over what is political, including the place
of men in women's lives, some feminists have more recently begun
to confront issues of difference among women. The late 1970s and
the 1980s also saw the emergence of a great feminist debate over
whether all women share similar problems because of their sex
or whether women experience different problems because of their
race and economic class and sexual preference. Black feminists were
among the early critics of what they perceived to have become a
movement that addressed the problems of women from a white
middle-class heterosexist perspective. By initiating what they called
a "politics of identity," they succeeded in calling attention to the differences among women, especially differences in women's forms of
oppression and access to or denial of privilege. They attributed these

differences to interlocking structures of domination, socially defined and constructed down through history in terms of race, economic class, and sexuality. Thus, they saw the necessity for a "politics of difference," through which all women could explore their various forms of oppression and privilege, and for a "coalition politics," through which women could become allies in fighting the various forms of women's oppressions and privileges. Whether and how white women respond to the calls of women of color for politics of identity and difference will affect all women's chances for collective empowerment, whatever arena of political action they decide to enter.

These developments in women's politics have moved me to seek answers to questions about how white women understand themselves as political actors both in their values about women's places in the world and in the roles they seek or the actions they take. How do they understand their political worlds? What values do they hold regarding relations with men and with other women? What forms of political action engage them, and why? How did they come to be the white political women they are? To readers with various interests in the endeavor of learning how and why some white women become different kinds of activists with different understandings of politics, I offer this map of the chapters that follow. In chapter 1, I present three sets of considerations preliminary to any standard political analysis: my basic assumptions about the political reality I am attempting to know better and my justifications for focusing these attempts on white female activists; my theoretical purpose and the significance of the study in relation to previous work in the field; my methodology and how it proposes to address the problems feminist theorists, among others, have found in scientific method.

Starting with chapter 2 and continuing through chapter 7, the women themselves come on stage to speak, often in their own words, of their lives from childhood to the times of my interviews with them. In these chapters I consider myself to be an interlocutor who also comments on the significance of what I am hearing and reporting to readers. In chapter 2, I present a full case study of Ann Strong, the oldest woman in the study, as a way to set the stage for presenting what I found to be significant aspects of development and engagement in the lives of the other twenty-six women in the study. At the end of chapter 2, I briefly introduce the other twenty-six. In chapters 3 through 5, I examine the women's political value development, specifically the values the women give to their sex/gender and color/race. In chapter 3, I examine the development during childhood of different patterns of gendered identity that appear to form the basis for these women's advocating feminism or antifeminism as adults. In chapter 4, I present the women's different understandings of "being a (white) woman." My use of quotation marks around this and other concepts indicates a recognition that different women attribute different meanings to these concepts. My use of parentheses indicates a recognition that some white women attribute more significance to the intersection of their race and gender than do other white women. In chapter 5, I examine what appears to be the culmination of the women's political development according to different gendered and racial identities in different forms of "feminism" and "antifeminism." In chapters 6 and 7, I turn to the women's political role development, first examining various patterns and paths of politicization and then examining the resulting differences in meanings that these women attribute to "the political."

In the concluding chapter, chapter 8, I return to my role as interpreter to discuss the significance of what can be learned from the life stories of these white political women. I hope that we all learn something of the variety of ways to engage the world politically from hearing and reading about the white political women who consented to be interviewed in the course of my own search for understanding. They necessarily must remain anonymous. These women receive my heartfelt thanks and respect for being who they are and for being willing to share their stories with a wider audience.

Parents and spouses may inadvertently become grist for one's political mill, and I owe debts of gratitude to mine: to my mother, Brenda Vivian Bisplinghoff Lowe; to my father, Erskine Havis Lowe, Jr.; to my first husband, Edward Oliver Fowlkes III; and to my present husband, Lawrence Everman Noble, Jr.

Many friends and colleagues have stayed the course with me from the initiation to the completion of this project, and I gratefully acknowledge their contributions and support. Early on, Roberta Sigel inspired me to take up the less-often used methodology of depth interviews when she offered pithy critiques of research in political socialization at annual political science meetings. My departmental colleague Mike Binford initiated me into the mysteries and requirements of depth interviewing and qualitative analysis. Chairman Don Fairchild and Dean Clyde Faulkner believed in the value of my work and stood by me throughout the project. Discussions with Larry Noble resulted in coining the term "countersocialization." Kent Jennings took a chance on my ability to complete an early paper on countersocialization based on the life stories of four of the women in this study, thus encouraging me to pursue my ideas wherever they might lead. Patricia Bell-Scott, Susan Carroll, Barbara Farah, Janet Flammang, Glenn Harper, Rita Mae Kelly, Patrice McDermott, Virginia Sapiro, and Sarah Slavin provided valuable feedback on other papers or on earlier drafts of various chapters. In particular, Susan Carroll and an anonymous reviewer gave close critical readings to an entire earlier manuscript and to a revised manuscript; to them I extend many thanks for helping me strengthen the organization and focus of the book. Likewise, I thank my editor at the University of Tennessee Press, Tana McDonald, for her encouragement and guidance, and the press's manuscript editor, Stan Ivester, for his careful work on the final text. I also thank Jackie Gaither and Faith Dugger, who painstakingly transcribed the interview tapes, and Alex Harris, who applied his computer skills to printing the first, second, and final versions of the manuscript.

I commenced work on the project, designing the interview schedule during the cold winter of 1981–82, in the Goldsmith Library of the University of London. As I began writing the book, certain women became my muses, mentors, and midwives: Linda Bell, Beverly Guy-Sheftall, Kay Hagan, Anne Harper, Shelby Lewis, and Gloria Watkins. Other women joined them to act as a life-support group: Linda Bryant, Carolyn Denard, Paula Dressel, Marymal

Dryden, Valerie Fennell, Naomi Lynn, Susan Ottzen, and Marsha Houston—as did the Pine River Chorus, Larry Noble, and Frances, a loving and much-loved cat. I began writing in space provided by Elizabeth Cates-Robinson in the Atlanta Center for Feminist Studies, and now a few years later, I am completing my final revisions in that same space; I am grateful to Libby for providing "a room of my own" in which to work.

The book is far from perfect, of course, and I take responsibility for the imperfections that remain. May they provide grist for others' mills.

WHITE POLITICAL WOMEN

Chapter 1

Preliminary Considerations

Political Considerations: Privilege, Oppression, and Power

In my study, white political women are at center stage. "Center stage" connotes theater. Indeed, drama will prove to be a useful metaphor for presenting and listening to living political activists in contrasting arenas tell the ways in which they have come to understand being women, being white, and being political. The women have been engaged either in electoral politics as Democratic or Republican party activists, representing a range of liberal and conservative stances, or in movement politics as leftist (predominantly Marxist) and women's community (predominantly Lesbian) activists. The women have been politically active in the Atlanta metropolitan area, though they hail from most regions of the United States. Their stories, taken together, constitute a multi-arena dramatization of women's political development from a variety of white women's perspectives.

Centering white women in a political analysis is both advantageous and problematic. *Centering* women means bringing them and their relationships with others into the foreground, not presenting them in isolation from others both similar to and different from them. Centering *women* yields the advantage of better illuminating the realities of political women's lives, lives that continue for the most part to be overshadowed by men's lives in a still predominantly white-male–dominated political science and society. Centering *white* women presents a problem in that such a focus reinforces the racial privilege that white women enjoy, consciously or unconsciously, in the study as well as the practice of politics, even as they come to consciousness of their gender-based victimization in a still predominantly white-male–dominated society. Because of this advantage and cognizant of this problem, I nevertheless have undertaken this study of white political women. More accurately, I have done so precisely because I believe an important political lesson about privilege and empowerment can be drawn from the juxtaposition of this advantage and this problem in these women's lives. In effect, these women present a political morality play. But before I can draw the lesson from their drama, I must prepare its ground.

First, some justifications of terms and emphases are in order, particularly of the use of "women" rather than "woman"; of the focus on "white women," a focus that is inextricably intertwined with the use of "women"; and of the meanings of "political." Breaking with earlier political science scholarship that purported to study "political woman" in contradistinction to "political man,"[1] I use the plural "women" rather than the singular "woman" to signify the diverse racial, ethnic, economic, age, and sexual statuses of the individuals so classified. The term "woman," frequently capitalized, suggests an essential and universally knowable female. But no sooner do I propose the term "women" than I face the challenge that "women" also suggests an essence that can be universally known, when in actuality "women," when used by white middle-class women, usually refers only to white middle-class women who are also probably heterosexual. This realization surfaces when someone refers first to "women" and then makes an addendum about, for example, Black women or poor women or Lesbians. Thus I declare my focus to be on *white women* and on the dynamics of their becoming, not on the static symbolism of universal "Woman" or universal "women." I should also note that women of working-class, middle-class, and upper middle-class backgrounds are included in this study, as are presumably heterosexual women and self-declared Lesbians.

I come, then, to focus on *white* women, at least those living in the United States, partly through my efforts to challenge the falsely presumed essentiality and universality of "Woman" and "women." I arrive at this point, remaining cognizant that I must not fall back into the trap of essentializing and universalizing "white women."[2]

I also declare my focus on white women in response to Black feminists who have raised my consciousness about my own privilege as a white academic and the role I will play in maintaining that privilege if, among other things, I am not explicitly self-conscious about my reasons for studying women without regard for their racial differences. It was after I had begun to study women and politics and to attend some of the annual meetings of the National Women's Studies Association (NWSA) that I came into contact with Black feminists and other women of color who challenged the racial hegemony of white women in NWSA. Women of color challenged white women to acknowledge our racial privilege and our role in maintaining racial hegemony and to do our homework on Black history, on African history, in fact on a host of topics we might never think to learn about from our racially privileged position in academe and in society generally.

Through conversations with certain Black women who in effect became my mentors, I began to understand why I should claim my identity as a *white* woman as these Black women had been claiming their identities as *Black* women. It is not that they told me I should do this—they are not the type to "give directions"—but that they raised my consciousness by sharing their own ideas about an inclusive feminism that struggles for liberation from all forms of oppression. From them I learned that *all* of us should be explicitly conscious of the political nature of our different identities under the systems of domination that have placed us in a variety of social locations with different political consequences.

These systems of domination, which form a structure I call "complex domination," shape an inclusive oppositional feminist perspective that frames my approach to this study of white women and that has been articulated in what has become a classic document: the 1977 "Statement" by Black Lesbian feminists of the Combahee River Collective. The Boston-based collective takes its name "from the guerrilla action conceptualized and led by Harriet Tubman on 2 June 1863, in the Port Royal region of South Carolina. This action freed more than 750 slaves and is the only military campaign in American history planned and led by a woman."[3] Reading the collective's statement helped me to crystallize my understanding and naming of complex domination. On the basis of several of their observations about the conditions of their lives, it is possible to posit the sources of their various oppressions in complex domination. From them we learn that these sources are not independent but interact to socially construct the realities not only of these women's lives but also of the lives of men of color and of white women and men.

Early in the statement, the members of the Combahee River Collective point to the multidimensionality and to the historical origins of their oppressions. They begin by declaring that they "are actively committed to struggling against racial, sexual, heterosexual, and class oppression, and see as our particular task the development of integrated analysis and practice based upon the fact that the major systems of oppression are interlocking. The synthesis of these oppressions creates the conditions of our lives." They then "affirm that we find our origins in the historical reality of Afro-American women's continuous life-and-death struggle for survival and liberation. Black women's extremely negative relationship to the American political system (a system of white male rule) has always been determined by our membership in two oppressed racial and sexual castes." In other words, they see themselves as having been and continuing to be oppressed not simply in terms of race *or* sex *or* class *or* sexuality but complexly in terms of all these dimensions "simultaneously." Thus they believe "that the most profound and potentially most radical politics come directly out of our own identity, as opposed to working to end somebody else's oppression."[4]

At the same time that they understand their politics to emerge out of their complex identity as working-class Black Lesbians under their unique combination of race, sex, and class oppressions, they also understand their need to work with "progressive Black men," with whom they "feel solidarity." Eschewing the sexual separatism of some white Lesbian feminists, they say, "We struggle together with Black men against racism, while we also struggle with Black

men about sexism." In other words, the politics of Black feminists—
even of Black Lesbian feminists—requires, in working to end their
own oppression, that they work in solidarity with, as well as challenge, people of other unique but related identities. Just as they
challenge Black men on their sexism, so they challenge white
women to recognize "racism in the white women's movement" and
to take responsibility for corrective actions, "which requires among
other things that they have a more than superficial comprehension
of race, color, and Black history and culture."[5]

This "politics of identity" advocated by the Combahee River Collective, then, is a dynamic politics of dismantling bit by bit in daily
political struggles the systems of oppression that, slowly and over a
long period of time, were put into place by those who have used
power to gain privileges at the expense of others. A consequence of
this politics of identity is to challenge the notions of essentiality and
universality that might otherwise adhere to systemic sources of oppression by pointing to the historical nature of the social construction of those systems and thus rendering them subject to change
through political action. By placing their politics of identity in the
context of historically situated systems of oppression, the Combahee
River Collective avoids the depoliticization that bell hooks warns
can sabotage a politics of identity if feminists lose sight of the political nature of their struggles. Consciously engaged in daily life
struggles that can result in both gains and losses, the members of
the Combahee River Collective or of any group of feminists similarly
engaged are unlikely to be able to settle into what hooks terms a
feminist "lifestyle" in a precariously secured woman-centered space.[6]

Discussing "problems in organizing Black feminists," the Combahee River Collective speaks of privilege in a way that suggests
that systemic privilege is another aspect of complex domination.
They say, "The major source of difficulty in our political work is that
we are not just trying to fight oppression on one front or even two,
but instead to address a whole range of oppressions. We do not have
racial, sexual, heterosexual, or class privilege to rely upon, nor do
we have even the minimal access to resources and power that groups
who possess any one of these types of privilege have."[7] Their refer-

ence to some combination of privilege in terms of race, sex, class, and sexuality—in effect, of interlocking dimensions of privilege—points to an elaboration of complex domination, which places at the bottom of the hierarchy poor and working-class Lesbians of color who suffer all the oppressions that result from a system that has been established to seize privilege for those in the favored categories of race, gender, class, and sexuality. To the top have risen those who have exercised power over others in order to dominate and thus enjoy all privileges simultaneously—the privileges that go with being upper/middle class and white and heterosexual and male. Between that social location in which dominance assures that all privileges are experienced simultaneously and that social location in which all oppressions are experienced simultaneously lie social locations that impose various conflicting combinations of categories of privilege and oppression. In these social locations may be found, among others, white women, men of color, and even some white men, of various economic classes and sexual orientations. It should be noted that, while the Combahee River Collective did not address oppressions related to ethnicity or disability or age, it would be possible to incorporate these and other markers of privilege and oppression into the interactions of the structure of complex domination.[8] Thus it has come about that complex domination has operated historically as a socially constructed, multidimensional, interlocking, hierarchical system of domination in which some men have gained privilege through oppressing women and other men and in which even some women have gained privilege through oppressing other women and some men.[9]

A few words are in order about how and why I assume complex domination to have been socially constructed. I posit that, over time and in particular geographic locations, humans have socially constructed systems of domination by attaching cultural and political meanings to several physical—that is, material—dimensions that they have deemed significant for their supposed effects on humans' functional capabilities in society. These physical characteristics, commonly understood to be "biological" and thus "natural" but whose definitions and meanings have been shown to be themselves socially constructed,[10] are sex, mode of genital relationship, skin color, and bodily relation to material production. In turn, these physical characteristics have come to be linked with categorical constructs that also have been put forward as "natural" and that incorporate expectations for dominant or submissive behavior: gender, sexuality, race, and economic class. The categorizations and their related relations of domination are well known: gender constructs men as "masculine" over women as "feminine"; sexuality constructs "heterosexual" as superior to "homosexual"; race constructs "white" as superior to "colored"; and economic class constructs "owner" as superior to "worker."

The categories of complex domination lend themselves to the stereotyping of people for purposes of domination, regardless of peoples' physical variations, even within one category, much less their diverse competencies and desires. But while complex domination historically has expected and attempted to enforce hierarchically ranked differences in thought and behavior, history also teaches that some people in various social locations have not cooperated with those expectations, even in the face of dire threats to their safety and security. Complex domination has never been pure in form or static in structure because some humans have always resisted other humans' attempts to dominate. Some humans have simply rejected the premises of complex domination that they are naturally inferior and must be submissive.

From the politics of identity initiated by the Combahee River Collective flows the "politics of difference" called for by Black Lesbian feminist Audre Lorde. For Lorde, not merely tolerating but recognizing and celebrating difference can become a basis for all women's empowerment. Lorde says difference must be "seen as a fund of necessary polarities between which our creativity can spark like a dialectic. . . . Only within that interdependency of different strengths, acknowledged and equal, can the power to seek new ways of being in the world generate, as well as the courage and sustenance to act where there are no charters. . . . *Difference* is that raw and *powerful connection* from which our personal power is forged." (emphasis added)[11] Lorde goes on to teach how we can turn into positives what complex domination has made the negatives of difference. She says, "survival . . . is learning how to stand alone, unpopular and sometimes reviled, and how to make common cause with those others identified as outside the structures in order to define and seek a world in which we can all flourish. It is learning how to take our differences and make them strengths."[12]

Lorde is speaking here to white women who have failed to recognize either how other women differ from them or how they differ from other women in terms of privilege, thus remaining "inside" the structures of power to cooperate with the oppressors. But she believes white women can decide to move "outside," in a manner of speaking, by challenging the structure—complex domination—that oppresses them sexually while it privileges them racially and perhaps economically.

As white women figuratively move "outside" the structure of complex domination, they are likely to encounter even more difference than they may have become conscious of "inside" their social location of combined privilege and oppression. Among others also moving "outside," they are likely to meet women of color who are different from them and different from each other, not to mention men of color and even white men. The politics of difference is not easy to negotiate. In fact, "moving outside" by ceasing to cooperate with a system that operates through domination and fear does not automatically place one in a position to make what Lorde calls "powerful connections" with others through relations of mutuality and trust.

Bernice Johnson Reagon contends that the form of politics required in a world that increasingly leaves us no place to hide from others who are different from us is "coalition politics." "You don't go into coalition because you just *like* it. The only reason you would consider trying to team up with somebody who could possibly kill you, is because that's the only way you can figure you can stay alive."[13] Some women might yearn to find a place where only those of "their kind" can come in and bar the door to others. This would be analogous to what bell hooks warned women against if they identified themselves as feminists of a certain kind and stopped at attempting to secure a woman-centered space in which to live a feminist lifestyle. But Reagon says, "There is no chance that you can survive by staying *inside* the barred room."[14] In that room, she says, it is possible to practice forming community, learning who you *could* be and how a transformed world *could* run; but in that room, which she calls "home," it is not possible to learn how to live with people different from you, and that is what she says we will have to do to survive into the twenty-first century. "Coalition work is not work done in your home. Coalition work has to be done in the streets. And it is some of the most dangerous work you can do. And you shouldn't look for comfort."[15] Coalition politics, according to Reagon, involves meeting others on their terms while presenting yourself on your terms, challenging others on whatever bigotry they spew out, while also learning from them what resources they have drawn on to survive as long as they have.

Some white women who cooperate with as well as some who challenge the system of complex domination participated in my study. Some have neither recognized their race privilege nor claimed to be sexually oppressed, while others have done both and are working to transform the still unjust system that privileges them on the basis of their color while it oppresses them on the basis of their sex. Herein lies the political morality play that I believe these white women present. Listening to these women should illuminate how white women can move from privilege to empowerment. The word "empowerment" is used here in contrast to "power" understood either as domination from a position of privilege or manipulation from a position of oppression. Whereas "power" is generally understood to operate in relations between persons positioned in higher and lower ranks, "empowerment" is intended to connote redirecting energy away from cooperating with the requirements of complex domination and toward working to accomplish objectives cooperatively with others and sharing resources while challenging one another's racism, classism, and heterosexism.

According to the political morality play, white women will not be able to leave positions of racial privilege until the structure of complex domination that confers racial privilege has been transformed.

But white women can be among those initiating that process of transformation when we begin to name and critique complex domination, to reject the legitimacy of and refuse to use racial privilege in order not to continue reinforcing the structure of complex domination. Empowerment for white women will begin to emerge as we join together to critique and refuse to use racial privilege, thus opening gateways through which to move "outside" the structure of complex domination. There we can meet halfway those women of color who likewise have been empowering themselves through resisting the oppressions of complex domination. Making powerful connections across difference, once understood negatively but now celebrated positively, can nourish the ongoing struggle for transformation and the ongoing process of empowerment, difficult as coalition politics can and will be.

My analysis of complex domination leads me to articulate that I am a white woman and, therefore, "inside" this social location. But even so, I have not experienced living in all the segments of this social location. As do the majority but not all of the women in my study, I consider myself to be middle class and heterosexual. Having been raised by a mother from the Midwest and a father from the South, I share those regional origins with many of these women. I am middle-aged whereas the women I have interviewed range in age from twenty-two to seventy-nine. As I have listened to these women respond to my questions and as I have drawn my conclusions about the meanings they give to their lives, I have tried to be alert to both our similarities and our differences even within this white female social location.

In speaking of white women, I am saying to women of color that I will not use the simple term "women" when my study involves only white women, because to do so would make it appear that I am assuming that what I find to be true of some white women's lives applies as well to the lives of women of color. I initially intended to include Black female party activists in my study, but all but one of the Black women I contacted by letter and then by telephone repeatedly turned down my requests for interviews. Their reasons had to do with hectic work schedules or with ill health, either their own or that of a family member for whom they had responsibility. It began to dawn on me that these reasons might be related to the oppressive conditions of the lives of Black women and their families in our racist society. After reading an article by Latina feminist Maria Lugones and white feminist Elizabeth Spelman[16] on the dangers for women of color being "studied," that is, objectified, by white academicians (which my university letterhead in all likelihood proclaimed me to be), I realized that these Black women might also be telling me that their priorities had to be elsewhere than giving three hours of their limited time to me.

By the same token, I say to white women that I will not claim that my understandings of the lives of the white women in my study will be representative of all white women's lives. What I will claim is that the white women I have interviewed lead lives that are similar in many, though not in all, aspects to the lives of other white women. I have chosen to seek the life stories of a limited number of white women in a limited number of types of observable *political* involvements—Democratic and Republican party activists and office seekers, leftist community activists, and women's community activists—as opposed to observable *social* or *economic* involvements. In other words, this is not a study of churchwomen or businesswomen but a study of political women. This is not to say that some of the women I interviewed are not religiously involved or business entrepreneurs. It does mean, however, that I chose each woman on the basis of some form of known political involvement rather than on the basis of some other kind of societal involvement or lack of any organizational involvement. Thus the understandings and explications that I draw from these women's reports of their lives will pertain to their political involvements, though certainly more than the political aspects of these women's lives could be studied and even perhaps will be divulged by my study.

The different meanings that white women give to "the political" will be a prime area to be explored in this study. I have already indicated that I included in this study of "political" women some who forego conventional politics for actions that others consider to be illegitimate—leftist organizing—or nonpolitical—women's community involvement. Conventionally, political scientists have used the term "political" to refer to the institutions and processes of government and public policy-making, institutions and processes that historically have largely excluded women. Through such a focus, which some contend is too narrow, political scientists until recently either have failed to include women as political beings or have included women but treated them in biased fashion.[17] By expanding the focus of "the political" to include so-called "social" movements that have challenged the conventional institutions of government and policy-making processes, political scientists can cast a wider net to include the greater numbers of women that have always been active in these forms of political engagement. Redefining "the political" can expand our understanding both of the organizational apparatus that governs and makes policy for society and of the process of societal change.

There is also a way to reconceptualize "the political" that implicates the structure of complex domination, which attempts to shape all aspects of our lives. Conventionally, political analysts have taken for granted the notions, which also carry normative implications, that politics operates in and is confined to a "public sphere" and that what goes on "in private" is, or should be, beyond the reach of politics. In capitalist systems, this "private sphere" includes both the family and the marketplace (as separate domains). In socialist systems the "public sphere" includes the state and the economy in the realm of production, that is, the political economy as one phenomenon; this "public sphere" rests on, depends upon, an assumed "private sphere" of domestic reproduction. In both types of systems, theoretically as well as practically, all women and some men have been left out of or extremely underrepresented in the "public sphere" and hence in political analysis.[18] These deletions have resulted from the interlocking of the "public/private" division of society with sex/gender, economic class, and racial systems with culturally specific forms that have placed all women and some men in the "private sphere," thus rendering them invisible to those who study "public" life. Furthermore, what has happened to people in the "private sphere" has tended to escape political analysis.[19]

Feminist theory questions the white masculinist perspectives of such political science. Can human society be neatly divided into public and private domains? Is "the political" confined to the so-called "public sphere" or does it pervade all aspects of life? How do women in their various social locations understand "the political"? In my study, I have turned the spotlights on white women involved in "conventional" electoral politics—Democrats and Republicans— as well as those involved in what the "conventional" term "unconventional" politics—self-defined Communists, socialists, Lesbians— with the expectation that they will provide a diverse array of ideas about the "the political" in all aspects of their lives, including the personal. These ideas will include but go beyond the definitions provided until recently by the discipline of political science.

I present the life-sketches and my understandings of the stories of these white political women, recognizing that their experiences will resonate with some experiences in each reader while contrasting sharply with others. It is my hope that these accounts will illuminate through similarities and empower through contrasts with others' lives. I also offer this work in the hope that it helps us to understand how sexism and racial privilege affect the lives of white political women and how some of these women address this sexism and racial privilege. This is the political morality play these women present. This is the political lesson I believe these women offer us as a necessary step in beginning to dismantle those systems of privilege and oppression that divide us all from one another. Having made these beginnings, amidst the differences that thrive even among white women, who certainly are not all alike, white women can then move on to make Audre Lorde's "powerful connections" and engage in Bernice Johnson Reagon's "coalition politics" with those women and men of color and with those white men who likewise have begun to dismantle the particular oppressions and/or privileges that shape their particular social locations under complex domination. It is from those connections that empowerment of all women and men can emerge. Finally, I offer this work not as a definitive statement but rather as a contribution to the ongoing dialogue among feminist theorists and activists of all persuasions who are trying to understand how we came to be, where we are going, and what we can do with this knowledge.

Theoretical Considerations: Who Possesses Authority to Know, and How Knowers Know

Discernable shifts in the study of political socialization and in women's studies have resulted in both fields' placing more emphasis on persons as political subjects possessing agency, rather than as objects, and on women as subjects capable of theorizing their own worlds, rather than as objects of others' theories. Consequently, as someone trying to understand white women's political activism in particular, I turn to selected white women activists in order to learn from them how they understand their own forms of politics in the context of their own lives as white women in the United States. Before explaining how I selected the women in the study, I want to review briefly how certain shifts in the study of political socialization and of women resulted in my particular approach to these women as subjects, both as political knowers and as political actors.

When I first began my study in 1981, I framed the research problem as one of trying to understand how women in general become political in the conventional sense of government and electoral politics, with emphasis on how women gain public office.[20] Thus I focused on women in electoral politics, and this focus directed me to two bodies of literature, one treating women and politics and the other treating socialization.[21] According to these two bodies of literature, females and males are understood to be socialized by agents external to their own persons—family, school, church, government, mass media—to societal roles appropriate to their sex. Feminine gender-role socialization is said not to prepare women to take on the role of politician, which is considered to be a role that converges with the masculine gender role. Thus, we have found few women in the role of elected public official.

Meanwhile, however, beginning in the 1970s, during the period of a reemergent women's movement that included an emphasis on the Equal Rights Amendment to the U.S. Constitution, women began to seek and gain elective office in greater numbers than ever before, though the percentage of women doing so was still small.[22] At first these increases were attributed to the efforts of women who in various ways had been socialized to believe that women should not be constrained in their political behavior by the feminine gender role but should seek participation in the "public sphere" equal to that of men.[23] According to this theoretical perspective, then, socialization to beliefs in women's expanded societal roles can explain the emergence of earlier female political leaders as well as those presently emerging. Yet scholars also recognized that women's socialization alone had been responsible neither for keeping them out of electoral politics nor for their achieving elected office in greater and greater numbers. The political structure itself, especially the political opportunity structure as determined by constitutional limits or lack of limits on terms of office and rates of incumbency, came to be understood as a major factor in shaping the flow and limiting the numbers of women that ultimately could gain office.[24]

It also became apparent with the emergence of the Stop-ERA movement that some of the women seeking and gaining political office opposed expanding women's societal roles and espoused feminine and masculine roles for women and men, respectively. One would think that women who want women and men to live by stereotypical gender roles would not venture into political leadership roles to achieve such a goal, and yet some women did and do maintain this apparent contradiction.[25] To explain the phenomena both of women in general and more specifically of feminist *and* anti-feminist women seeking and holding public leadership roles I introduced the concept of "countersocialization."[26] In an attempt to balance the approach to women as individual subjects with an approach that recognized women as objects within hierarchical power structures, I defined countersocialization in terms of its content on two dimensions—roles and values—and posited that "members of groups defined as dominant or subdominant on the basis of sex and race may nevertheless strive to develop their own modes of action, or subdominants may strive to occupy roles reserved by tradition or law for dominants, because the individuals have developed self-concepts and/or values that run counter to dominant sociopolitical norms."[27]

In contrast, socialization, in this scheme of things, would refer to the acceptance or internalization of roles and values appropriate to one's place, subdominant or dominant, in hierarchical societies through a developmental process of self-denial promulgated by the various agents of socialization. Thus, for example, women of any race, as members of a group subordinate to white men as the dominant group in society, could be of at least four possible types derived from crossing the role and value dimensions of socialization and countersocialization within the arena of electoral politics. According to the resulting typology, fully countersocialized women would support feminist *values* as well as seek the *role* of public office; they would be ambitious feminists. Fully socialized women would oppose feminist *values* and would not seek the *role* of public office; they would be unambitious antifeminists. Some women, however, would be socialized on the *role* dimension but countersocialized on the *value* dimension; they would be feminists not interested in seeking or holding public office. Other women would be countersocialized on the *role* dimension but socialized on the *value* dimension; these would be the paradoxical ambitious antifeminists noted above.[28]

Conceptually, countersocialization moved the study of political socialization into a more explicit concern with learning how some people come to resist oppressive systems of domination. Thus, countersocialization could describe the process by which people in various social locations of complex domination break out of subdominant roles either to seek entry into leadership roles in the conventional political apparatus of electoral politics and governmental policy-making or to create alternative forms of politics. Among white women, as among other such groups, would be included those who enter electoral politics to take a place in the dominant political order and those who enter movement politics to challenge the dominant political order.

But the term itself, "*counter*socialization," suggests only the negative move against complex domination, whereas the concept includes a positive move as well. Political movements embody critique as well as creative vision and practice. This double process of critique and vision came together in the women's movement in the liberatory process of consciousness-raising.[29] Thus, in this study I have replaced the term "countersocialization" with the term "consciousness-raising." In effect, I have elaborated my original definition of countersocialization by expanding the hierarchical context of the process into complex domination and by using consciousness-raising to explicate how people might move into opposition to expectations for values and actions under complex domination. "Socialization" then becomes a term to refer to the process by which people learn to cooperate with the expectations of complex domination. I use "socialization" and "consciousness-raising" interactively to explicate the politicization process of the women in the study.

Students of political socialization have, for the most part, conceptualized the process in ways that make objects of the selves being politicized. In this process, persons are acted *upon*, influenced, molded. The family, the school, the peer group, the mass media have been considered to be the major agents of the sociopolitical system, which requires that each new member be fit into the ongoing roles and institutions of that system.[30] There is, however, another way to conceptualize the process: selves as *subjects* acting *with* others.[31] And some students of political socialization have begun to focus on how individuals shape their own self-development[32] and on the role that family and other relationships play in an individual's development.[33] What is important here is that the emphasis shifts from the individual per se and others' influences on that individual to the person embedded in and acting in social networks. In this study I have approached the women's political development from the perspective of the social self-development model.

Early students of political socialization also focused mainly on childhood learning,[34] but after a decade or more of studies of schoolchildren from the earliest grades to high school,[35] it was becoming clear that childhood could be only the beginning of political learning. Most students of political socialization were unprepared for the outbursts of political protest by Black college students and some of their elders, antiwar protesters, and women of diverse races and classes and ages throughout the 1960s and 1970s. Were such values learned in early childhood?

Clearly something other than childhood socialization to the ongoing political processes was at work. Activists in all these movements spoke of consciousness—Black consciousness, class consciousness, feminist consciousness—meaning that they were becoming politically conscious in a critical mode—conscious of racial injustice and oppression, of imperialism and neocolonialism, of sexual discrimination and oppression. "Politics as usual" came to be understood by these activists as part of "the problem." And so students of political socialization had to conclude that political learning can take place throughout life.[36] In other words, it has become clear that some do become *politically socialized* to conventional forms of political engagement, if not during childhood then during some time in adulthood, while others turn to more "radical" forms of politics as a result of *consciousness-raising* experiences during some period in adulthood. Various women in this study present evidence of early childhood socialization influencing adult forms of politics as well as consciousness-raising experiences in the years since childhood.

Politicization, whether through socialization or through consciousness-raising, presumes persons, selves, that become identified by themselves and by others as capable of political action. Because I have chosen to emphasize the self as subject acting with others to become politicized, I want to elaborate on the nature of self as subject that becomes identified as a political actor through knowledge of self and others. I contend that it is in the process of becoming knowing selves through the recognition of standpoints, as illuminated by sociologists Alfred Schutz[37] and Dorothy Smith,[38] that persons may also become political actors of one kind or another.

Let me begin with the idea of self as embodied social being, as self-in-society, with two dimensions—a curious, seeking, creating "I"-dimension and an objectified "me"-dimension.[39] Given this understanding of self, we can understand consciousness emerging, the self *becoming* identified, as the "I" becomes critically aware of the "me."[40] Consciousness recedes as the "me" overrides the "I." The mix of "I" and "me" and hence one's quality of identification (self-identified or other-identified) and one's degree of consciousness depends on the "attitude" one takes. "Attitude" can be either what Schutz defines as the "natural attitude," that is, not doubting but accepting that things are as they seem, or the critical attitude of doubting and questioning.[41] One's ability to be critical, according to Smith, depends on the extent to which one stays embodied, that is, stays in touch with one's bodily senses and feelings in the material world.[42] Thus it is, for example, that the members of the Combahee River Collective can experience and name their oppressions as multiple and simultaneous. In other words, consciousness-raising as process begins with the engaged, embodied self-identified "I" doubting and questioning the other-identified socialized "me," what society is making or has made of the "me" and why. The conscious self-in-society emerges in the tension between that self's bodily experiences and that self's interpretations of individuality and the sociality of existence.

Consciousness vitally affects how one understands the relationship between one's world as experienced through the bodily senses and the world in the abstract as interpreted or theorized and thus how one acts with others to change one's world. Smith disagrees with Schutz's approach to theorizing. According to Smith's reading of Schutz, men as theorists, who distinguish themselves from non-theorists, theorize the abstract world by "leaping" conceptually out of the everyday world into the "world of science," from which they presumably can make a disinterested explanation of how the ordinary world operates.[43] In contrast, Smith, in effect, conceptualizes theorizing as consciousness-raising in everyday life. She contends that women, any women, can critically theorize their own lives *from within* the very world that, as described by Schutz, has been designed to support and serve the scientific theorizing of men. According to Schutz, men as theorists are expected to suppress "interest in that setting [everyday life] . . . [which is] organized in a division of labor that accords to others [women] the production and maintenance of the material aspects of a total process."[44] In other words, Smith challenges the normative setup that supports men's doing science and women's taking care of men who do science. Smith contends that women can know and explicate their own lives from within their own everyday worlds. Thus it is, for example, that members of the Combahee River Collective can identify themselves as multiply and simultaneously oppressed Black working-class Lesbians, can apprehend the organization of the world as it oppresses them, and can name the structures of domination that oppress— racism, sexism, classism, heterosexism.

Smith suggests further that consciousness-raising results in bifurcated consciousness because it involves women's locating a "line of fault" between each one's actual experience "prior to its social expression," and its definition according to societal forms of consciousness. It is "that line of fault along which the consciousness of women must emerge."[45] It is through the possibility of the two-dimensional self and bifurcated consciousness that women can emerge as ever more conscious of themselves as active subjects in what consequently must become a transformed world, one no longer masked and left in place by the "natural attitude," but one continuing to be created in response to whatever critiques of past and present conditions are developed. In the case of the Combahee River Collective, their group consciousness-raising emerges as their politics of identity: their naming of oppressions, the critique they make, and the actions they take to secure places in the world for themselves on their own terms. Self-consciousness becomes group consciousness when each shares her doubts with others, who also share their doubts, and together they come to critical understandings of the social relations that are causing the disjunctures with what they perceive to be their own experiences.[46]

Consciousness and self-in-society emerge, according to both Schutz and Smith, in the context of—and thus depend upon—one's place, one's social location, one's standpoint in the world. Smith refers to women's social location *as* "the standpoint of women."[47] Nancy Hartsock similarly argues for a "feminist materialist standpoint" as an epistemological device that grounds knowledge and action in women's experiences, which are necessarily different in many ways from men's experiences because of the sexual divisions of labor, the social relations of production and reproduction.[48] The use of the term "standpoint" is significant because it means that the basis of knowledge and action, which includes consciousness and its knowledge-content, is a material grounding in the body-as-engaged in the ongoing physical (natural and humanly constructed) world. One's perspective from that *stand*point is informed by what one senses, not just through the "mind's eye"—one's *view*point—but through all the senses of the "body's eye."[49] This is to say that we are, or can be, more than reasoning beings; we are, or can be, historical reasoning, feeling, and acting beings. While feminist standpoint epistemology, especially as developed by Nancy Hartsock and Dorothy Smith, has drawn its fair share of criticism,[50] I intend to retain it and to push it around another turn in my study.

Note that, in line with Sandra Harding's discussion of feminist standpoint theorists, Hartsock *is*, as Harding states, working out of a Hegelian-Marxist framework, in contrast to Smith, whom Harding also places within the Hegelian-Marxist framework, but who herself says she is using "a limited aspect of Hegel's [master-slave] 'parable.' "[51] Using Marxist method, Hartsock shifts the focus from class to gender as the basis for domination. This projects the unfortunate implication that all women exist in a sex-class dominated by all men in a sex-class. The posited feminist materialist standpoint then implies that women as a group can socially reconstruct reality in their interests, a valuable idea for women. But the crucial problem lies in avoiding a reconstruction that itself becomes ideological as some women come to believe that other women are attempting to reconstruct reality for all women. The problem becomes more evident when it is acknowledged that women themselves are divided by barriers, among others, of race, class, age, and sexuality.

Smith is more eclectic than Harding notes, using Hegel and Marx to critique her fellow sociologist Schutz's phenomenology of the lifeworld. Smith uses Hegel's master-slave relation to make the point, similar to Hartsock's, that the labors of women, among others, directed as they are by those in dominance, obscure the sources of the "conditions of ruling" from the rulers themselves. Thus, she can say, "There is a difference between forms of consciousness arising in the experience of ruling and those arising in the experience of doing the work that creates the conditions of ruling."[52] Her critique results in her insistence that theorists stay bodily engaged in the everyday world while they theorize. The latter form of consciousness enables women to doubt that everything is as it seems and to theorize while still engaged in the everyday world. According to Smith, it is only the theorist who stays grounded in the bodily engaged standpoint who can know the sources of the conditions of ruling. To know and theorize these sources is of special interest to women, since they have been the ones so often silenced in the conventional mode of scientific theorizing.

At this point, Smith's "standpoint of women" brings us to the same problem that Hartsock's "feminist materialist standpoint" brings us. The problem is twofold: both standpoints, and the knowledge developed therefrom, emerge in and for a whole social location, or whole class, defined only in terms of sex and gender. "Women's social location" and "sex-class," without further elaboration of differences among women, mystify the individuality of women in their social existence.[53] Further, the implication is that knowledge from the "standpoint of women" or from a "feminist materialist standpoint" is universalized to all women regardless of the differences among women. But because Smith, unlike Hartsock, works out of a Schutzian framework, albeit critically from Hegelian and Marxist perspectives, she opens the door to the possibility that women can maintain their unique individuality, their "I"-ness, while engaging with other women in group consciousness-raising and the politics of identity. I believe the Schutzian framework provides a way to recognize both the imposed and the inherent differences among women that will require us to speak and write of the standpoint*s* of women.

To show how this is so, let me now situate the Schutzian idea of standpoint in the world understood as a structure of complex domination. In a multidimensional hierarchically structured world, different persons may develop different perspectives on and understandings of "reality" depending on their social location in complex domination. Thus, in a society characterized by complex domination, groups of women consigned by the rules and values of such a society to their various social locations would be expected to be capable of locating particular combinations of Smith's "lines of fault," which in turn would reveal different standpoints from which to understand, critique, and resist the forces of complex domination as they affect women in each of their social locations. For example, the Combahee River Collective could be seen as speaking from the standpoint of Black working-class Lesbians.

If we stopped here, we would still face the problem that some women could be perceived as constructing reality for all women in a particular social location. Thus, people in just one of many possible social locations, for example, Black working-class Lesbians, would still be presumed to share the same standpoint and thus know the world in the same form as a shared reality, when in fact there might be, and probably would be, differences both in experience and in consciousness, even among this particularly identified group of women.[54] The Schutzian framework, however, suggests that each embodied self possesses uniqueness and individuality and engages the world from a unique standpoint. Schutz posits that, upon entry into the world at birth, each person takes up and occupies a unique place, Here, in a time shared with contemporaries, Now.[55] Thus, Schutz's social self can be understood to incorporate the potential for the "I" dimension, for individuality, by being born to take up that unique place in the world, that Here, that no one else can occupy, while also sharing Now with contemporaries, who along with the already living and dead constitute the historical sociality of existence.

As persons come into the world, they also enter into socially constructing reality each from her or his own particular standpoint in one of two ways. Either, following Schutz, they take the "natural attitude" and assume like perspectives from different standpoints,[56] thus accepting what others tell them is so—that is, they become socialized, fitting into always already socially constructed reality—or they question authority, reveal to chosen allies their own interpretations of their own experiences and needs, and socially construct with those allies another reality, shared though not necessarily consensual, through consciousness-raising and political action. If they follow the model proposed by the Combahee River Collective, Audre Lorde, and Bernice Johnson Reagon, this other social construction of reality would proceed, not by accepting the world as given, but by engaging in the politics of identity, the politics of difference, and coalition politics.

Note, especially, the dangers in assuming, as Schutz says men do, like perspectives from different standpoints, especially if reality is structured as complex domination. For those maintaining the "natural attitude" in subordinate social locations, the dangers of oppression increase as the social locations are constructed of more negatively valued characteristics. To the extent that the "I" is submerged in favor of the socially objectified "me," the self becomes confined to what is intended to be a powerless position vis-à-vis those who came before and had the most say in constructing society. Most of the women in this study rejected at least some of what would have been expected of them under complex domination. It is these women who have suggested to me that, even within a particular social location of complex domination, each of us stands at a unique standpoint in the world. To the extent that we become conscious of our respective standpoints, we each possess unique perspectives from which to engage with others, both those in our own particular social location and those in other social locations, in social constructions of reality through politics of identity, difference, and coalition.

Methodological Considerations: Selecting Women as Subjects, and Interpreting the Meanings They Give to Their Lives

The women in this study present a variety of ways to think about being women and to engage in politics. By no stretch of the imagination do they or I claim that they represent all possible ways to be women or to be political. In an earlier stage of the study, designed to search for evidence of countersocialization among female political activists, I selected the white women engaged in electoral politics at random from ambitious and unambitious Democratic and Republican party activists who had participated in an earlier survey study of county party officials.[57] As noted earlier in this chapter, I attempted to include Black female party activists who had been involved in the earlier study, but I failed in those attempts. I had found in analyzing the data from the earlier study that party identification was strongly related to support for the ERA,[58] and I used that support as an initial indicator of feminism. Within the arena of electoral politics, then, I selected these women to represent four possible types of activists that would be expected to develop through socialization and/or countersocialization: ambitious and unambitious feminists and antifeminists.

Through contact first by letter and then by telephone I was able to arrange interviews with twenty-one women. I tape-recorded all interviews and had them transcribed. Four interviews were unusable because of malfunctions in my tape recorder, leaving seventeen activists to represent electoral politics. By 1982, when I began interviewing, two of the ambitious women had achieved state legislative office. I then added two other white female legislators from the Atlanta area to bring to four the number of officeholders in the study. Among the unambitious party activists were women who had become less active in their party organizations and more active in interest group or advocacy politics, including the women's movement, especially the effort to ratify the ERA, the Stop-ERA effort, and the Moral Majority. At this point I had interviews with nineteen white female activists—seven Democrats and twelve Republicans—of varying degrees of feminism or antifeminism.

Since all of these women had been chosen for their involvement in conventional electoral politics, I decided that for contrast I should also interview women involved in more radical movement politics. Such women would help me to explore the larger meanings of "the political" and of consciousness-raising to which my work with countersocialization and studies in women and politics and in feminist theory were beginning to point. Lacking systematic surveys of women so involved but drawing on personal contacts, I chose four white leftist community activists, predominantly self-identified Marxists, and four white women's community activists, predominantly self-identified Lesbians, each of whom had been organizationally active in the Atlanta area during the 1970s. I interviewed the leftist women in the summer of 1982 and in the spring and summer of 1983 and the women's community activists in the summer of 1984. Thus my study includes women who have been active politically in many ways—as officeholders, office seekers, party activists, issue activists, leftist and women's community activists—and who present diverse antifeminist and feminist perspectives.

The interviews, which averaged two and one-half hours in length, were conducted in the various women's homes or places of employment. The same questions were asked of electoral and movement activists. The interviews were structured to cover several areas of theoretical concern: present political involvements; employment history; marital history; child-care responsibilities; conceptions of "the political"; relative merits of holding office versus working through groups or movements; life-history—characteristics of self and parents (mothers, fathers, mother- and father-surrogates) in childhood family; siblings, relations with siblings, mother, father, other family members or friends, teachers, other memorable influences (events, books, ideas); significance of race and gender in growing up; initial interest in politics; values pursued in politics; personal qualities suiting one for politics; motivations for political involvement; organizational involvements; ambition or lack of ambition to hold elective public office; conditions for pursuing office or pursuing other political concerns; meanings and significances of "being a woman" and "being feminine"; discussions of why more women have not been in office and how to change that; women's issues; the civil rights movement; the women's movement; meanings and significance of "feminism."[59] These areas of theoretical concern arise from extant studies of women and politics, socialization and counter-socialization, or from my concern to understand white women's consciousness of privilege and oppression under complex domination.

My analysis in this study is based on portions of these interview materials and on general historical treatments of conditions in the United States relevant to the various life spans of the women interviewed.[60] Lest some readers misunderstand how I present and interpret the political worlds of this group of white women, let me clarify my method of analysis. The form of my analysis is inductive, qualitative, and "grounded" in the everyday lives of the women as described by them.[61] Working from the responses of each woman and comparing responses to a particular question or set of questions across women, I develop categories for general concepts, such as family structure, feminist or antifeminist consciousness, identity as a white woman, and understanding of "the political," on the basis of the women's language. Thus, for example, based on what the women tell me in response to questions about what feminism means to them and whether they consider themselves feminists, I develop several categories of feminist and antifeminist consciousness. I name these categories in ways that I think describe the different patterns of meaning these women give to the concept in their own language. The women in this study suggest the categories of "male-defined feminine-ism," "antifeminist people-ism," "women's rights feminism," "Marxist-feminism," and "women-centered feminine-ism."

Having inductively developed categories for the various concepts used to shape the analysis, I proceed to discuss relationships between concepts. Thus I seek patterns of relationship between the various ways of understanding being white women, being feminists or antifeminists, and being political. The general propositions that result from these discussions are intended to explicate the various meanings that *these women* give to their political worlds and the various dynamics that shape their political actions. It should be noted that if other white women or women of color, or men for that matter, were added to the study, the categories, relationships, and propositions could change by becoming more specified. That is the nature of grounded inductive analysis. The explication changes *in scope* as greater numbers of "types" of actors are brought in. In contrast, deductively developed theory must be "tested" with data collected for that purpose and can change for lack of confirmation in the testing process. Unconfirmed hypotheses call for the reformulation of propositions and hypotheses and the collection of new data to test new hypotheses. My purpose is not to test theory but to present and explicate the political worlds of the diverse white women in this study.

Dorothy Smith makes a useful distinction between "theorizing," either in the deductive or the inductive mode, and "explicating." In a discussion of feminist methodology, she says:

> Methods of thinking could, I suppose, be described as 'theories,' but to do so is to suggest that I am concerned with formulations that will explain

phenomena, when what I am primarily concerned with is how to conceptualize or how to constitute the textuality of social phenomena. I am concerned with how to *write* the social, to make it visible in sociological texts,
in ways that will explicate a problematic, the actuality of which is im-
manent in the everyday world.[62]

In effect, Smith is calling for social scientists to come down from the
pedestal of scientific theory into the everyday lives of themselves
and their "subjects," who themselves possess agency in shaping and
completing the meanings that social scientists detect through their
studies. She continues by suggesting that feminist social "scientific"
method become, in a sense, a form of interpretative literary criticism when she says,

A sociology for women must be conscious . . . that its meaning remains to
be completed by a reader who is situated just as she is—a particular
woman reading somewhere at a particular time amid the particularities
of her everyday world—and that it is the capacity of our sociological
texts, as she enlivens them, to reflect upon, to expand, and to enlarge
her grasp of the world she reads in, and that is the world that completes
the meaning of the text as she reads.[63]

Thus, these women's stories and my explications, interpretations, of
them will be useful to the extent that readers can apply what we
are saying to the problematics of their own lives.

Though I began this study with the idea that I would select
women to represent theoretical types of activists in electoral politics
and in movement politics, I concluded well into the study that the
women I had asked to share their life stories were telling me much
more about the singularities and particularities of their lives than
about the essentiality and universality presumed by the selection of
theoretical types. And yet in reading over the transcripts of their
taped interviews I could find similarities as well as differences
among the women that suggested different patterns of being women
and of being political. Some of the differences sprang from the differences in types of political engagement that had I specified as my
starting place for analysis and that the women themselves had chosen or constructed for their own purposes. Some of the differences
sprang from the different historical periods in which the women

grew up and from the different forms of family structures indicated by their descriptions of their childhood families.

These different patterns of being and living suggest different forms of sociopolitical reality that these women have taken part in constructing, consciously or unconsciously, in the courses of their lives. By interviewing each woman and using her responses to help me understand her as a "white political woman" within her everyday world, her "reality," I have—in the final analysis, following the suggested methodology of Dorothy Smith—approached each woman as a subject in her own right, engaged in her own unique standpoint at the juncture of her own place and time—her unique Here and social Now—within an ongoing sociopolitical world.

In approaching each woman, I have assumed that our—the women's and my—everyday world is socially constructed, meaning not that it is rigidly consensual but that, in Smith's words, such reality is "social . . . arising in an ongoing organization of practices that continually and routinely reaffirm a world in common at the most basic grounding of our life in the concrete daily realities as well as in more complex social forms. Our world is continually being brought into being as it is and as it is becoming, in the daily practices of actual individuals."[64] My role as presenter of these women's lives as political activists is, therefore, a dual role of interlocutor and interpreter. My objective as interlocutor is to bring to center stage what Smith calls the "concrete daily realities" in the women's own words that they shared with me in our interviews. My objective as interpreter is to explicate what Smith calls the "more complex social forms" that these women's life stories suggest. The result is an array of politicized realities and forms that constitute what feminist activists/theorists have begun to call politics of identity, difference, coalition, and, ultimately, reality.[65]

Chapter 2

Ann Strong Sets the Stage

The curtain opens just after the turn of the century on a plantation in the Deep South. It was in that time and place that Democratic party activist Ann Strong was born, the first of two children. When she was seven years old, her father died; and a few years later, she moved with her mother and younger brother to a large city north of her birthplace but still in the same region. Her mother's two sisters had already gone to the city to teach school, "and the family sort of came together up there." She describes an extended family network, on her mother's side, of aunts and uncles and cousins living in or near the city. "I was told from the time I can remember that I owed the world a great deal because I had been fortunate in my parents' family, and that they had always stood for the best. They were active in the community." Strong says, "[My mother] worked because my father didn't leave much." When he died he left a "good-sized plantation, you know, but everything was mortgaged. Cotton was practically nothing. My father's gin burned, and he was one of those that felt you didn't have to be insured."

Her mother was well prepared for returning to paid employment, having finished high school and one year of college. "She worked her way through," and taught school before she married. She was the daughter of a Methodist minister. "They grew up poor. I would say plain living and high thinking." In fact, Strong says her mother "worked until she was seventy-four years old," and died at the age of ninety. Like her mother, Strong finished high school and one year of college before she married and became active in local politics. In Atlanta, where Strong and her husband later moved in connection with his business, she finally returned to college, finished college and earned a graduate degree, and took a job to earn the money necessary for home nursing care for her mother.

Strong initiates and exemplifies a pattern common to the women in this study who were born and reared in what I call female-centered families, in which a mother or mother-surrogate becomes the venerated mainstay of the family. In this study, most of the women who grew up in this form of family lived in rural or small-town settings, at least for a good portion of their early childhood years. Strong remembers her mother as "a very strong person, a very feminine person. She was a small, attractive, very intelligent person." After Strong's father died, her mother "tried to get along as long as she could without working because it was very difficult for a woman to work and keep house in those days." They were still living on the mortgaged plantation but with very little money. Strong's mother finally went to work when Strong was twelve years old.

The mother-daughter relationship was "very, very close," though the dead father was not forgotten. In response to a question about any influence her younger brother might have had on her, she says, "No, I don't think so. My mother was a very strong influential person, and just the memory of my father and things she told me about him had a great influence." Strong's mother was an intellectual. She told Strong

> not to take cooking and sewing at school. She said, "You'll learn that anyway, and I can teach you." And she said, "Take Latin." So I took what was called a Latin Classical course, which was a college-oriented course—four years of Latin, three years of French, . . . and algebra. . . . She was always a reader, and we were always readers. We were taught to love books and to enjoy school, and the teachers were supposed to be wonderful people.

Strong remembers helping her mother do the wash on Saturdays. "And those were the days when we didn't have washing machines. And she would recite poetry to me. In fact she wrote some poetry. She was quite a philosopher."

What would Ann Strong's mother have most wanted her to be? Strong thinks what her mother wanted for her had nothing to do with a career. "That was beside the point. My mother, as I said, was very feminine. I guess if she had been wealthy and had lived back in the nineteenth century, she would have liked for me to have a salon, a place for intellectual gatherings, something of that kind. But as it was, she just wanted me to have a full life, to develop all the resources that I had, and then to do whatever I wanted to, but to have the time to do it. And really that is what I followed."

Ann Strong grew up to be a feminist as well as what I call a "Wise Elder Woman." As the oldest woman in the study and the only woman to have been born before World War I, her case also initiates and exemplifies the interaction between type of family structure and period of growing up that appears to explicate why some of these women grew up to advocate feminism while others became anti-feminists. Perhaps, more than anything else, her having been born into an entirely different generation sets her ideas of "being a woman" apart from all the other women's ideas. Yet her rather complex understanding of being a woman also captures some of the ideas held by other women in the study, those born later in the period between the world wars or in the postwar period. Some of her ideas are reminiscent of the nineteenth century and earlier, as when she voices the very traditional conceptions of womanhood that would be expected of someone of her race and economic class. But some of her ideas clash with such tradition, as when she says that women as persons should have equal rights with men. In fact, her ideas about women exemplify, and probably derive from, the Janus-faced feminism that emerged in the early twentieth century,[1] during the pre–World War I period in which she grew up.

Nancy Cott writes that the "appearance" of this feminism "in the 1910s signaled a new phase in the debate and agitation about women's rights and freedoms that had flared for hundreds of years."[2] One of Cott's major objectives in delineating the origins and meanings of feminism as distinct from the earlier "woman movement" is to show why the word "feminism" should *not* be read back onto the earlier history of the struggle for women's rights. Though feminism emerged during the last years of the woman suffrage movement, Cott says "the new language of Feminism marked the end of the woman movement and embarkation on a modern agenda. Women's efforts in the 1910s and 1920s laid the groundwork and exposed the fault lines of modern feminism."[3] Modern feminism's agenda would include seemingly paradoxical components: a concern for equality between the sexes, or at least "opposition to ranking one sex inferior or superior"; a belief that women's condition and therefore status are not naturally or divinely ordained but "purposefully shaped" and therefore capable of being changed; and a belief nevertheless that women constitute a biological as well as a social group that must recognize its shared condition and work together to effect change in women's unjust status.[4] Thus, "Feminism asks for sexual equality that includes sexual difference. It aims for individual freedoms by mobilizing sex solidarity."[5]

Like other women in the study who equate "being a woman" with being "persons" and whom I therefore call "Women Persons," Ann Strong begins with the idea that she is herself, and she adds that she is always interested in improving herself: "Well, I've never wanted to be a man. In fact, I've never wanted to be anybody [else]. I've never envied anybody. I rejoice in whatever talents people have, and I would like to be more talented myself. I'd like to be smarter. I'd like to be prettier. I'd like to be better educated. I'd like to have more money. I'd like to be a better cook, a better housekeeper. All those things I'd like to do better than I do." Then, echoing the women in the study who call themselves "Ladies," she states her very traditional ideas about women's special roles that allow them to perform what she believes are vital community volunteer roles: "I think there are certain roles that women [occupy], women have certain qualities and so on. And I really in a way deplore the fact that women feel that they *have* to go into business or they have to work because I think they're needed to spend their time doing what I do. And I think it's just unfortunate that we don't have women who can do a lot of the things, the Cub Scouts and the Girl Scouts and the volunteer work as well as other things, things like I do."

Next, as a harbinger of the younger women in the study who speak of the restrictions they have experienced because of their sex and whom, therefore, I call "Women Made, Not Born," but also still echoing the "Ladies," she voices the idea that women must have rights, *but* without losing their privileges:

> I think everyone should be free to do whatever he wants to do. I'm a libertarian in the sense that I think everyone should be free. But I think women should have all their rights and all their privileges without having to give up anything. I don't see why women should have to give up a home life just in order to be able to vote and be free to do all these—not only vote, but I mean have all these things, full equality [the same] as men. Of course, I was very fortunate in this. My father was very much a feminist in his day. And my husband is very much a feminist. . . . I don't see that women have gained, for instance, by being able to go out and get a job. I don't see any real gain in that. She's always been able to do that.

Then she returns to the traditional conception and presents it as an ideal to take the place of making women choose *either* home *or* career outside the home:

> I think it's ridiculous that people feel that you have to choose between making a home and having a career. . . . But my ideal is when a man makes a living, and a woman keeps a home, and of course ideally you have children, which we weren't fortunate to have. . . . And there are multitudinous interests in running a lovely home and all the influences that go with it. And then being able to do a lot of things during the day that her husband doesn't have time to do. And then helping him in the things that he wants to do outside. Working together on the outside interest that they both, hopefully, would be interested in; if not, that each one is interested in separately. . . . My idea is that it will be much more difficult to do something new in the world of ideas [her conception of politics] with all the women working full time. My mother is a case in point.

She says that her mother "was able to influence me and maybe a few people that she came in contact with. But by the time you work all day and keep house at night, you don't have much money, as most women don't who work. And even if you have a husband, . . . very few husbands share and share alike in housekeeping." Remembering her mother leads her to envision a second form of the ideal world:

> Maybe the time will come when they [husband and wife] will go into the kitchen together and walk out together, you know, that kind of thing. He

runs the vacuum cleaner while she does something else. But that doesn't happen often. And it means that there's just not much time anymore for those ideas. Go home and read for a while. If you go out to meetings and things like that, who's going to stay with the children? Who's going to see that their homework is done? And so I just think it's going to be more difficult.

Strong believes that this ideal world will be long in coming.

Very much exhibiting the marks of having grown up in a period when modern feminism was emerging, Strong considers herself "a feminist. That doesn't mean that I'm against men. I just believe in equality. I believe in justice for everybody." I respond that some women see feminism as militancy and bra-burning; she replies, "That's kind of a red herring. And that's one of those things that you just throw out just to make people, to turn them all off. . . . That's so ridiculous. I don't see how any intelligent people could even swallow that kind of thing. That's demagoguery."

As Strong's interview unrolls, she becomes for me a "Wise Elder Woman" with whom I explore mysteries presented by other women in my study. With her, I skip my question about "being feminine" and ask her to expound upon the women to whom she alluded when discussing the problems she had faced in politics: "those women . . . who don't bother about the ERA." In the course of discoursing on this issue, without my asking, she touches on the other questions relevant to "being a woman," "being feminine," and receiving positive and negative treatment on account of sex and race.

Talking about "those women," she says, first speaking as if she were they and then speaking as herself in response to them,

They've never had any problems. What they've done, they've just gone right ahead [and done]. Well, I think there are very few women in business that can say that. I've been in business, I mean, worked in offices, and I've seen too much. My mother went through some of it. And I've seen too much where superior women have been working under inferior men and have had to take all sorts of stuff, everything from sexual harassment to all kinds of little sexual overtures, you know, propositions and stuff like that.

I ask her if she has faced that. She replies, "Yes, I did. I had men try to put their hands on my breast and try to proposition me. And here

I was, a perfectly respectable, religious, obviously a decent young woman, who rushes in where angels fear to tread. Don't think it's just the loose-living women, you know. That's what they say, you know, that you've done something to encourage it. That's not true. That is not true."

Having addressed the question of negative treatment on account of sex, we then talk about why these women do not support the ERA. This discussion leads Strong to talk about women's lack of what is today called feminist consciousness in comparison to what is today called Black consciousness. In the course of this discussion, Strong demonstrates her awareness of the barriers constructed on the basis of positive and negative treatment on account of sex and race, though she refers to the treatments of others and not to her own experiences. Speaking of the women who have made it to high positions, she says, "Maybe they have been unusually fortunate, unusually aggressive, maybe even unusually talented, let's face it, attractive in some ways. And when they've gotten there, they couldn't have gotten there without seeing some of the things that you and I've seen. And when they've gotten there, they think of themselves as an elite. 'I've made it. I'm special.' " I add that some will say, "Well, I'm aware that women have problems of certain kinds, but I've accomplished what I've done on my own. And so can they." She responds, " 'So can they. They ought to be stronger. They'll be better women for it. That will make them stronger if they have to overcome these obstacles.' But why should obstacles be put in front of women that are not put in front of men, just as a matter of pure justice?"

I ask her why she thinks some women do not even perceive the obstacles. She attributes that to their not wanting to acknowledge obstacles because they believe that they do not have the strength to compete out in the world:

> There are some women who don't have the strength to stand on their own and who feel that if they had to compete in the whole world of women standing on their own, they would be kind of left out. They'd rather hang on to this idea of being a clinging vine, the dependent ["being feminine"]. And this gives them a sort of old-fashioned glory in itself, [to believe] that their husbands want them this way. And a great many

people still look up to that idea. Whereas if we have the other way, they'll be back numbers.

In effect, she is articulating an obstacle to feminist consciousness-raising that is developed more fully later in the study in the chapters on "being a woman." This obstacle is a lack of awareness that the dominant social construction of woman as necessarily dependent is deceptive and is meant to prevent women from recognizing their strengths. But Strong is also perceptive about why "those women" do not recognize their potential. The world that they grew up in did not expect or prepare them to be self-sufficient. It is no wonder that they "cling" to husbands that, luckily, bring in income and, along with income, status. These women understandably believe that, if they were to be "displaced" from their marriages, they would be hard pressed to go into the paid workplace, unprepared as they are. They would indeed end up as "back numbers," either in a low-paid job or as candidates for welfare.

Strong then launches into comparing what will have to happen for women with what she believes had to happen for Black people to gain self esteem. Again she role-plays, using the language of the oppressor and then reverting to her own language.

> And another thing I think is the perfectly same phenomenon that certain Black people have . . . if they had been helped by white people, and they still looked to this person as a kind of sponsor: "this 'big nigger' made it. He was a rare one, a special case. And there's no way that we can [make it], this little nappy-headed Black," and so on. They couldn't even see themselves as being educated. And the pretty people were the white women and the beautiful people, and that was a different world, and they couldn't see themselves like that. And it took a long time to get the sharecroppers and the maids and the people doing needlework to feel that they could. . . . But I think it's the same today, some of the women probably feel that same way, that they couldn't, if it were equal, they couldn't find their place among those women [who did make it].

As someone who was born and raised in the Deep South, during the era of Jim Crow, she has good insight into what feminists today, both Black and white, call the problem of internalized oppression.[6] Thus, Ann Strong encapsulates a version of feminist consciousness that includes both the feminism of the period in which she grew up as well as the more recent consciousness of internalized oppression on the basis of gender and race.

Concerning the double vision that Nancy Cott has shown to be the hallmark of the feminism that emerged in the period in which Ann Strong was growing up, it was a form of consciousness that could hold two contradictory notions of "woman" in tension. On the one hand is the idea that a woman has capabilities that she can develop to the fullest. Strong's mother had done that, even while working to support her family. On the other hand is the idea that such self-development requires time and that the way to secure that time is through a traditional form of marriage. Strong grew up to believe that the way to secure that time is through a marriage in which the husband earns the household income while the wife pursues her community involvements: "being a lady and using all my feminine instincts and intuition, not feminine wiles, but all that is best in a woman's thinking mind. It may or may not be different from a man's. How do you know? I only know my own." Marriage to a husband who is the household breadwinner leaves the wife the time necessary to manage the couple's household and to pursue her ideas through the political arena. Thus, Strong's notion of "being a woman" can hold in tension both the ideas of femininity, including not pursuing a career, with the ideas of strength and abilities, just as Cott suggested that the newly emergent feminism was a form of consciousness that allowed women to follow seemingly contradictory lines of thinking and acting.

But feminism, even that which emerged early in the twentieth century, also requires that women not pursue their needs and wants, their "self-interest," simply as individuals but that they also recognize themselves as members of a group unjustly excluded from certain endeavors on the basis of their sex.[7] In order for women to be able to work together for feminist-directed change, women must value one another as "sisters" in the struggle. So it would seem that one way women might begin to learn the value of other women would be through growing up in a female-centered family in which much-loved women played central roles. Whether that recognition of women's value by other women would develop into feminist consciousness would depend on other developments along the life path, but at least such a family form appears to lay the ground for such developments in the future.

Though "mother" or significant other women central to a woman's childhood family may interact with the status of feminism in a particular historical period to lay a basis for a woman's later feminist development, it is probable that "father" or significant other men will also play some kind of role, if for no other reason than that the dominant culture in the United States has posited a requirement for the presence of "father" along with "mother" to constitute "the family." At least, this is the ideal image of family portrayed in that dominant culture. In Ann Strong's family, her father played an important role that was cut short by his death. His feminism seems to have reinforced Strong's admiration for her mother after his death.

He lived long enough to be remembered by her, and fondly; in addition, she noted that her mother told her of her father in ways that influenced Strong's development. She remembers her father in positive terms:

> He was tall, had grey eyes, fair skin, black hair. He was merry-eyed. He was a lusty sort of person, [but] very deeply reverent. I told someone once if I were a sculptor and I could do a statue of reverence, I would do his back and shoulders because when I think of reverence, I think—we used to have family prayer at evening meal—and I can remember him, his kneeling down and seeing his back. That's just as vivid to me. I can see the place before the fire and my brother in his little red chair and me in my little wicker rocker, and his kneeling and saying the prayer. . . . He was active in politics. He liked to keep up with everything that was going on. . . . He loved to hunt and fish. And he was a good neighbor. He didn't hold grudges. . . . He was a peace-maker.

She says her relationship with him was "very close because I was the oldest. My little brother was two and a half years younger than I was, and in those days that meant a lot of difference when you were that young. And he used to take me fishing with him. Of course, he would put the worm on my hook, and if the fish got tangled up or a little hard to get, he'd help me with it. I always got credit. He'd come home and tell them about my catching the fish."

Strong says that no other family members particularly influenced her, since her mother's and father's influence was so great. "They were really different from all the members of their family, just as my husband is different from a lot of members of his family." She herself appears to have been "different" from those around her. In response to my question about how she would describe herself as a child, she says:

> I never felt that I quite belonged to most of the children. I played. I enjoyed playing, . . . but I enjoyed playing games, particularly if they were complicated, and I enjoyed exercise. I still try to walk a mile a day and I do yoga. I like to exercise. I was a good basketball player. I was on the state championship team at my high school when we won the state basketball championship in 1922. But I'll just be honest with you. I guess I was a misfit. I tried to have friendships, . . . but I always felt that I was holding something back from these people because it was something a little bit too precious that they would not, that they would trample on.

Strong appears to have had a feminist sense of self from a very young age, and she protected herself from being overridden by others. That is not to say that she was a social isolate. She played with other children; she played a team sport in high school. She married and became actively involved in women's organizations and local politics. But she carried a strong sense of self and her own ideas into the public community arena—backed by a "very strong, very intelligent, very feminine" mother, memories of a loving feminist father, and a network of extended family members actively involved in the community. She has maintained a steady similar course down to the present.

Where Strong's father appears to have played a central role was in motivating her to become political in the sense of entering local politics as party activist and advocate of what she considers to be just causes. Her father provided a model of political principles that she has followed throughout her life; she sums these principles up by the term "justice." Though he died when she was seven years old, she remembers enough of him to believe that she was a kindred political spirit with her father.

Strong's feminist consciousness and political activism also appear to have developed in interaction with her racial consciousness. She does not speak explicitly of racism and white privilege, as do the youngest feminists in my study. She does, however, exhibit awareness of and distaste for the racial prejudice and discrimination that were rampant in the Jim Crow era in which she grew up. This was a period of *de jure* racial segregation in the South so that in her young adulthood any work with Black women across racial lines would bring her into noncompliance with white supremacist prescriptions for and proscriptions of master-servant race relations. Thus, she experienced conflict with her mother over not being able to invite to a party, in public, a little Black girl with whom she was allowed to play in private. Also in private, her mother, and her father while he was alive, never expressed "any prejudice, hatred— the idea of something like the Klan would just be the most abominable idea of anything in the world." Yet her family "didn't go along with" her interracial activities in public, that is, in the local community after she married. She learned to act for racial integration through the United Methodist Church. "You see, we were now part of the whole northern, southern Methodist Church, [which] put out this literature: 'Making a friend across racial lines is a step forward.' I took it seriously." She says this set her apart from her family and from her friends, but it has not stopped her from acting on her beliefs when and where she sees fit.

Strong indicates that she did not get active in politics until she married. She says that it was difficult to get involved if you did not support the local political machine. But her husband's family, like her own, was anti-machine, and she found her way into anti-machine politics along with her husband. For her, this involved belonging to the local chapter of the League of Women Voters and starting a Black voter education project. Black women asked her to work with them on voter education in their community because she had earned a reputation for interracial cooperation through her work in the Young Women's Christian Association. She got involved in Democratic party politics during the campaign of an anti-machine reform candidate for the U.S. Senate. When she and her husband moved to Atlanta, she continued her party work with the local county party. Her first campaign in Atlanta was John Kennedy's run for the presidency.

Now, as a longtime political activist, Ann Strong thinks of "the political" as a process within which she has fought the powers-that-be as she crusades for her causes. She leads into my question about the political by talking of her long interest in politics:

> I've always been interested in politics. In the long run, you know, ideas about doing things are, like somebody said, like fire balloons in the night that go out among the stars. Until you get them into politics. Eventually everything—people talk about politics being dirty and all that stuff—but it all gets into politics before it's done.
>
> [How would you define the political?]
>
> It ends in getting laws passed and implemented and executed. It's part of the things that we're obliged to live by. But it starts down with people being elected and what people demand of government, what they want— the grass roots and the special interests and the lobbyists, and all that. And in a democracy an informed electorate is absolutely essential. And an honest electorate, and honest elections. And, of course, that's very difficult to achieve.

In more recent years she could have run for a seat in the state house, but if she had run, she would have lost as a single-issue candidate. In the process, she says, she would have "betrayed my party by getting somebody else elected that they didn't want." She chose to stay out of electoral politics so she could "raise hell" on "what I believe in." Thus, she has placed herself outside officeholding but inside an advocacy relationship with officeholders who she believes can one day be educated to support her cause.

The Twenty-Six Other Women in the Study

Ann Strong's story sets the stage for presenting twenty-six other women in the drama to come. I set out here brief descriptions of each woman as she was engaged in politics at the time of her interview. I present the women as they will be analyzed in the next chapter, in groups according to the type of family structure in which they perceive themselves to have grown up.

In the first chapter, I framed the stage for the ensuing drama as the social location of white women defined by the terms of complex domination in order to draw attention to several interrelated problematics of identity, values, and action that white women have faced and still face in the United States today. Three such problematics for white women concern questions of identity: as women in relation to other white women and to white men, as white women in relation to women and men of color, and as political actors in a dominant culture that has been slow to recognize women's political capabilities. Some answers to these questions emerge in chapters 3 through 7 as I examine different aspects of the women's development according to the pattern set by Ann Strong. From birth and growing up in a particular form of family in a particular period of history characterized by emergence or submergence of feminist movement, to becoming political in the sense of becoming feminist or antifeminist women with whatever degree of consciousness of racism and white privilege, to becoming political in the sense of engaging in electoral or movement politics—the white women in the chapters to follow will tell life stories of considerable diversity.

A fourth problematic concerns a question of overall political objectives: are white political women likely to continue "politics as usual"? This form of politics has been loath to question the comprehensive simultaneity of privilege and oppression as organized under complex domination, though some singular aspects of racism, sexism, classism, or heterosexism have been addressed through this form of politics. Or are white political women preparing to question the "reality" of complex domination and to enter into alliances with feminists of color who have initiated politics of identity and difference? In chapter 8, I "re-assemble" the women to show how they have variously combined their identities, values, and actions to suggest different models of "white political women," some of whom engage in "politics as usual" and some of whom launch a "politics of reality." I conclude by sketching the political morality play about privilege and empowerment that I believe the women present in this study.

Growing Up in Female-centered Families

Ann Strong initiates the pattern for white women growing up in female-centered families. While Strong was the only woman in this
study to have been born before World War I, three women—Sally
Martin, Arlene Pringle, and Edith Hammond—grew up in such
families in the period between the world wars, and three—Susan

---

**Table 1. Women in the Study, by Perceived
Family Structure and Historical Period of Birth**

Female-centered Families

Before World War I
  Ann Strong—Democrat
Between the world wars
  Sally Martin—Democrat
  Arlene Pringle—Republican
  Edith Hammond—Democrat
During and after World War II
  Susan Murphy—leftist community activist
  Annie Witt—leftist community activist
  Tillie Zadar—women's community activist

Male-centered Families

Between the world wars
  Bridgit Malone—Republican
  Ella Washburn—Democrat
  Audrey Nelms—Republican
  Lorraine Reilly—Republican
  Lavinia Ravenel—Republican
  Dulcie LaFontaine—Republican
  Maryanne Thayer—Republican
  Sybyl Jensen—Republican
During and after World War II
  Kate Greene—Democrat
  Adrienne Stone—Democrat
  Gretchen Bright—women's community activist

Murphy, Annie Witt, and Tillie Zadar—grew up in such families during and after World War II (see table 1).

In her mid-sixties, erstwhile Democratic office-seeker Sally Martin is married, mother of two, grandmother of two, and employed as an executive secretary.[8] She was born in the West North Central region but grew up in the South Atlantic region. She ran for state legislative office in a special election called for a vacated seat several years ago because "a couple of people had been nagging me to run for the city council, and I really didn't want to run for the city council." But when a state office came open, she ran for that and lost. "It was fun, but it was really no fun to lose. It's fun to do the work, but it's not fun to have spent all that for nothing." She is no longer involved in the county party organization, though she does work for particular candidates during election campaigns. Her overall approach is not to get involved unless asked to do so.

Republican party activist Arlene Pringle, who was born in the East North Central region but grew up "all over," is in her mid-sixties. She is married, the mother of five, and the grandmother of nine. She is less involved in party organizational work now because her

Table 1, Continued

Non-centered or Mixed Families
Between the world wars
    Elizabeth Latimer—Republican
    Linda Helms—Republican
    Betty Mason—Republican
    Bess Shumaker—Republican

Male-dominated Families
During and after World War II
    Nancy Harding—Democrat
    Hazel Beecroft—leftist community activist
    Barbara Bergen—women's community activist
    Fran Daly—women's community activist
    Maria Montgomery—leftist community activist

husband and she, since his retirement, have bought a small business that keeps them busy six days a week. She mainly contributes money to direct-mail solicitations. "Since I can't give as much time as I used to, I just feel like my money's got to [compensate]." She is also heavily involved in grass-roots lobbying via group-directed letter writing for Stop-ERA and Citizens Choice. She would not herself seek public office though she says, "I would like to see some of the things that I would do if I were in office come about. But I don't know if I would be willing to take the punishment you have to take in office."

Democratic party activist Edith Hammond, who was born and grew up in the South Atlantic region, is in her mid-fifties, married a second time, and has no children. She is no longer involved in her county party organization, but she has been appointed to serve on a state board. She has been associated with the labor movement since she "went to work . . . at a very early age." She has been involved in countless election campaigns, but presently she seems to have drawn back from that kind of involvement. She considers her work political, however: "I think all work is political." She is not interested in running for office—she believes that she would be "badgered" if she were in the public eye—but feels more effective working behind the scenes.

Leftist community activist Susan Murphy, who was born and grew up in the East South Central region, is in her late thirties. She is also in her second marriage and has one child. She is a lawyer who has also remained active with the group of former Communist Party–Marxist/Leninist members still involved in community organizing around various issues. She is still trying to come to terms with why the group disintegrated, but she has not given up on socialism. In fact, she wants to see electoral work become a viable option for socialist organizing. She wants "to build organizations and institutions that can give the people in this country more control over their own lives." She believes what is "desperately needed in this country is a third political party and the right kind of candidate." And, yes, she would be willing to run for office as a candidate for such a political party, but she sees that party as one of several organizations—"radical women's organizations and farmers' organizations and the trade unions . . . and an army"—that are needed to "have the power to impact on this system." She does not see such organizations as alternatives to the system but as grass-roots structures to replace the present system.

Leftist community activist Annie Witt, who was born in the South Atlantic region but grew up "all over," is in her early twenties. She is a college student who also works thirty hours a week as a secretary in a labor law firm. She says she is constantly involved in leftist political discussions at work. On campus her major political involvement is with the student women's committee, which she chairs.

Women's community activist Tillie Zadar, who was born in the South Atlantic region but grew up in the Pacific region, is in her early twenties. She lives with a housemate, is a college student, and works as a member of a community media collective. She characterizes most of the other members of the collective as "leaning left but not feminist" in contrast to herself and the other radical Lesbian feminist on the staff. She has been involved in a local Lesbian feminist group as well as a local women's peace group and still supports these groups by working in fund-raisers or going to protest demonstrations "because they need the numbers." She did some volunteer work for the 1984 Geraldine Ferraro campaign, but presently she is devoting most of her energies to her school and media involvements. She considers all these involvements as political, though "just now I'm kind of in a dormant stage. I go back and forth. . . . I know people who are members of six organizations and go to meetings every night. I've never been like that."

Growing Up in Male-centered Families

Eight women grew up in male-centered families in the period between the world wars: Bridgit Malone, Ella Washburn, Audrey Nelms, Lorraine Reilly, Lavinia Ravenel, Dulcie LaFontaine, Maryanne Thayer, and Sybyl Jensen. Another three—Kate Greene, Adrienne Stone, and Gretchen Bright—grew up in such families during and after World War II (see table 1). Male-centered families, as explained more fully in the next chapter, are those in which fathers or father-surrogates are remembered positively as fun-loving persons in contrast to mothers or mother-surrogates who are remembered negatively as restrictive disciplinarians.

Republican party activist Bridgit Malone, who was born and grew up in the Middle Atlantic region, is in her early sixties. She is married, the mother of three, and involved in her church and in a Republican Women's Club. When asked about her present involvement in her county party organization, she indicates that her responsibilities are less now than in the past and she likes it that way. She does work for particular candidates and says that next year she will probably be drafted to be "chairman [of the county nominating committee]. . . . For some unknown reason I seem to have the permanent job of being nominating committee chairman for this act."

Democratic party activist Ella Washburn, who was born and grew up in the South Atlantic region, is in her early sixties. She is married, mother of two, grandmother of two, and daughter of a still-active ninety-year-old mother. She works as an executive secretary but is beginning to look toward retirement. She has become almost totally uninvolved in party organizational activities, though she still works in her Democratic congressperson's campaign. She puts most of her energies now into promoting passage of the ERA, from organizing rallies to arguing women's equality with the people in her daily life. She neither is nor has ever been ambitious for public office.

Republican party activist Audrey Nelms, who was born and grew up in the East North Central region, is in her early sixties. She is married and the mother of three. Since she is employed by a nonpartisan government agency, she no longer may hold party office. She does, however, get involved with Republican candidates' campaigns during election times. When interviewed in 1977, she expressed an interest in running for a city council post, but now she has come to a realization that she cannot do this, even though this is where she would feel more effective politically.

Republican office-seeker Lorraine Reilly, who was born and grew up in the East North Central region, is in her mid-fifties. She is married, the mother of six, a member of a Republican Women's Club, and heavily involved in the county party organization. She is captain of her precinct, area captain of five precincts, and a member of the county party executive committee. During election time she involves all the family: "when the literature comes in that you have to put out in the precinct, we all sit down on the floor, we all get it together, and then we all go out and just put it out." She eventually would like to challenge her incumbent state representative when that person appears to be losing district support.

Republican party activist Lavinia Ravenel, who was born and grew up in the South Atlantic region, is in her mid-fifties. She is married, the mother of one, and is working in her husband's business as a secretary until they find someone to replace the secretary who left. She is still chair of her precinct and gets involved in campaigns at election time, but she says, "I'm not as active as I was because I don't have to stay at home like I did then, so I just don't have as much time." Though in 1977 she expressed an interest in running for a state legislative seat, she now says she has no aspirations to run for office. "I think there's a lot of people that's much more capable than I would be."

Republican officeholder Dulcie LaFontaine, who also was born and grew up in the East South Central region, is in her mid-fifties. She is married, mother of three, and grandmother of three. Active in her church, she also is working toward a college degree. As a state legislator, she considers herself full time and "the closest connection [her constituents] have to government." She maintains ties with many groups in her district— from schoolchildren and retired people to engineers and those concerned with drug and alcohol abuse.

Republican party activist Maryanne Thayer, who was born and grew up in the South Atlantic region, is in her early fifties. She is married and has no children, but she does have primary responsibility for the care of her mother, who is in a nursing home. She is also very involved in her church and is trying to organize a group there "for adult children of aging parents." Because of this involvement she is less active in her party organization, though she still gets involved periodically in election campaigns.

Nearing age fifty, Republican Sybyl Jensen, who was born and grew up in the East South Central region, is married, the mother of four, and a state legislator. As an officeholder, she says she is involved throughout the year during and between legislative sessions with committee work, other legislators, and constituents who, she says, call at all hours of the day and night.

In her early forties, Democratic office-seeker Kate Greene is the mother of three. She was born and grew up in the South Atlantic region. She has just finished a college degree and is considering entering law school. She is heavily involved in women's and party politics, having held leadership positions in both kinds of organizations. She is ambitious to hold office at some time in the future and is biding her time until the right opportunity opens up for her.

Nearing age forty, Democratic officeholder Adrienne Stone, who was born and grew up in the Middle Atlantic region, is the mother of two. As a state legislator, she does committee work during and between legislative sessions, works on getting her own legislation through the lawmaking process, watches out for "bad legislation," takes calls from constituents and directs them to the officials that can help them. She also serves on boards, speaks to groups, and seems "to be approached much more often on research projects [such as this study] than the men in the legislature."

Women's community activist Gretchen Bright, who was born and grew up in the South Atlantic region, is in her mid-thirties. She is divorced and is beginning a transition from being involved in a women's collective business to spending more time writing and conducting workshops on approaches to self-knowledge. She considers all these involvements to be political. Given her political involvements, she is consistent in eschewing public office as a way to seek her political ends. She says that when she was younger she was "fascinated by the existing political system and electoral politics." In her idealism she believed it was possible in the 1960s and 1970s to "get behind the right person." But her experiences "working in city government . . . being involved in the behind-the-scenes role of electoral politics" taught her about the "corruption" of the "individual's integrity" that is necessary to achieve political office. "I mean, writing speeches for politicians is a pretty surreal experience." With that view of the personal destruction required to succeed in electoral politics, "married to my overall growing perspective of the patriarchy and what the system is really designed for, I don't feel a need to work in the system." She wonders if she should vote in the upcoming presidential election where "the choices are between a nominal Democrat [Walter Mondale] and Reagan . . . between disasters." But in the final analysis she doesn't "take it real seriously."

Growing Up in Non-centered or Mixed Family Structures

Also growing up in the period between the world wars were four women whose families could be classified neither as female-centered nor as male-centered. Elizabeth Latimer and Linda Helms grew up in what I call shared-discipline families. Betty Mason and Bess Shumaker grew up in families that began as male-centered but later became female-centered (see table 1).

In her mid-fifties, Republican Elizabeth Latimer, who was born and grew up in the West South Central region, is married, the mother of two, and a state legislator. Her constituents are concerned about local problems, many of which can be directed to state government and some of which must be addressed to the local government. She works on appropriate state legislation and otherwise directs constituents to the government officials who can address their particular problems. She also works on her committees, goes to meetings and gives speeches, and edits a newsletter for her district. She was applying the address labels to her latest issue throughout our interview.

Republican party activist Linda Helms, who was born and grew up in the South Atlantic region, is in her early fifties. She is married and the mother of three. Though still active in a Republican Women's Club, she is less involved in local party politics because her retired husband is on a fixed income and she has had to devote more time to a business that she runs out of her home. She has held many party offices, but she says she would never want to hold public office because she is timid and has "very bad stage fright. And it terrifies me to stand up and speak. It would terrify me to be in political office where I would have to be in front of people. That's one reason. The second reason is because I felt my first responsibility was to my family, and if I were serving in political office, I couldn't fulfill the responsibility." Thus, she has opted to work to influence the way public officials vote on various issues, and she contributes to political action committees such as the American Conservative Union and Citizen's Choice.

Republican party activist Betty Mason, who was born in the Middle Atlantic region but grew up in the South Atlantic region, is in her early fifties. She is married, the mother of five, involved in her church, employed as a regional office manager, and heavily involved in various state and local party executive committees and in the upcoming gubernatorial campaign. She says she would run for office "in a heartbeat . . . with no question at all, no reservations," except that she already has too many other commitments and no time to run for office. Furthermore, she believes she can be "possibly more influential not holding an office than you can be holding an office. . . . I'd rather just do my own thing behind the scenes."

Republican office-seeker Bess Shumaker, who was born and grew up in the West North Central region, is in her mid-forties. She is married, the mother of three, and a business partner in a family business. She is also intensively involved running election campaigns for particular candidates, serving on her party's county executive committee and serving on a county board, which is an appointed public office. She has run for a seat in the state legislature and lost; she does not rule out running again if the opportunity is right for her.

Growing Up in Male-dominated Families
Finally, five women grew up in male-dominated families during and after World War II: Nancy Harding, Hazel Beecroft, Barbara Bergen, Fran Daly, and Maria Montgomery (see table 1). Male-dominated families, as explained more fully in the next chapter, are those in which fathers or father-surrogates are remembered as both loved and feared because they both organized family fun and meted out discipline, while mothers receded into the background as the steady servants to the household.

Nearing age forty and the mother of two, Democratic office-seeker Nancy Harding, who was born and grew up in the West South Central region, teaches high-school social studies. In contrast to her earlier intense involvement in county party politics and numerous state legislative and local election campaigns, she is now totally alienated from and uninvolved in organizational politics. The birth of her children demanded most of the time she previously devoted to politics, but she is not willing to spend good money for child care in order to continue being used as a "go-fer"—"go for this and go for that"—by the sexist men of the party and campaign organizations. She does not want to put any more energy into "hopeless causes," but she still harbors a desire to run for a seat on the school board.

Leftist community activist Hazel Beecroft, who was born and grew up in the Pacific region, is in her late thirties. She is married, has two children, is a graduate student, and works as a secretary. She says that she is less organizationally involved now than in previous periods, partly because the movements in which she has been involved have become quiescent for the time being, but she is still very group-oriented. She is active with a women's group on her campus. She continues a long-term involvement with a small group of public utility shareholders who attempt to raise political issues, such as stopping the building of nuclear power plants, at the yearly meetings of the company stockholders. Her shares of stock are a birthday present from an aunt whom she characterizes as "progressive." She also is active in solidarity groups that form around U.S. foreign policy in Central America, South America, and South Africa. She rejects seeking and holding public office as ways to pursue her political ends because "I don't think those are real effective institutions." She does acknowledge that local government is closer to the people, and she does think it is good when progressive people have been elected to city councils, but she cannot see herself getting involved in electoral politics.

Women's community activist Barbara Bergen, who also was born in the Pacific region but grew up "all over," is in her early thirties. She lives with two housemates and is totally involved with the Lesbian community. She considers her whole approach to living to constitute her political involvements, "from where I buy my food to what sort of marches I go to in the streets." For example, she and one of her housemates have formed the "Hungry Dykes' Buying Club," which takes orders for wholesale natural foods from "a lot of other women and one man in the community," then picks up and distributes the food. "It's a way of supporting a cooperative, getting natural foods at cheap prices, and eating well." She also is intensely involved in the women's peace movement and is part of a women's collective business.

Women's community activist Fran Daly, who was born in the East South Central region but grew up "all over," is in her mid-thirties. She is involved in a women's collective business, which is the center of her political life. A major political concern for those involved in the collective is creating and maintaining a "nonhierarchical, transformative work experience." Her politics also involve living with a female housemate—she is "out" as a Lesbian—and raising a child. She is also involved in the women's peace movement. I interviewed her shortly before her local group left for a peace encampment.

Leftist community activist Maria Montgomery, who was born in a Central American country but grew up in the South Atlantic region, is in her late twenties. She is a graduate student and is involved in progressive student and women's groups on her local college campus. She is also involved in an informal network of former Communist Party–Marxist/Leninist members who are trying to regroup since that party became defunct. She is in her second marriage and is the mother of two preschoolers. Her major concerns are her family, her studies, and her political work, all of which involve linking issues off campus with activities on campus, from anti-Klan actions to organizing observances of International Women's Day. Regarding public officeholding, she says laughingly, "I used to think all the really important decisions are made in the Tri-Lateral Commission meetings. . . . But I've changed my view on it because . . . what I call electoral work in this country, because of its traditions, is very important." She believes that the work has educational value, and "you *can* win some reforms. . . . I think you have to be aware that they're limited." The educational value comes in showing people what socialist politics can accomplish, as in city councils in California, Washington State, and Vermont. "You've got to show them what kinds of things can be done if different people with different interests were in power." I ask if some day she might run for office, and she responds that "it's not impossible." As she sees the development of Marxist-Leninist political philosophy in this country, there is a turn toward making office seeking and officeholding part of a larger group strategy to bring revolutionary change to the country, and she herself might be one of those who seek public office to show people what socialism is about.

The lives of these activists engaged in electoral and movement politics converge at the time of the interviews on a single place, Atlanta, but the past lives of these women span the twentieth century and the geographical land mass of the United States and beyond. Though activists who grew up in the South predominate (sixteen of twenty-seven; three of these were born outside the South), activists were born in all four regions of the United States. The party activists are much more likely than the movement activists to have grown up in the same place where they were born. This phenomenon can be explained in part by three of the movement activists' fathers having made careers in the military services. Finally, there is no party sectionalism evident among the party activists. Democratic and Republican activists alike are likely to come from any region. Thus, although this study is set in a southern city, it is intended to be not a study of white southern women but a study of white political women. That is, the purpose of my study is not to determine how region affects form of political engagement but to understand the meanings these activists give to being white political women. In the final analysis they are all similar only in their physical appearances—being white and being female—and in the happenstance of their present geographical location.

Chapter 3

History and Family Lay the Ground for Becoming "Political Women"

When the women in this study were born, from the turn of the century down to the early 1960s, any turns they made toward becoming political—especially toward running for office or organizing leftist or feminist movements—would have branded all but Ann Strong as unusual at the least. Even Ann Strong, in her early twenties a charter member of her local chapter of the League of Women Voters and an active member of the Young Women's Christian Association, was in a small minority of predominantly white middle-class women engaged in such activities, although, through the 1920s and 1930s, increasing numbers of women Black and white, working class and middle class, would surpass the numbers of women that had been involved in politics during the nineteenth century in movements for the abolition of slavery and for Black and woman's suffrage and through numerous women's and general membership organizations.[1]

Those women who turned to working in political parties for candidates or to advocating causes through women's organizations would have been, and were, depoliticized in their public image by the concept of "voluntarist," meaning performing the nurturant auxiliary role in "the (white) man's world of politics" or at most crusading as altruistic "do-gooders." Implicit in these conceptions of women involved in "man's political world" are assumptions about the basis for women's politics. Before the passage of the Nineteenth Amendment, women without the vote were considered to lack any instrumental reason for engaging in politics, since the Founding Fathers fashioned the citizen role around voting and the original states reserved the voting privilege initially for white men of property.[2] After the passage of the Nineteenth Amendment, Black women still were excluded from the suffrage in many states, mostly in the South, by state laws and constitutions. White women still were considered to lack any instrumental reason for engaging in politics beyond voting because for the most part they lacked economic clout, either individually or as a group. They might organize their numbers and express their demands and grievances, but without economic clout they had little hope of exercising any "real" power in a system of "men's politics" to which they had come only lately.[3] With politics construed as an arena in which men, especially white men of property, could pursue their rational (economic) self-interests, what possible reasons could women have for entering this arena but voluntarily "helping" men pursue those interests? At the most, perhaps women's involvement would result in "better (more moral)" public policy for all concerned.

So how is it that some of the women in the study grew up to engage in what they themselves characterize as "political," though others have labeled them "volunteers"? How is it that these women entered politics as subjects and as agents of their particular types of political change? How is it that others of these women grew up to challenge sexual stereotyping by running for office, holding office, and organizing movements and actions to empower women? For some answers I begin by examining their self-development in the childhood family. In this chapter I focus on the gendered aspect of social self-development shaped by interpersonal relations beginning in the childhood family. We will then be in a position to hear in succeeding chapters how gender has shaped each woman's understanding of "being a woman" and claiming feminism or antifeminism as a political stance.

Without treating self-development in childhood family and beyond historically, I would not be able to make sense of the relationships between early childhood family structures and later forms of feminism and antifeminism in the women in this study. The scholarship in women's studies has documented historical emergences and submergences of critical consciousness of capitalism, racism, and patriarchy. A strong socialist movement emerged around the

turn of the century in the United States, accompanied by the rise of
modern feminism as distinct from "the woman movement" and the
woman suffrage movement, movements which began in the nineteenth century[4] and which had roots in political thought going back
at least to the early fifteenth century in the writing of Christine de
Pisan.[5] The beginnings of the modern Black civil rights and Black
nationalist movements also can be traced to this period at the turn
of the twentieth century, with Ida B. Wells's Anti-Lynching Crusade
and the founding of two organizations, among others—the National
Association for the Advancement of Colored People and the Universal Negro Improvement Association.[6] This is not to say that these
and other movements during this period formed a unified attack on
perceived injustices against Black men and women and white
women of diverse economic classes. But women were vitally active
as members and leaders of the organizations that were at the cen-
ters of these movements, whether the organizations were confined
in membership to one race or sex or class or attempted to integrate
memberships across race, sex, and class barriers. Remember that
this is the period in which Ann Strong grew up, and she exemplified
white women who, though then relatively small in numbers, exhibited the feminist and anti-racist values of that era.

All of these movements, but not all of these organizations, went
into decline with the coming of the "Red Scare" that followed news
of the Bolshevik Revolution in Russia. During this period of retreat
from radicalism after the end of World War I, any antiestablishment
movement in the United States became suspect of being "communist." Woman suffrage was finally gained, though largely for white
women only, with the passage of the Nineteenth Amendment. But
feminism, socialism, and Black consciousness lost favor as rallying
cries, and social reform organizations in general turned to the slow
grind of lobbying national and state governments for piecemeal
change in the courts and legislatures.[7]

In the period between the world wars, the contradictions that
Nancy Cott suggests had been held in creative tension under the
rallying principles of modern feminism broke loose from one another
to emerge as two alternatives for achieving women's rights. One al-

ternative, which emphasized equality without regard for a person's sex, was to seek an amendment to the U.S. Constitution guaranteeing that equal rights would not be abridged on the basis of sex. The National Woman's party took the lead in the effort to get the ERA through the constitutional amendment process. The other alternative, which emphasized differences between the sexes, was to maintain existing and seek additional legal safeguards for women's "special protections and privileges." What became known as the U.S. Department of Labor "Women's Bureau coalition" took the lead in this effort.[8] The protectionists held sway over the advocates of the ERA until the late postwar period. In the early 1960s, President John F. Kennedy's Presidential Commission on the Status of Women succeeded in moving the focus of the debate to equal rights as a goal without advocating or opposing a particular strategy, including the ERA. Meanwhile, under pressure from the Kennedy administration, Congress finally passed the Equal Pay Act of 1963.[9]

With the exception of the Black civil rights movement, which accelerated again in the late 1950s, it was only toward the end of the 1960s that the early twentieth-century progressive movements resurfaced for renewed rounds of consciousness-raising and mass mobilization of activists: movements for Black Power, women's rights, and women's liberation; movements of the New Left; a peace movement against the war in Vietnam. Except for occasional attempts at coalition for staging national demonstrations, these movements would continue in dialogue but not in unified strategies for bringing about "justice."

Like Ann Strong, the white female activists in my study were born into families that developed into one of three major or two minor forms during the three distinct historical periods that I have just outlined—pre–World War I, between the world wars, and post–World War II. I call some family forms "major" because they occur for sizeable numbers of women in my study in contrast to the two "minor" forms, which occur only for two women each and will not be included in the analysis to follow.[10] I will describe the major forms of family structure in a moment. At this point it is important to note that this finding is significant in that "the family" in studies of political socialization has, more often than not, been assumed to be of one form—the nuclear group composed of the role sets of wife/mother/houseworker and children dominated by the husband/father/breadwinner.[11] Kent Jennings and Richard Niemi, however, treated this "dubious assumption" of male dominance as a hypothesis to be tested in their study of high-school seniors in the mid 1960s.[12] They found that affective relationships, measured by items about closeness to one or the other or both parents, explained some of the socialization process in families, especially for girls.[13] And they concluded that women were much more significant in the political enculturation process than had been expected; they stated, "If one could imagine a world inhabited only by grandmothers, mothers, daughters, and girlfriends, the prospects for political continuity would be greater than they now are."[14]

Jennings's and Niemi's findings about the importance of affective relationships with women in the political socialization of girls could be read as running counter to some feminist theorists' explanations of how the institutions of society produce and reproduce gender. Feminine gender dictates that women develop into beings submissive to masculine men and presumably not become politically inclined. Especially provocative have been the studies beginning with those of Dorothy Dinnerstein and of Nancy Chodorow, the latter using object-relations theory, on the hypothesized effects of mothering, as contrasted to fathering, in the first months of children's infancy until about age three.[15] Sandra Harding provides a useful overview of that use of object-relations theory, which grows out of Freudian psychoanalytic theory.[16] Equally provocative have been the theoretical analyses of how language structures gender, beginning in each person's infancy; these studies proceed out of a Lacanian psychoanalytic framework.[17] Given the Eurocentric origins of the Freudian and Lacanian theories of psychosexual development and genderization, I think it is safe to assume that those theories are relevant to the infancies of the women in my study. Yet those studies also assume "the family" to take the form of the male-dominated nuclear group with the mother assigned primary responsibility for infant care and child care. And those studies do not take historical context into consideration. Perhaps this assumption along with historical context should be examined. Certainly the women in my study suggest such examinations.

It should also be noted that, when Jennings and Niemi speak of continuity in the socialization process, they mean the transmission of similar attitudes and behaviors from one generation to the next without specifying whether those attitudes and behaviors support or oppose dominant social norms. But later, they suggest that "the family and schools are unlikely candidates as major *sources* of change in the political culture, at least in the American case." Rather, they look "to rather unpredictable events and circumstances outside these traditional sources . . . for an explanation of changing socialization outcomes."[18] In their next study, Jennings and Niemi develop elaborate explanations of continuity and change that take historical "period effects" into account as sources of changed outcomes in young peoples' socialization.[19]

The women in my study, however, suggest an amendment to the proposition that change is generated outside the family. These women's stories suggest rather an interaction between childhood family structure, as perceived by these daughters, and historical period, with mothers in a certain type of family predisposing daughters to become feminist agents of change and fathers in a certain type of family predisposing daughters to become antifeminist agents of continuity. Similar to Jennings and Niemi, then, I find some mothers to be significant in the politicization of their daughters. But what emerged in my interviews when I asked these women to describe themselves, their mothers and their fathers, and their relationships with these two parents is considerable emphasis on a division of labor in affective and evaluative relationships. Not surprisingly, the parent who disciplined, whether mother *or* father, tended to be less liked and therefore less linked to later outcomes supporting continuity or change than the parent who was perceived as strong and competent or fun-loving.

I developed the forms of family structure primarily from the descriptions these women gave me of themselves, their mothers or mother-surrogates, their fathers or father-surrogates, any significant other family members, and their relationships with any or all of these family members.[20] Note that these women provided their descriptions from memory, and it is quite possible that later self-development shaped recalled perceptions. I cannot and do not claim to have uncovered *causal* relationships between childhood family forms and adult political leanings. I can and do claim to have discovered theoretically interesting relationships that call for further inquiry into the hows and whys of the relationships. In the discussion that follows, I provide some possible explanations to link childhood family forms with adult political leanings.

If I had conducted the study with men as subjects, I would have asked male activists to describe their childhood families from the perspectives of sons in their respective families. Different forms of family might emerge from such a study. Indeed, different forms of family might emerge from a study of other daughters in the families of the women in my study. In other words, my delineation of family structure is based on the perceptions and reports of particular daughters in particular families. "Family structure" is not a concept intended to cover objective households; I use it to refer to subjective perceptions of particular family members.

I have named the three major forms of family structure to emerge in this study female-centered, male-centered, and male-dominated. The women in female-centered families remember their mothers, or sometimes grandmothers, in loving, even adoring terms. They remember their fathers, or male father-surrogates, in much less glowing terms, usually because these men were perceived as the hard disciplinarians, unreasonably restrictive toward their daughters in their daughters' estimations. The women in male-centered families remember their fathers in adoring terms as social and fun-loving. In contrast, these women remember their mothers, who more often than not played the traditional housewife role, as the restrictive disciplinarians. The women in the male-dominated families remember their fathers as both adored and feared because they were fun-loving as well as the strict disciplinarians. These women remember their mothers as passive or "even," stabilizing the family circle in the wake of the actions of the dominant man of the house. Interestingly, no women in this study remembered mothers in both adoring and fearful terms and fathers as passive, a configuration that would have been termed female-dominated.

Family structures appear to have affected daughters' identification as women through female family members or through male family members. Those who identified through female family members I call "female-identified women," meaning identifying oneself in relation to other women and implying that women are centered and used as sources of support and evaluation in one's own life, even in the context of a dominant male-centered society. Those who identified through male family members I call "male-identified women," meaning identifying oneself in relation to men and implying that men are centered and used as a source of standards for women in society. Female-identified women were much more likely than male-identified women to become feminists in their post-childhood years.

Different forms of family structure tend to be found in certain historical periods and to be emergent in rural or urban settings, thus suggesting their relationship to economic sectoral change as the United States transformed slowly from a rural to an urban nation. In the present study, Ann Strong, who was born into a rural setting in the South at the turn of the century and grew up in the years before World War I, first describes the female-centered family. In agricultural settings, some of the women in my study report that their mothers and grandmothers played obviously significant parts in production and gained some status thereby. A rural economy relied on women as well as men, and this societal integration of roles in the farm household presumably laid the basis for socializing the children of the household, daughters as well as sons, into members of society that could think and feel and act in ways appropriate to the needs of the society. This is not to say that the rural culture of the United States supported fully egalitarian roles for women and men in society but that women in that culture seem to have played recognizable productive roles in society. The female-centered family structure continues to be found in later periods, in rural settings during the period between the world wars but also in urban settings during the postwar period.

The male-centered family in my study is almost entirely an urban form, first appearing in the period between the world wars, but also continuing for three women born during or soon after World War II. In urban and therefore industrialized settings before World War II, some of the women in my study describe families in which the men and women played more distinctive roles in production. Men were the recognized "breadwinners" for the family, while women stayed at home to perform the unpaid and therefore less recognized but necessary services of husband care, child care, and housework. Again, this family structure reflected the needs of an economy, in this case a capitalist industrial economy, in an urban culture that also imposed a more distinctive division of labor by sex than did the rural culture.

The male-dominated family appears in my study for women born during and after World War II. Most of these women grew up in cities, and the fathers of many of these women moved their families often in connection with their careers, military or otherwise. After World War II, the urban industrial setting overshadows the rural setting in the lives of the women in my study as well as in the United States generally. The women tell stories of growing up that evoke the postwar culture described by Betty Friedan in *The Feminine Mystique* and by Cynthia Harrison in her history of women in the postwar period: "Government planners had defined the major postwar domestic problem as the readjustment of sixteen million [male] veterans, and they believed that readjustment would come sooner if the vets found their girls as they had left them, not as independent working women."[21]

A striking interactive relationship between family structure, historical period of childhood, and development of feminist or antifeminist consciousness emerges in the analysis that follows.

Becoming Advocates or Opponents of "Feminism"

Growing Up in Female-centered Families
In the previous chapter I presented the singular case of Ann Strong, who grew up in a female-centered family in an era, before World

War I, when modern feminism—as distinct from the earlier woman rights movement—burst forth upon the scene in the United States. Strong appears to have consciously grown up as a feminist, because in her discussion of feminism and being a woman she states that her father was a feminist, as is her husband, who grew up in the same place and time as Strong.

Three women grew up in female-centered families in the period between the two world wars. This was a period when feminism declined abruptly because of its connotation of leftist radicalism. Two of these women, nevertheless, claimed to be feminists at the time I interviewed them in the early 1980s. Presumably, growing up in female-centered families resulted in the emergence of female-identified women. When a feminist movement reemerged in the late 1960s, such women apparently were predisposed to support that movement and to claim the name of "feminist."

The same would appear to be true for another three women who were born and grew up in female-centered families in the postwar period. One of these women was born just after the end of World War II and grew up before the feminist movement reemerged. The other two women were born in the early 1960s and so were growing up as the feminist movement was reviving and spreading. The oldest of these latter three women was in the process of integrating feminism with her Marxism when I interviewed her. The younger women were confirmed feminists at the time of my interviews with them.

Growing Up between the World Wars. The three women who were born in the years between 1918 and 1941, a period, as earlier noted, which saw the demise of feminism, all grew up on a farm or in a small town. All lived in female-centered families, in which the mother or a grandmother played the central role while the father was absent or the father or man who replaced the father was strongly disliked. These women grew up in families similar in form to Ann Strong's with the exception that Ann Strong's father was remembered fondly after his death and his influence was felt through these fond memories. The two women who grew up in the South, Sally Martin and Edith Hammond, as adult women would claim "feminism," while Arlene Pringle, who grew up in the Midwest, would reject "feminism" in her adult years.

Sally Martin was born right at the beginning of this period in the West North Central region on land staked out and claimed by her mother:

> She was in college [in the South Atlantic region] when my father, my future father, came to the school. He had been [in school] and then went out to the Midwest and came back with this great news that if you go there and live on the land, you can own 144 acres. And my mother heard it and it sounded good to her. So she took off for [the Midwest]. She went with another girlfriend, but we sort of lost track of the other gal. She . . . filed a claim, lived on that land, and you have to occupy it a certain amount of time in order to claim it. But she was teaching school in another part of [the state]. She would get on the train, go home on the weekends, and live in this little shack on this 144 acres, cold, twenty degrees below zero, no central heat, and she lived there by herself. She was out there for six or so years before she married my father.

Martin's father, who was a preacher, died when she was three years old, and her mother moved with her seven children—there had been nine but two died—back to the South Atlantic region, where the whole family farmed for a living quite successfully. They lived with the father's sister and her husband. Martin, the youngest of the seven children, reports that she had a "happy" childhood full of hard outdoor farmwork and indoor housework and a social life centered around her church.

Arlene Pringle was born a year after Sally Martin in the East North Central region. Since she did not designate the name of a city in her response but rather a region of a state, I assume she was born in a small town. She grew up "all over—Dallas, St. Louis, Louisville, Milwaukee, Pittsburgh." Her father was "an estimator, what they would call now a purchasing agent" during the Great Depression. "He was always one city ahead of us; . . . he would get a job, and then we would move." She does not remember much about her father while she was growing up, but her mother graduated from high school and worked in her own father's print shop before she married. When Pringle was born, her mother devoted all her time to her only child, sewing all her clothes and later entertaining Pringle's friends:

"she chaperoned a lot of teenage parties." Pringle does not "remember doing without a great deal. I certainly never missed a meal." Later, speaking of her mother and of herself as a child, she says she was given voice and piano lessons. "I guess I was spoiled; . . . even in the depression years I guess I was pretty privileged."

Edith Hammond was born in the late 1920s and grew up in a rural setting in the South Atlantic region. Her "father's family was wealthy at one time," but when she and her older brother were growing up, all the family—father, mother, children—worked on the farm; "we were very poor." Her mother attended school through the ninth grade, and her father attended through the eleventh; "out of nine children he was the only one that did not have a college education." Hammond's mother died when Hammond was twelve years old, and she moved into a small nearby town to live with her grandmother and her father's two sisters; her aunts were schoolteachers.

As children all these women report that they were closer to their mothers than to their fathers. Though there are of course variations in the ways that each woman describes her particular set of mother-father-daughter relationships, Sally Martin presents an exemplary case. Martin says her mother "was a really wonderful person, very practical and somebody who just did what she needed to do. She was marvelous." But Martin does not remember her mother as a "dominant" person; she was capable but not dominating in her way of doing things. Martin is clearly proud of her mother's homesteading experience and the fact that when her husband died she worked for the family's living on the farm owned by the deceased husband's sister and the sister's husband. Martin's relationship with her mother was "wonderful. She had that time for everybody. How she did it, I'll never know, but she really did have time, somehow or other, to spend with us, the children, individually and collectively." Like Strong's mother, Martin's mother encouraged her and her siblings to love school. She read to her children every night. She encouraged Martin to get as much education as possible and told Martin "you be whatever you want to be. You *can* be whatever you want to be." Martin does not remember anything about her father other than his having been a preacher. Her uncle became the father figure when her family moved to the farm. However, she "didn't like him very much. But he *was* the male. And of course I had my brothers. My oldest brother . . . probably functioned too as a male that knows everything and can do everything, making all the decisions." In fact, she did not like her uncle or her aunt because of the way she was disciplined. "My aunt and uncle both were much more severe, had much stronger and more stated do's and don'ts—no dime novels, no reading, no funny papers, no this, no that." She "resented" their rules and voiced her resentment to her brothers and sisters, but she followed the rules for the most part. She describes herself as a child as "very strong and healthy. I did a lot of outside work. I had good emotional support from my mother and brothers and sisters."

The early lives recounted by Sally Martin, Arlene Pringle, and Edith Hammond reinforce the idea that female-centered families lay the groundwork for the later emergence of feminism among the daughters, if the daughters are growing up during a period in which feminism as a movement has been derailed. Adoration of the mother by the daughter appears to be important in this process, since one must like and be comfortable working with other women if one is to become a feminist. Sally Martin reported such an attachment to her mother. Edith Hammond, likewise, was much closer to her mother than to her father, whom she seems to have disliked intensely. When Hammond's mother died, Hammond's much beloved grandmother took her mother's place. Arlene Pringle did not report a close affectionate attachment to her mother; herein may lie one reason for her deviating from this group of feminists.

Another element in the process of developing into a feminist is the emergence of a strong confident self, one resistant in thought if not in action to others' demands for certain prescribed behaviors. Again, Sally Martin to a lesser degree and Edith Hammond to a greater degree exhibited such selfhood. Martin tells of how she resented her aunt's and uncle's discipline. Hammond reports that she never did what other people wanted her to do. Arlene Pringle, on the other hand, submitted herself in obedience to her mother's requirements, though such public performances frightened and sickened her to the point of developing an ulcer in later life. She reported that her mother "preferred that I do things that would be elevating like piano and voice and things." Pringle says that she liked her music but "I never liked performing particularly. I'm very self-conscious, which I guess is a kind of a supreme egotism, afraid that you're going to be judged badly. Just like with this tape recorder." She was referring to my tape recorder. I replied that I would never have known that it was making her nervous. She said, "That's why I have an ulcer."

Thus it seems that female-centered families in which the daughters adore and identify with strong competent mothers or grandmothers provide sustenance to the development of a strong sense of self. Positive feelings for women, both self and others, lay the groundwork for the emergence of feminist consciousness when a feminist movement breaks forth once more.

Growing Up after World War II. Three women in female-centered families were born and grew up in the years following the end of World War II. Susan Murphy was born soon after the war ended; Annie Witt and Tillie Zadar were born in the early 1960s. Only these last two women, the youngest in the study, grew up during the period when the contemporary feminist movement had become active again. All three would claim some form of feminism as young adults.

Susan Murphy was born in a small town in the East South Central region soon after World War II ended. She grew up there and then in the country near by, where her family moved when she was eight years old, "the same place that my parents and my grandparents and their parents grew up." Her father graduated from high school and then went into business as a livestock dealer. "He was a child of the depression. His family lost everything. He really bootstrapped himself up to be a successful man." Her mother also graduated from high school and then "had a year of college. . . . And she dropped out of college because it was too threatening to him [Murphy's father] for her to continue school and him not to be able to."

Annie Witt and Tillie Zadar were born in the same South Atlantic state. Annie Witt's father made his career in the U.S. Navy, serving as chief officer on various nuclear submarines, so she grew up "all around"—Washington, South Carolina, Virginia, Connecticut, and Hawaii. She considered Hawaii, where she moved at age 13 and attended school through the eleventh grade, to be the place where she "consciously" grew up. When her father retired and went to live in the Deep South, where she graduated from high school, she returned on her own to Hawaii after graduation. Her parents since have returned to live in Hawaii. Her mother was a housewife for most of Witt's growing up years, but she returned to college in the late 1970s to get a college degree in home economics and now works as a Mary Kay cosmetics salesperson.

Tillie Zadar's father, a physician, served in the U.S. Navy before setting up his private practice in a city in the Pacific Northwest, where he moved his family when Zadar was six months old. Both of his parents were dentists. Zadar's mother, on the other hand, who earned a college degree in political science at a prestigious midwestern university, came from a poor Yugoslav immigrant background. Zadar says that her mother "was always kind of ashamed of her folks. She never talked about them when I was a kid. I was always pulling teeth to get stuff out of her about them because they were peasants." Her grandparents, aunts, and uncles on her mother's side came from Yugoslavia. Some of them mined in the West or logged and then bought a small farm in the upper Midwest. They were all Catholics, but of "two factions": some were disaffected from the "corrupt" church as it was run in the old country and were "leftist" in orientation. Her uncle was arrested and jailed for some of his "Wobbly" (Industrial Workers of the World) activities. But her mother's family were what might be called "bourgeois" in contrast to what Zadar called the "leftist" faction: they were very proud when their daughter married a doctor and moved into a "nice house in the suburbs." Some were equally put out when she divorced her husband many years later.

In effect, Annie Witt and Tillie Zadar grew up as feminists, much as Ann Strong, who grew up during the emergence of modern feminism in this country. Both were much closer to their mothers than to their fathers, against whose ideas and restrictions they struggled with the support of their mothers. Susan Murphy's case is more complex and shows the significance of grandmothers for overriding the expected effects of what otherwise would have been a male-centered family.

Susan Murphy begins by describing her mother as "very beautiful, very attractive physically," and "extremely capable." But Murphy notes something that always interested her about her mother: "My mother didn't have friends. My mother's life was completely wrapped up in family, and she didn't seek out [other women friends]. I have this vivid memory. We moved from a little town out into the country when I was eight years old. And my mother was so relieved not to have neighbors. She didn't like neighborhood gossip. She didn't like sitting down at the table with other women." Murphy contrasts herself to her mother by saying "but that was always interesting to me that she didn't because I'm someone who is, friendship has been very important to me in my whole life, and I continue to have good women friends today. You know, like nothing's better than to sit down at the table and gossip. I mean, we usually talk about our families, not who did what and that sort of thing."

Murphy describes her relationship with her mother as a "power struggle." She knows now from talking to her mother about those years that the relationship was difficult for both of them, "but it was so bad at one point when I was thirteen that I went to live with my grandmother rather than stay at home." She says that everything that her mother excelled in—sewing, cooking, managing a large house, bookkeeping, she, Murphy, was not good at and was not interested in doing. Murphy's mother has told her, since Murphy has grown up, that "when she first had me, she expected me to be perfect. I was her first child. She had made the comment a number of times that it was a big surprise to her that I was as active, if not more active physically, than a lot of the little boys in the neighborhood. I get the impression that that was an embarrassment to her. I was very much a tomboy, climbing and tearing my dress and was never quite put together right." Furthermore, her mother disagreed with what she called Murphy's "everlasting dissatisfaction of life." She did not understand how Murphy could want to get away. "She felt there was something unhealthy about this quest that I had and the fact that I always had my nose stuck in a book and I lived in a dream world and wouldn't get in touch with reality."

To hear Murphy talk of her father is to learn where she may have gotten her ideas of "getting away" into the "world out there," though the thing she heard most from him was the importance of being as pretty as her mother. Her description of her father, in contrast to her mother, comes out in her discussion of the importance of music to her:

> Well, I think that what it meant to me when I was a little girl is that music was life. My father played the banjo. And in my father's and mother's relationship, as strained as my relationship was with my father, to me, he sort of stood for life and world and he was a big man. He was out there, and he played the fiddle, and he played the banjo, and he cracked jokes, and he laughed, and he went in the world and had friends and was respected among people. And she sort of stood for keeping everything the same and conservatism and holding back. And so when I was very young, this rolling banjo, you know, and this man belting out this song was just the greatest thing in the world.

But for all her admiration for her father's talents, she finds it difficult to describe their relationship. She knows that he had a "tremendous impact" on her life, and "he is a very smart man. So it's like I admired him from afar, and longed for him to appreciate me, but it never quite happened." I asked her what he most wanted her to be. "Pretty, like my mother, and I really think that's the way he expected his daughters to be." She did not consider herself to be pretty, and she believed she failed him by being the "intellectual tomboy." She describes a recent scene with her father in the hospital: "He was sitting up talking to me, and he was talking to me about some other young girl who was in the hospital. And he said, 'You know, she's the daughter of so-and-so, and her mother was the prettiest girl in the county, and she is too,' you know, and it just brought back all that stuff again."

Given these experiences with her mother and father as she was growing up, but not according to their expectations of her, it becomes clear why her grandmothers were so important in reinforcing her selfhood and her love of doing things with other women. She says both her grandmothers were very significant in her life because they were such opposites. One was the intellectual and the organizer:

> My mother's mother had been a school teacher. For her day and age she had intellectual achievement. She started the first, they were called Tomato Clubs, in my county, which was the forerunner of the 4-H Clubs, and a home demonstration club. She brought a canner in and organized four women in the community to get their tomatoes together and can. She was very active in her church and in the women's clubs.

The other grandmother was musical and fun-loving:

> And my other grandmother, my father's mother, worked in a shirt factory. She was a round, roly-poly, totally accepting, totally loving woman who loved to square dance and go out to wrestling matches, go to dinners on the grounds [of the church] up in the country. She was just full of life, absolutely full of life.

Murphy believes her grandmothers overrode the negative signals she was receiving from her parents:

> I was the first grandchild, and both of those women adored me. Whatever qualifications or doubts or whatever my parents had, I think the fact that I have the self-confidence or whatever I have today came from my grandmothers because I could do no wrong. And they were proud of me. They came to everything that I ever did. They bragged about me, and they had pictures all over the house. And they took a lot of time with me. They were both storytellers. They encouraged me to tell them stories. The one grandmother, my granny, who was the square dancer and loved the music, sang and played the piano by ear. And so she really affirmed a lot of that in me. And the other grandmother affirmed the active me. She was not so beautiful herself. In fact, I think I probably look a lot like her. She was much more a woman whose life was about doing something. And I think those women had a tremendous impact on my life and that I have them to thank for the fact that I have the capabilities that I have.

Murphy also credits her teachers in grade school and high school, though none in particular, for affirming her self and her actions. And finally she speaks of the importance of books, especially biographies of women, in her life. Her favorites were Amelia Earhart and Louisa Mae Alcott, "not because of what they did when they grew older, but because of what they were like as children. Both of them were tom-boys."

Susan Murphy, Annie Witt, and Tillie Zadar all present stories of young girls who, with the loving support of mothers or grandmothers, develop strong selves through struggles with opposing fathers, or mother in the case of Murphy. That each young woman pitted her will in words and actions against authority figures attests to the emerging presence of a strong self. Murphy, growing up in the period before the reemergence of the contemporary women's movement, would not become a feminist until she had worked her way through civil rights and Marxist movements. But Witt and Zadar, coming of age during the contemporary women's movement, translated their familial conflicts into feminist consciousness as a matter of course, taking their mothers with them part of the way, though both say that they are more radical in their feminism than their mothers.

To summarize, the daughter's family became female-centered for one of two reasons: the father became absent through death or divorce, or the father or father-surrogate became disliked because he took the role of strict, sometimes harsh, disciplinarian. In contrast, the mother or grandmother emerged as a strong, competent, and much-loved, even adored, figure who became the daughter's affective anchor and mainstay. I have suggested during this part of the analysis that daughters who grew up in such family structures identified as young women through what they considered to be positive affective relationships with strong loving women. Such daughters became female-identified women.

The consequences of such identification were at least two. First, in the context of the larger society, which continued to be centered upon and even dominated by white males, young women nevertheless learned that they could assert their innermost selves to think and feel and act in ways not always condoned by the larger society. Second, they gained the capacity to identify with other women and to work with other women. In a historical period in which feminism was devalued, such capacities among and desires of women would not be named "feminist" and might in fact go unnamed. But in the event of the emergence or reemergence of a feminist movement, such capacities and desires could arise out of latency into full consciousness as some form of feminism. In historical periods in which feminism was an acknowledged possibility for advocacy, women growing up in female-centered families would be predisposed to join such movements forthwith.

Growing Up in Male-centered Families

Eight women tell stories in distinct contrast to the six of seven women who grew up in female-centered families to become feminists. These eight women were born into male-centered families, for the most part located in cities, in the period between the two world wars—when feminism was in public disrepute. Presumably these women emerged as male-identified women. To a woman, these eight rejected feminism for themselves. Only one told of being converted late in life to feminism—when her daughter met sex discrimination while trying to establish credit, first as a married woman and later as a single mother. This woman's conversion came after the contemporary feminist movement had moved into full swing.

Another three women also grew up in male-centered families, but these women were born during and after World War II. After attempting to be what they called "good girls," that is, marrying and in two cases having children, these women divorced their husbands and became feminists, though not necessarily in that order. In all cases these women, living and changing in the midst of the contemporary feminist movement, appeared no longer able or willing to repress their innermost selves in service to their husbands.

Growing Up between the World Wars. All but one of the eight women who grew up during this period in male-centered families will emerge as antifeminists during the height of the contemporary women's movement in the early 1980s. Bridgit Malone was born shortly after the end of World War I in a Middle Atlantic state. She was raised there by Irish immigrant parents. Her mother died in childbirth when Malone was five years old. Her stepmother also came from Ireland and was educated there. "I don't think high school . . . even in this country people didn't [finish high school].

They got out and went to work." Malone's stepmother, whom she called mother, was "very smart." Before marrying Malone's father, she was a telephone operator and a companion to the wife of a public figure. Malone thinks her father probably finished grade school before he left Ireland at the age of sixteen. When Malone was growing up he was a house painter and a member of a union. Before that he worked on the railroad.

Ella Washburn was born a year after Bridgit Malone in a South Atlantic city and grew up there. Her mother and father had "very little education." Washburn's mother was a housewife "devoted" to her six children. Her father grew up on a farm and farmed before coming to the city to learn how to be a barber. Eventually he became the owner of two barber shops and was "very successful. We enjoyed a good life for a long time." But the depression "took everything we had," and her father turned to drinking for a long period of time. "It's a horrible thing to go through. We were the family on the block [whose] lights were turned off, our water was turned off, everything. . . . There was no money to pay bills, and my father was drinking on top of that."

Audrey Nelms was born a year after Ella Washburn in a city in the East North Central region and grew up there. Nelms's father finished the sixth grade and was a self-employed salesperson and very active in the American Legion. Her mother finished eighth grade and was "a good housekeeper and very fussy about the house." She went to work as a department store salesperson during the depression and finally got involved with the American Legion Auxiliary. Nelms was encouraged to follow her interests in the Girl Scouts and in learning a musical instrument. Her father rented a studio in which she herself could give music lessons. Nelms seems not to have suffered during the depression. Nelms says that her sister, who was seven years younger, "was a depression baby, . . . and I think maybe that shaped her life more than it did mine, because now material things seem to be very important to her while they're not for me."

Lorraine Reilly was born near the end of the 1920s in a city in the East North Central region and grew up there. Her mother finished the eighth grade, and her main involvement was "working and taking care of the family and the house and very little outside activities [except] she used to love to go to baseball games." She died when Reilly was nine years old. Reilly's father finished the sixth grade and worked as a supervisor for a subsidiary of a large utility. After her mother died, Reilly's father did the work of both father and mother, even down to washing and ironing the clothes or later sending them out to be washed and ironing what Reilly was not able to iron.

Lavinia Ravenel was born in the same year as Lorraine Reilly but in vastly different circumstances. She was born in a small town in the South Atlantic region and grew up there. Her father, who took a business course after finishing high school, became a railroad executive. He also "owned lots of property and big farms, and we didn't live on the farm, but we would go to the farm." Her mother finished high school and married Lavinia's father at age sixteen; she devoted herself to the care of her children and husband and was involved in her church and her bridge club. She was a very good cook who prepared picnics for her family when they went to the farm and food for sick neighbors. The family also had a full-time maid.

Dulcie LaFontaine was born a year after Lorraine Reilly and Lavinia Ravenel in a city in the East South Central region and grew up there. Her mother was one of fourteen children born to a French woman whose coal-mining family brought her to the United States as an infant. The family of LaFontaine's grandmother was well-to-do, but by the time LaFontaine's mother was growing up in this same location, the family had fallen on harder times; and LaFontaine's mother had to drop out of high school to go to work. LaFontaine's father was the youngest of eight children, his mother having died in childbirth when he was three years old. He had a hard life with no family support for his getting an education even though he was a "brilliant man," an honor student who also had to drop out of high school to go to work as a bookkeeper. Still he seems to have provided adequately for his family until he became ill, and then LaFontaine's mother went to work as a salesperson in a department store. She worked on commission and "made good money."

Maryanne Thayer was born in the early 1930s in a South Atlantic city and grew up there. Both of her parents had college educations; her father was a minister in a church that served as a community social center, and her mother prided herself on being the minister's wife. "She thought ministers' wives shouldn't work because she felt they should devote their entire time to the husband's occupation." As a child, Thayer was involved in basketball, swimming, tennis, horseback riding, "the usual." She says that she was born during the depression, "and there *was* a lot of poverty as I remember, [but] it didn't affect me *too* much."

Sybyl Jensen was born in the mid 1930s in a small town in the East South Central region. She grew up on the college campus where her father was a professor. Her mother finished high school and was employed before and during her marriage as a secretary, bookkeeper, and finally as head of a public authority that oversaw all the local utilities. Her mother was also involved in her church, civic activities, and several bridge clubs.

Bridgit Malone sets the pattern for male-centered families. Malone characterizes herself as a child growing up as having had a rough time during her preschool years because her mother died in childbirth when Malone's youngest sister was being born. She says her father said he never forgave himself for that. When he remarried, she did not always get along with her stepmother, though she seems to have grown to love her and calls her "mother" throughout the interview. Otherwise, Malone says, she was talkative and friendly; and she still is, she and I laughingly agree.

Her mother nicknamed her "Bridgit Friendly," but it was her father to whom she talked. Her father said he would miss her after she married and left home. Before that, she "would get up in the morning and sit and have breakfast with him and sit and chat and carry on and break my neck getting to the subway to make the train." Her sisters were not like that. In fact, later she learned that they were jealous of her; they thought she was the father's favorite. She describes her father as "very happy-go-lucky, a fun-loving person." It turns out that she learned later that he kept this role for himself by assigning the stepmother the role of disciplinarian: he

was "strict, too, . . . [but] the reason I say my mother gave the orders was because he would tell her, and she'd give the orders. . . .
But he had a terrific sense of humor, . . . and he loved to play jokes
on people . . . and loved to sing and dance and enjoy himself." Malone
respected her stepmother; she perceived her as "exceptionally
smart," and she was a hard worker, cooking and washing and
starching and ironing endless numbers of white midi blouses that
were part of Malone's Catholic school uniforms. But she seemed not
to have received the kind of adoration that Malone accorded her father.

Malone has described a family structure in which the father, or
other chief male figure, moves to center stage as the fun-loving *bon
vivant* while the mother, or other female figure, steps over into the
less likable role of disciplinarian. This is not to say that such mothers are unloved, but it is to say that such fathers seem to play a
greater role in shaping their daughters' identities as male-identified
women. In male-centered families, young girls may learn early to
focus on the man, or more generally men, as the natural center of
women's lives. Male-identified women, in turn, appear to be less
likely to form close bonds with other women in ways that predispose
them to become feminists when the issue arises.

The other seven women in this group generally describe their
families in ways similar to Malone's family. Lavinia Ravenel is particularly exemplary in showing how centering on a loving father of
the family may be generalized to other males in a woman's life.
Ravenel, in remembering her father, goes on to speak of a series of
other revered men in her life: "My daddy was absolutely one of the
finest men that ever lived. Both of my brothers were. I know that
I've got the best husband in the world. He is really a prince of a guy.
And our son is." All of this came in response to the question, "How
would you describe your father when you were growing up?"

Ella Washburn, the only woman in this group to identify herself
as a feminist at the time of our interview, shows how a woman can
change her male-identification to include other women. Her daughter is the one who turned Washburn's attention to the ERA, which

she now adamantly supports. Her daughter had problems getting credit both when she was married, living in a small town and teaching, and after she divorced and returned to her hometown. Her daughter's plight opened Washburn's eyes

> to all the discrimination in the world against women. And I have to admit that I've not always been that way. I can remember making the statement many years ago, when a friend of mine and I were staying at home, taking care of our children, raising a family, doing all the things that a woman "should do." She and I both said, "Well," when the women's movement first started—if you go back and recall when the women's movement first started, we did not get the true picture of what it was all about. All we got was it was a bra-burning thing, and that's the furthest from the truth of all things that the women's movement stands for. . . . And she and I both said, "Oh, gosh. We've just never had it so good." And then as I began to learn what it was all about—and I still, one of my biggest arguments is, "Look, I have a good husband. He's a good provider. He's always been a good provider. We get along beautifully. We have a great relationship. Not every woman in the world has that. I'm lucky." But I'm not going to say I'm not going to get out and fight for another woman to have it. There's too many women in this world who have been left.

Washburn notes something that will conflict with what the other women in this group will say about feminism, that the women's movement was *not* about bra-burning and was *not* anti-men but was pro-woman, pro-rights. Washburn seems especially to identify with older women who have become "displaced homemakers" when their husbands have divorced them, and this identification helps her to discount the untruths about bra-burning that other women believe and abhor.

Audrey Nelms, on the other hand, shows how a woman's male-identification can work against her claiming to be a feminist when she comes into contact with other women who criticize men and men's ways and seem not to accept her for her different experiences and beliefs. Nelms's father supported her in her musical interests when she was growing up. She, being the daughter of an avid American Legionnaire, joined the Waves during World War II, something that was considered unusual for women to do in those days. In general, her father seems to have supported her in doing things that society otherwise would have frowned on young girls' and women's doing. She worked for the Girl Scouts for a time after she was married, and she says that she felt that organization was discriminated against in the distribution of community monies. Moreover, they were "never given credit for the talents and the skills, the management skills that have come out of that organization."

Nelms seemed a candidate for the women's movement when it began to emerge in the 1960s. She favored the reforms in the credit laws.

> But there's something about the women's movement, and I think it might go back to some of my religious values. I have not felt mistreated by my husband or by men in the church. So I can't agree with what they're saying about that. . . . The man *is* the head of the household. But he also has the instructions to treat me just as he would want to be treated himself. . . . At one time I *was* interested in it [the women's movement] while I was with the Girl Scout Council. There were several staff members interested in it. I went to some meetings. And I asked one of the leaders if I accepted the man as head of the house, if I enjoyed being a mother, being a housewife, would I truly be accepted. I feel that her answer was not sufficient, and then I dropped it, and I've never been interested in it since.

The conception of feminism that she brought away from those meetings and from some of the reading she did was that it was about "bra-burning" and "a hatred toward men." Given her positive experiences with her father and later with her husband, in addition to the reinforcement of her religious beliefs about men's place and responsibilities, she was not willing to join a movement that she believed had changed from working for legal reforms to hating men.

Growing Up during and after World War II. Of the three women that grew up in male-centered families in this historical period, two grew up in the South and one grew up outside the South. This group of women is different from the earlier group that grew up in male-centered families: they became feminists. The suggestion is strong that this difference can be traced to the historical period in which they grew up. These women followed a path similar to the eight who preceded them. Then, as did Ella Washburn, when the contemporary women's movement emerged in the late 1960s, these women acted in ways that seemed to respond to an inner self long repressed through the process of becoming male-identified. In the context of the women's movement, they transformed their identities to embrace women—some also maintaining their ties with men—and became feminists.

Kate Greene was born in the early 1940s in a South Atlantic state and grew up there. Her mother finished high school, married, and devoted her time and energies to caring for her family. According to Greene, her mother was a "terrible cook" but she sewed a lot and was very involved in her church. Greene's father finished college and then taught mathematics and engineering for a major utility.

Adrienne Stone was born in the early 1940s in a Middle Atlantic state and grew up there. Her mother finished one year of college, married, and became a homemaker. Her father finished college and took over his family's business. Both of her parents came from affluent families that owned large family businesses, and Stone herself grew up in affluence.

Gretchen Bright was born in the late 1940s in a South Atlantic state and grew up there. Her father dropped out of school after finishing the eighth grade, did military service during World War II, and went into the construction business with his father-in-law. Her mother finished high school and two years of business school. She also was "the first woman in [her state] to get a pilot's license." During her marriage to Bright's father, she held part-time jobs from time to time but otherwise stayed home to take care of her family. The childhood that Bright describes was not easy since both parents became alcoholics, her father in reaction to "some pretty devastating experiences" during the war and her mother as the "enabling co-alcoholic," terminology Bright has learned in doing research into the whole problem of alcoholism in families. She says she has since realized that "at some point my dad started drinking, to compensate from coming back from the war, starting his family, and one thing he always said was that all he wanted was peace and quiet. . . . He wanted a house in the suburbs, he wanted the kids, a carport with the two cars, and he was not so intensely upwardly mobile, but he did have a sense of status that he wanted."

I said earlier that the families of these three women *can* be classified as male-centered. There is no question that the mothers were the disciplinarians, Greene's mother teaching harshly through moral precept, the others not so harshly. But there is a sense in which each of the fathers is flawed. These fathers do not stand out as thoroughly fun-loving types that jollied their families along in the period between the wars. World War II and the postwar period seem to have scarred the men and somehow changed the family dynamic. Stone remembers her father as supportive of her but more supportive of her brother. Greene says that her father was submissive to her strict authoritarian mother. "He spent an awful lot of time in a basement workshop. He built our first TV set and that sort of thing. And that was his escape. He would just come straight home, sit down and have dinner and go straight to the basement and never got very involved with me." Her relationship with him was "standoffish" though it seems she would have liked it to be a closer one. She would go down in the basement and "hang around." But he was not forthcoming. "He never did say much except 'Don't touch that. Leave that alone.' It wasn't much fun down there considering the cold." It is as if Greene yearned for a more fun-loving father, but he was not able to satisfy her yearning. And Bright remembers her father as schizoid: "There were many things that I really loved about him; . . . he had an extremely good sense of humor, . . . he made friends very easily and was gregarious." But there was his other side that was withdrawn and untrustworthy:

> By the time I was six or seven, there was a sense that I couldn't trust him and I couldn't trust his consistency, and that I needed to protect myself from him. Because looking back on it now, I know that there were times of his anger or his withdrawal or his ranting or raving or whatever, that he didn't even remember. And so like as a kid, I would go through experiences with him that were extremely disturbing to me and then the next day he wouldn't even remember. He would act as if nothing had happened, and I began to doubt my experiences.

Later, as a teenager, she would confront him directly and try to get him to stop drinking, but all she got was negative responses.

Perhaps it is not so strange, then, that when the women's movement reemerged, these women were no longer so strongly male-identified—assuming they had been—that they could not assert themselves as feminists. All of them had tried to be the "good girls" their parents seemed to want: they married, and Greene and Stone had children. But all either married and divorced before they became feminists—Greene and Bright—or after they became feminists—Stone. Stone is particularly good at showing how she became feminist in reaction to her parents' trying to shape her life to their expectations:

> I think I had these concerns and I think I always felt misplaced until the women's movement came. I was so thankful to see it. You know, I was from a small town—you had one set of friends. You couldn't go off and find yourself, whatever. And then when they started writing these articles and I read them, I said, "Oh, my goodness, they're out there." It was a relief. . . . I was out of college. I remember it being around when I was in graduate school. It wasn't formed enough for me to say, "This is what women do now, Father and Mother." You know, there was not enough consciousness. But it just didn't come early enough for me.

She says that she and her husband were "the in-between generation." They married and started their family in the period "before and after the birth control pill. And I think that for whatever reason, it was always on my mind. And then when the women's movement came out, I had a place to channel it." What started as inchoate reactions to Stone's parents' directions became fully conscious for her once the movement surfaced.

To summarize, the next major form of family structure to emerge in my study was the urban-based male-centered family, which emerged in the period between the world wars, when feminism was in disrepute. Bridgit Malone set the pattern for this type of family in which a father or father-surrogate took the role of fun-loving worldly man while the mother or mother-surrogate took the role of in-house disciplinarian. Note that the women in these kinds of families took—or, as in Malone's case, were delegated—a distinct role of *some* power: they were recognized as ruling within a narrow space, the household, over a well-defined population, the children. What the women in my study suggest happened in their self-development was that as daughters in such families they learned that they could seek and, before the outbreak of World War II, get almost unconditional love and affection and downright fun from their fathers or father-surrogates. Any misbehavior on the daughter's part would be taken care of by the mother or mother-surrogate. In other words, another woman would do the negative work of disciplining while a man would become the source of positive support and encouragement. Daughters in such families would be inclined to identify as women who expect men to be the positive center of their affective life in contrast to women who would serve as negative forces to be contended with. I have called such daughters male-identified women.

The consequences of such identification were at least two. First, young women learned to seek and expected to get approval and support for their thoughts, feelings, and actions from the men who would populate their lives. In a white-male–centered and –dominated society, during a period when there was no visible mass feminist movement to dispute such arrangements, such women thus learned to abide by the formal and informal rules of that society, rules that are intended to keep women in their various places. Second, such women were not likely to identify with other women in a way that would lead them to join a collective form of political action designed to challenge society's negative treatments of women.

In historical periods when feminist movements emerged as opportunities for advocacy for women, male-identified women would be predisposed to view such movements as challenging the white male system and therefore anti-male and to be shunned. The only women to break out of this pattern besides the older Washburn were the younger women, born during or after World War II. The fathers in these postwar families seemed not as capable as the prewar fathers of giving consistent positive support and encouragement to their daughters, while the mothers in these families did continue the pattern of strict discipline of their daughters. These women attempted to replicate their childhood family structure in their marriage families, but for various reasons the replication failed in the context of a reemergent feminist movement, which these women joined.

Growing Up in Male-Dominated Families during and after World War II

Five women, who were born during or after World War II and grew up in the postwar period, some moving from place to place, in male-dominated families, became feminists during the 1970s and 1980s in response to the reemergence of the contemporary feminist movement. In all of these cases the feminist movement appears to have been a crucible in which problematic relationships with overbearing fathers and passive or rebellious mothers produced a basis for feminist self-transformations from male-identified to female-identified women.

The male-dominated family seems to resonate with the marriage families of predominantly white middle-class suburban housewives described by Betty Friedan in *The Feminine Mystique*. This was a form of family that evolved in the postwar period to serve as receptacle for the women who were at first cajoled and then forced out of paid wartime jobs back into low-paid "women's work" or unpaid housekeeping jobs under the guise of the togetherness of the happy family.[22] What the women in this study suggest is that the "feminine mystique" was a phenomenon fairly specific to a certain historical time and race and economic class, not the universal phenomenon that some early women's movement writings seemed to suggest.[23] This would explain why some women would find a critique of this type of family the source of their liberation, while others, perhaps older white women or women of color, would find this sort of critique foreign to their own lived experiences.[24]

Nancy Harding was born in the early 1940s in a West South Central state. She says she grew up "all over" the state because her father covered politics for a national news magazine, and the family moved around with him during some periods of her childhood. Her father, who had an M.A. in political science, came from a wealthy family long involved in state politics. In contrast, her mother came from a broken family; *her* father had moved around putting up oil rigs and finally became an alcoholic. Harding says her mother had a "rotten life" growing up. Harding's mother finished high school and two years of college and then married Harding's father, thus moving up the economic ladder. She became a homemaker: "Well, actually she was not. Our house was always a mess. She was a super cook, never sewed, did anything. Her whole life was reading. My father finally in defense got a maid."

Hazel Beecroft was born in the mid 1940s in the Pacific Northwest and grew up there. Her father had a college degree in engineering and was a civil engineer.

> And he had a real ability to make lots of money in a short period of time, but he had no ability to go from day to day. So he was always starting a business, making lots of money, going off and doing this and that. He started an international business one time and traveled to Japan and Africa and did this whole thing. And, you know, I don't know whatever happened to him. But he made lots of money. And then there were whole periods of time when he didn't make lots of money. I guess you would characterize him as very eccentric. He had a hard time getting along with people. And as he got older, he just got crazy. So by the time, when my sister had to get married, I mean everything just fell apart, you know, and it was drugs and drinking, violence. . . .

Yet he also took his family to the opera and ballet and theater. "He was intellectually stimulating." Her mother, who graduated from high school and went to business college, was a housewife who went to work as a secretary when Beecroft was in high school, apparently as a way to bring a more stable income into the household.

Fran Daly was born in the late 1940s in the East South Central region but grew up "all over the world" on Army bases in the United States, Japan, and Germany. Her father made his career in the U.S. Army, entering as a draftee just out of high school during World War II, earning a college degree in the Army, and retiring as an officer. Her mother finished high school and became "an Army wife."

Barbara Bergen was born in the early 1950s on an Air Force base on the Pacific Coast. As the child of an Air Force officer, she grew up "all over" before moving to Georgia, where her father retired. She considers the years she spent in Norway—grades one through four and six through ten—to have been very influential on her growing up. Her father, who finished high school and retired as a career officer, was assigned to Norway on NATO tours for both of those periods. Bergen's mother is English, having come from a farm background; she attended the English equivalent of high school and received secretarial training. After marriage, she became a housewife.

Maria Montgomery was born in the mid 1950s in a Central American nation. Her father left her mother when Montgomery was one year old, and her mother took her two daughters back to the United States to live with her parents in a small rural town in a South Atlantic state, where Montgomery grew up. Within a few years, Montgomery's mother remarried. Montgomery's stepfather was an accounts analyst with a high-technology communications firm. Montgomery's mother remained a housewife for a few years and then "rejected" that role. She had been the first child in her own family to get a college education, and she went to work, first teaching typing in a Catholic school and then directing a program in continuing education for women at a local community college.

Nancy Harding sets the pattern for the women who grew up in male-dominated families. As a young girl she says she was "just silly, never had a thought in my empty head. I had, we had a real good childhood, and we grew up, you know, very secure. My parents had a very stable marriage, and my brother and I were close enough to be friends." Polio was a big threat in those days, and until the polio vaccine was developed, Harding says her mother kept her children confined to the house during the middle of the hot days of summer. "No swimming pools. No restaurants. No public places. I guess from about March or April until about October, [it was], you know, bars on the windows type thing." So she read a lot. Weekly trips to the library to get more books were the only public outings allowed. Then in high school and college her interests turned to boys and having a full social life.

Meanwhile, the civil rights movement erupted on the scene, and her father was very involved in covering the movement in the

Southeast. She describes him in heroic terms during this period of her life:

> I was vaguely interested in politics because my parents were liberal Democrats. They were very concerned about civil rights. . . . The Klan in Alabama for a long time had "Wanted" posters, and he was on the face of one of these "Wanted" posters. They had him, in some school in Alabama, holding the hand of this little Black girl walking through this mob of, you know, jeering white people throwing things and shouting obscenities. . . . And when he would go to Birmingham, he couldn't stay in hotels and stuff . . . because I mean literally it was that dangerous for him. And I admired that, obviously.

And so her father enters into her description of herself as a teenager.

Her father also enters into her discussion of her mother. She says that her mother "was rabid about me taking care of myself and being able to support myself." Harding attributes this great concern to her mother's mother having been left by *her* husband and having to take care of herself. But Harding's mother could not take care of herself when Harding's father died. Fortunately for her, he left her well off economically, but emotionally she was not prepared. "My mother has been nothing since then. Her whole life was him, and he did everything and he managed everything. . . . My father was fairly chauvinistic toward my mother, and they had a very traditional marriage. He would have had a fit if she wanted to work. . . . But he wasn't that way toward me."

Harding describes her mother as "passive" in her "life-style" and "in terms of relating to my father." But "in her views and so forth she's not at all passive." Politically, Harding says her mother was very liberal, and as we shall hear in a moment, the entire family— father, mother, daughter, son—engaged in raucous political discussions. But in relation to her husband, "she thought he was just it; the whole universe revolved around my father." In describing her relationship with her mother, Harding almost immediately begins to talk of her father: "We were pretty good friends. But my father—I mean, I had a healthy fear of my father in the sense of discipline. My mother was just kind of a joke. My father made us behave. He was the stern and the tough. And I just kind of ran over her, really.

I didn't take her very seriously, I guess." Harding seems to have modeled her behavior toward her mother on her father's behavior toward his wife.

Harding describes her father in the same adoring terms we heard from her earlier:

> The most self-confident person I've ever known. Very sure of himself. Any group he took over—if there were fifty people, my father, I mean without seemingly putting forth any effort, would then become the center. Everybody liked him. He had ten thousand stories to tell. He was very vocal, good with words. He really was a born politician. . . . I admired him tremendously. And everybody did. He was in command of everything. An amazing person.

But her relationship with him was not all fun. He was also the disciplinarian, and "we battled constantly; . . . both of us were very strong willed. And I would do things, now I don't know why. If I was going on a date, I had to be home by eleven. I'd go out of my way to get home by twelve just because he told me eleven." They also would argue about ideas.

> When I was a kid growing up, it was more about what I could do. Later on, when I was older, high school and college, and I started becoming interested in ideas, we clashed constantly over ideas. And at the dinner table, my mother was that way. . . . Dinner was all four of us shouting and battling over whatever, Vietnam, whatever the issues were. And we all, I mean, nobody took offense at it. It was just the way it was.

She tells of how the family would often divide over issues: it became she and her father against her brother and her mother. "My mother and my brother are the tender-hearted, and my father and I were more realistic. You know, they'd get real upset over somebody getting their feelings hurt or something. And we were more callous about it. Later in life it evolved into the two of us against the two of them." In other words, family disagreements over political issues were expected, and much of the fun of the relationship came in debating the issues. But there was no debating the structure of the family unit. The father loomed large in domination over his wife and children, and this domination was made palatable by his heroic stature and his ability to become the center of life at home or at social gatherings.

The path from dominant male hero's daughter to feminist is by no means direct. Some of these daughters have passed through way-station marriages in which husbands take the place of dominant fathers while the daughters also attempt to play their mothers' perceived roles of submissive wife. Harding is most explicit about this process because of what she has learned in therapy:

> I had my marriage structured the way my mother and father did, except for my working, and I role-played my mother. And they had a tremendously successful marriage. And I thought that would work for me, for my whole life. I used to buy this Cinderella stuff about, you know, one man could, you know, my Prince Charming, and here he is sitting eating dinner. He's made for me and all that shit. Well, we had a lot of problems in our marriage, and I found myself isolated. I hadn't bothered to make friends, and it went on for years. And I might as well tell you we're separated right now. But I discovered women. I mean I needed people. I went in therapy. And since then I've started discovering women friends, and I'll never be isolated like that again. And one of our contentions in our marriage now is that I won't devote myself to him. You know, I won't. Somehow I got into a dependent role, and that will never happen to me again. Never in my life, not until the day I die. I have to be my own person, and it's going to cost me my marriage, I guess, to be my own person, but I don't have any choice. I have to find out what's me and how to take care of myself.

Ironically, Harding's mother's stress on Harding's taking care of herself has finally emerged to take priority over the other strong message Harding received from her mother and her father as to the "proper" way to structure a marriage. Harding's self has broken through and joined forces with women friends so that never again will she let herself be cast in a dependent role.

The other women in this group are a bit different. Leftist feminists Hazel Beecroft and Maria Montgomery have the examples of previously "steady" mothers who have asserted themselves by rejecting the role of traditional housewife in response to dominating husbands and have entered paid employment. For both Beecroft and Montgomery, radical leftist politics have preceded their feminist politics, and they have married men likewise involved in radical leftist politics. Beecroft has married a man less heroic but also steadier than her father, a husband who seems to have grown with her over the years. Montgomery, after one failed marriage, likewise has married a man who has been willing to share household and child-care responsibilities. Fran Daly and Barbara Bergen, on the other hand, have never married, though Daly did have some boyfriends, and both came out as Lesbians in the course of becoming feminists. By the time all of these women were making their turns toward feminism of some kind, the women's movement was well under way in all its various modes. And these women apparently began their turns in reaction to ambivalent rather than consistent signals they were receiving from all-powerful men whom they both admired and feared.

To summarize, the third major form of family structure that emerged in this study was the postwar urban-based male-dominated family. Nancy Harding set the pattern for this form in which a father or father-surrogate took both disciplinarian and *bon vivant* roles while a mother or mother-surrogate took a passive submissive stance in relation to the man of the house. Note that in this form of family structure, the father became the dominant affective center of the family, dispensing both positive support for and negative restrictions on the daughter, while the mother faded into a dependent service role. This type of family structure appeared to transmit numerous conflicting signals to daughters who received no consistent basis for what apparently became a tension-filled male-identified womanhood. In the background loomed the specter of what the daughter as woman would be expected to become—a subservient wife and mother modelled on her own mother. In the foreground loomed the almost bigger-than-life father, the Hero, her mother's Prince Charming, from whom the daughter learned she could expect to receive support and encouragement and a good time. But it seemed that this "love" was conditional. Father was also to be feared because he disciplined, and when he disciplined, it seemed that his love and support might be withdrawn.

Surely a mixture of contradictory signals and behaviors would affect young women's self-development, perhaps by leading them to construct a bifurcated persona in which interior thoughts and feelings would not necessarily be reflected in external actions. In historical periods in which feminist movements break out to criticize a society that privileges white men over all others, women experiencing such bifurcated selves might become tortured by the recognition that they have been subjected to male domination and that such male domination is wrong in a society that gives what must be only lip service to the notions of liberty and equality for all. But such women might also become hopeful that they can grasp the opportunities feminist movements provide for women to throw off the shackles on their external behaviors and bring their actions into congruence with their until-now repressed inner thoughts and feelings. For such women, "the personal" indeed becomes "the political." We shall meet such women again in chapters 6 and 7.

Some Further Thoughts on the Role of "the Family" in Self-Development

In light of what we have heard from the white women in this study about how different family forms developed in different historical periods and in different geographical—that is, rural or urban—settings, we must ask if assigning mothers primary responsibility for infant and child care, what might be called "primary mothering," necessarily always reproduces gender. Either it does not; that is, primary mothering took place in all the families described by the women in this study, but not all these daughters grew up to support the notion that women should make men the center of their lives; or it does, but the effects of primary mothering are overridden in some cases by subsequent influences. The women in this study suggest that there is more than one form of affective structure in nuclear families. Further, they suggest that the affective structure of the family, which in turn appears to be influenced by both historical period and rural or urban base, can have an effect on whether daughters later accept "traditional" feminine belief patterns or grow up as or become "feminists" who reject such genderization.

What we cannot know from my study, because these women cannot report from memory how their mothers related to them in infancy, is whether these differences were initiated in infancy or developed after that period. If the differences were initiated in the period of infancy, and if primary mothering was a common occurrence for all the women in the study, then the suggestion would be strong that primary mothering itself may take different forms in different historical periods and may differ in rural and urban settings. Certainly more research is called for to address such possibilities.

Whatever the case for primary mothering in the period of infancy and very early childhood, women's growth and development do not stop there. And women's growth and development within the family, whatever its form, surely must not go unaffected by the structure of the larger society of which the family is only a part. What the women in my study suggest is that the affective structure within the family can mirror women's and men's relative statuses in society during particular historical periods in rural or urban settings and thus can affect daughters' subsequent self-development. I have already suggested that different forms of family, having developed in relation to specified historical periods and economic sectoral changes, may have influenced these women as daughters to become female-identified or male-identified and, depending on the occurrence of feminist movement within a historical period, to become feminist or antifeminist in their political tendencies.

A major implication that the feminist object-relations theorists draw from their explication of Freudian psychosexual development is that parenting within the family should be restructured so that fathers or father-surrogates share infant care with mothers in order that daughters and sons can experience both women and men as powerful loving figures from the very beginnings of their social relations as newborns. But will such fathering within a reconstructed family setting make any more difference than primary mothering in daughters' and sons' gender development if the larger society continues to be gender-differentiated, placing more "value," however defined, on men's lives than on women's lives?

During the 1980s, as the U.S. economy has continued to develop, now placing more emphasis than ever on service and management occupations, women of all ages, races, and economic classes have begun to perform waged or salaried work in the labor force in addition to unpaid housework. Women have again become recognized as key "breadwinners" either as single mothers or as equal married partners in the household, and some men have begun to perform their equal share of housework. The time may be closer upon us when women will also be recognized as valuable productive members of the labor force, equally so with men, but that recognition will not come as long as the paid workplace remains race/gender discriminatory and segregated and as long as housework also remains women's primary responsibility.

What do such developments portend for the affective structures of families today? How will such structures affect girls' and women's, and boys' and men's, race/gender identities and political inclinations? Only future research can answer these questions, but the theoretical proposition to examine must be that women's and men's psychosexual development within the family household is affected not only by how mothers and fathers treat children but also by how mothers reflect women and how fathers reflect men in the larger society. The quality of those reflections will depend on the relative statuses and powers of women and men in society.

Chapter 4

Understandings of "Being a Woman" Shape "Politics of Identity"

For women, engaging in the world as a political activist must necessarily emerge out of engaging in that world as a woman. I say "necessarily" because the dominant political culture in the United States historically has differentiated "being a woman" from "becoming political." Thus, under complex domination, *any* woman who has "become political," whatever her race or economic class or sexuality, has had to negotiate two sex/gender barriers: one to consciousness that she herself can act politically and the other to recognition by others that she can act and does act politically.

How a woman negotiates these sex/gender barriers to political consciousness and political engagement is further affected by her social location in "complex domination." From this perspective, she must also negotiate barriers that include, in addition to sex/gender, her race if she is not white, her economic class if she is not upper or middle class, and her sexuality if she is not heterosexual. These barriers may be perceived as singular or as intertwined. Thus, for example, a female person who identifies herself and is identified by others explicitly as a "woman" but not also explicitly as "white, heterosexual, and middle class," might proclaim sex discrimination as "the" obstacle for her and all other women to overcome. In contrast, a female person who identifies herself explicitly as a "poor Black woman" may perceive the barriers to her very existence to occur at "the intersection of race, sex, and class." She may proclaim that, for her and for women like her, the struggle must proceed simultaneously on several fronts—not only against sexism, but also against racism and perhaps even against capitalism.[1]

Any movement to eradicate one or all of these barriers to women's political engagement must also address these same barriers as they divide women from one another. This is not to say that differences among women should be dismissed. It is to say, following Audre Lorde, that the various privileges and oppressions that the dominant culture has used to differentiate women must be recognized and somehow transformed into sources of empowering diversity among women.[2] Thus, for example, in order to enter into political alliances with women different from her in terms of race or economic class or sexuality, a white middle-class heterosexual woman, similar to some in this study, would have to enter into a "politics of identity" through which she might come to understand how her privileges are linked with other women's oppressions. She might come to understand that (1) sex discrimination has abridged her individual rights at the same time that (2) racial, sexual, and class privileges, even if now recognized by her personally, have complicated any attempts she might make to forge political coalitions with Lesbians of any race or class, heterosexual women of color of any class, and white heterosexual working-class women, (3) all of whom are subject to oppressions not only because of their sex but also because of their race and/or class and/or sexuality.

In other words, women, who may be characterized by different combinations of race, class, and sexuality, would be expected as women both to understand themselves in different ways and to perceive that others treat them in different ways. Thus, the ways that the female activists in this study understand themselves as white women and perceive that others treat them as white women should have some effect on how they understand "feminism" and "the political" and thus the form of political engagement they have chosen to undertake. Hence my focus in this chapter on how these white activist women think and feel about "being a woman." Empirically their skin color and sex allow them to be placed into categories known in the dominant culture as "white" and "female," but these physical similarities do not translate into conceptual sameness. Different meanings of "being a woman" emerge not only out of their different interpretations of their own experiences but also out of their different interpretations of others' behaviors toward them.

Thus I asked the women about the *meanings* to them of "being a woman" and "being feminine." I also asked if they had *experienced* negative and positive treatments on account of their race and sex. Some of the women themselves brought in the additional dimensions of age, class, and sexuality as they responded to all these questions about "being a woman."

Sandra Lee Bartky's phenomenology of feminist consciousness[3] provides a way into analyzing "being a woman" and how different understandings of "being a woman" ground different forms of feminism and antifeminism, the subject of the next chapter. Midway into Bartky's analysis it becomes apparent, when she introduces the concept of privilege, that by "women" she must mean white middle- and upper-class heterosexual women, and in my presentation here I make explicit the implications of her very suggestive analysis for the intersection of gender, race, class, and sexuality in the lives of white women. In effect, Bartky's analysis implicitly assumes the existence of "complex domination." For Bartky, feminist consciousness is both process and content; that is, the process of consciousness-raising is part of the outcome that becomes the content of consciousness. Thus, a key aspect of feminist consciousness is the capacity for consciousness-raising. Bartky identifies three positively interactive elements of the *process* of consciousness-raising and two sets of contradictory elements of the *content* of feminist consciousness.

The process of consciousness-raising involves multiple moments, which, I would suggest, do not necessarily occur in a linear order. The moments are: becoming aware of conflicts or contradictions in one's existence in the everyday world, recognizing possibilities for changing oneself and the world in ways that resolve the contradictions, and having visions of what ought to be as those possibilities are actualized. The content of feminist consciousness is multi-layered, dynamic, and interactive. In the context of "complex domination," for white middle-class women it involves, when fully emergent, a dual consciousness of double contradictions.

One contradiction turns on a positive tilt: at one and the same time, such women become aware that, cast as "victims" in the dominant social reality, they are placed in a weak position vis-à-vis white middle-class men. Marilyn Frye's analysis of Lesbian existence[4] suggests that those the dominant culture terms "homosexual" women may experience themselves cast furthermore as nonexistent, though they may also wish to remain invisible for reasons of self-preservation. But when these women, heterosexual or homosexual, become aware that this dominant social reality is deceptive, that they in actuality do not have to accept such definitions of weakness or nonexistence, this recognition releases energy to throw off these definitions. Heterosexual women who reach this level of consciousness transform "weakness" into strength. Homosexual women transform "nonexistence" or invisibility into strength by "coming out" as Lesbians. From such transformations comes the strength to struggle against the systemic oppression of what has become recognized as *deceptive* dominant social reality.

The other contradiction turns on a negative tilt: at one and the same time, heterosexual or homosexual white women cast as weak or nonexistent players vis-à-vis white men may become increasingly aware that they nevertheless are race-privileged vis-à-vis women and men of color, regardless of class and sexuality, and class-advantaged vis-à-vis white women and men of classes below the middle class, regardless of sexuality. Heterosexual women may also become aware that they are privileged vis-à-vis homosexual women of the same race and class. Awareness of privileges of whatever kind in the face of sexual victimization produces "confusion, guilt, and paralysis in the political sphere."[5] How can one be victimized while privileged or vice versa? This is the double bind for white women under "complex domination." What if one does not want to give up those privileges? What if challenging oppression in terms of sex results in losing privileges conferred with race and/or class and/or sexuality? This double bind is different from the double bind that women of color face. For them, experiencing multiple oppressions can *prevent* a clouding of the issue of oppression. The problems come rather, as the Combahee River Collective notes, in doing something about the oppressions without access to the resources that go with privilege. The phenomenon of "guilty victim," therefore, renders the process of emerging into feminist consciousness different for white women in comparison to women of color.

The women I interviewed express a myriad of ideas and feelings about "being a woman." And yet there do appear to be underlying patterns, similar to what Bartky has described, that distinguish different forms of consciousness of "being a woman." At one end of what seems to begin as a spectrum, or perhaps a single-ply thread, is a woman who calls herself a "lady"; she values her privilege and denies any form of victimization or guilt because of that privilege. At the other end of what becomes a multi-ply thread is the "white woman in America" who says that, in spite of "the patriarchy's" devaluation of women, she is coming into her own powers as a woman through her interconnection with all living things. On the way from privileged "ladyship" to "empowered womanhood" can be found among the women in this study five distinguishable forms of consciousness of womanhood: (a) positive-only expressions of enjoying "being a woman," "woman" being one who is a "lady," a good wife and mother; (b) positive-only expressions of enjoying "being a woman," "woman" being one who is both a good wife and mother as well as a good businesswoman or politician—enjoying the "best of both worlds"; (c) positive-only expressions of enjoying "being me" or "being a total human being"; (d) consciousness of unresolved contradictions between various positive and negative aspects of "being a woman"; and (e) consciousness of living in "two worlds" in conflict and of engaging in ongoing struggles for women's integrated lives. Interestingly, none of these women expressed negative-only conceptions of "being a woman."

If there are underlying patterns that distinguish different understandings of "being a woman," some are more clear-cut than others. The most distinct clusters of women are those who call themselves "Ladies" or "Ladies with Best of Both Worlds" or "Women/Persons" or "Women Made, Not Born." All of these women seem to be most "at home" in electoral politics. Then come other women in electoral or movement politics who seem to be engaged in unique standpoints from which they are collectively struggling to transform their political worlds. I have called these "Women Spinning—Women Together, Threads, Networks." Listen now to the women as they respond to the questions about "being a woman," "being feminine," and receiving negative or positive treatments on account of their sex/gender and color/race.

"Ladies"

Three women—Lavinia Ravenel, Linda Helms, and Bridgit Malone—expound upon the joys of womanhood. They seem never to have experienced any problems *as women*. In fact, Ravenel and Helms attribute their positive experiences as women to the privileges of ladyship. Malone simply has never seen "being a woman" as an issue. Both Ravenel and Malone seem affronted by the questions and the very thought of my making an issue of "being a woman."

Ravenel is particularly emphatic in denying that she has been a victimized woman: "I think it's the best position in the world to be in. And I have never, ever, ever felt like I was discriminated against because I was a lady. . . . I wouldn't change places with anybody." To her, "being feminine" means "conducting yourself in a manner that people would respect you as a lady." I ask if that is important to her; she replies:

> Very, very, very. . . . I like for people to open the door for me. I like for people to be polite to me. And I want to be polite to others. And I have known young girls that the men would start to open the door, and they'd jerk the door open. They didn't want to be helped. I want to be helped. I like for the fellows to help me. I like for [my husband] and [son] to open the door and help me in the car. And I like for them to push the door open when I get to the place.

Helms and Malone continue in this vein, additionally celebrating women's "special role," as Helms calls it, in the family. Helms says she "would not be a man" if she had a choice, and she has "never wanted to be a business woman, a career woman." Malone says, "I've enjoyed being a mother, enjoy being a wife. I've enjoyed my children. As far as just being a woman per se, I have never felt that [it's] that important one way or the other. I guess I got across what I mean, right?"

Neither Ravenel nor Malone say more than a short "no" to each question about negative or positive treatment on account of sex and race, though Malone does seem to get a glimmer of how others *have* made her sex an issue when she realizes she has received positive treatment as a woman. She says, "No. [*pause*] The only time I can think of is when they elected me as first vice-chair of [a county organization] because they thought that it was about time they had a woman. Okay? Now that could be, right? Because that was mentioned, you know?"

But Helms's responses to the questions about positive and negative treatments on account of sex and race are more explanatory of how "Ladies" may respond to such treatments. If she has been confronted with contradictory experiences concerning her capabilities and society's deceptions about those capabilities, she has consciously lowered her consciousness in response to those contradictions. Concerning whether she has received negative treatment on account of sex, she says: "I don't think so because I never attempted to do anything that wasn't open to me. . . . I have been put down as a Republican. . . . But I can't remember ever having been put down because I was a woman. If I have, I've forgotten it." Concerning negative, and including positive, treatment on account of her race, she says, "Well, just being in the majority race and being white, I don't think I've ever been put down because of that. However, I think we're seeing much reverse discrimination, . . . not just Blacks but a lot of minorities were given special preferential treatment because they were minorities." But positive, special treatment on account of sex is another thing: "Yes. I think women have special privileges because they are women. And I think gentlemen treat ladies with special deference because they are ladies. And I like that. I like to have a car door opened for me, a door opened for me because I'm a woman." I ask about simple courtesies. She replies, "I think women receive many courtesies because they are women, but I would not receive them if I didn't act like a woman." Helms's understanding of "being a woman" suggests that "ladyship" is highly privileged but narrowly limited and rightly so. She implies that, if one pushes beyond the limits set on women, one will quickly lose the narrow but high place reserved for ladyship.

"Being a woman" and "being feminine" are virtually synonymous for the "Ladies." Both concepts mean not simply "being" but *acting out* a "special role." Helms makes the connection that "good" behavior begets "good" treatment in return. If women act like ladies, in a feminine manner, then men respond gallantly by acting as gentlemen, especially opening doors for ladies.[6] But even among the "Ladies" there is a slight gradation of consciousness of privilege and possible victimization. Ravenel, somewhat defensively, refuses to discuss any possible negative or positive treatments related to her race or sex. Malone, more matter-of-fact than defensive, says "no" to the questions but shows a glimmer of recognition that she was picked for a leadership position because of her sex. Helms is also matter-of-fact in her responses, but unlike the other two she answers at length. Her responses have the effect of explaining how all these "Ladies" maintain their identities: they do not push beyond society's boundaries for women. They "forget" any "put downs" they *do* receive as women. They appear to accept without questioning, in fact to expect, their privileged "majority" racial status.

"Ladies with Best of Both Worlds"

The next three women—Lorraine Reilly, Bess Shumaker, and Sybyl Jensen—enjoy, as do the "Ladies," the role of mother or wife. At the same time, unlike the "Ladies," they seem to pride themselves on being able and wanting to play roles they understand to belong to men, from playing sports to running businesses to wielding political power in a political party or in state government. To capture their enjoyment of double role sets, I have named them "Ladies with Best of Both Worlds."

Bess Shumaker and Sybyl Jensen are both exuberant in proclaiming their enjoyment of "being a woman." Jensen breaks into her version of a show tune in response to the question: " 'I like being a girl.' I really do. . . . I like being taken care of. Yet, I like to be independent. There are a lot of times when I [say] 'Please, I'd rather do it myself.' But I just never had any problem being a woman. I can't conceive anything else. I mean I like it. I like being feminine." "Being feminine" is simply another aspect of "being a woman," "doing all the mother and wife and female-type things, yet still having enough tensile strength to get out into what used to be conceived as the man's world and accomplish some things that way too." Shumaker adds, "Basically I guess it means that really I got the best of both worlds. I mean, I run my own business, I'm in politics, [I've] been married to my husband for twenty-five years and he still opens car doors for me. I've got it *all*. Of course, I'm a fortunate woman. I'm very aware of that." Reilly refers to women in athletics in explaining the meaning of "being feminine," which has to do with being heterosexual, not with being athletic: "Somebody not feminine, well, I don't know. You see women in sports, but if they're women, they're still feminine. I mean, the only thing is if someone is not feminine, I would say they're queer."

None of these women say they have received positive treatment on account of their race, though Shumaker gives a hypothetical response: "If I were in a situation and I felt that I was here and a Black lady was here and if I felt that I was getting special consideration because I was white, I would object to it. That's rudeness." None of these women say they have received negative treatment on account of their race; and interestingly, they interpret the question to mean negative treatment of whites by Blacks. Reilly, for example, says, "I've gone to Black Caucus luncheons, and they treat you just as if you're one of them, really. . . . Race has never been really an issue with me." In other words, they do not exhibit consciousness of the privilege that society has conferred on them by virtue of their whiteness.

But, having ventured into "politics as a man's world," they are aware of having received both negative and positive treatments on account of their sex. All three tell stories of negative treatment by men in their political parties or in the legislature, though they say that is mostly in the past. Reilly says, "Well, I tell you some of the things you face are some of these men don't think women should be in charge in things, that they're scatterbrained or they can't do this. . . . Sometimes I'll get angry with my husband, and I tell him,

'You ought to be happy that I'm not pushing for ERA, or boy, you'd really be in trouble in this house.' " She goes on to say, "But I guess the women in between all of us have showed them, so there isn't any more [problem]." Shumaker tells of having gotten her friend, Jane, elected as district "chairman" in her party by engaging in "a tremendous power struggle" with the men and not backing down. But Shumaker believes such "male chauvinism," as she calls it, is "inbred" and not really men's fault. "It's been going on for centuries, you know." By the same token, she believes women's charm is a natural endowment. Jensen illustrates how these women use positive treatment on account of their sex to advantage. She says, "I think that I have gotten special treatment on account of my sex more often than I have the other way around, and I've enjoyed that. I just sort of eat it up with a spoon. . . . I've gotten favoritism because of my sex because they perceive me as being a lady and they enjoy helping me because of that. And they have been very helpful." As an example, she tells about male legislators who changed their behavior when she began attending committee meetings as a new legislator. They chewed tobacco, but they started leaving the room when they had to spit.

For the "Ladies with Best of Both Worlds," the identity that includes a union between "being a woman" and "being feminine" has expanded to include a third term, being "like men" in certain ways. Reilly, Shumaker, and Jensen all suggest that women can do all the "female-type things" as well as what men can do. They celebrate their ability to live in two worlds—of dependence and of independence, in effect to be both "feminine" and "masculine." Femininity, therefore, is no constraint on behavior. Rather, it allows "ladies" to enjoy the "best of both worlds"—meaning men's as well as women's worlds.

Having expanded their horizons to include "the men's world," these women acknowledge having encountered negative in addition to positive treatments on account of their sex. But they see that as no contradiction because that is what such women know to expect. If they cannot change some men's hearts, they can at least stand such men down "man to man." Shumaker and Jensen also enjoy gentlemanly behavior toward them, and use their femininity to advantage if need be. Just as to them their sex is not an issue—they as "strong" women have taken care of that—so to them others' race should not be an issue. In so claiming, they fail to acknowledge that historically the dominant culture has conferred privileges on whites and degradation on Blacks. And a contradiction remains buried: in accepting the special treatments that go with ladyship, these women undercut their notion of individual merit regardless of gender *or* race.

"Women Persons"

The next five women echo various ideas put forward by the "Ladies" and the "Ladies with Best of Both Worlds," but three new ideas enter the picture to distinguish this larger cluster of women. They believe that times have changed; they emphasize their individual personhood over their womanhood; but some also suggest that in certain ways women may be better than men. Some emphasize their personhood by saying that being a woman means being "me" or being a "total human being." Others imply their personhood by denying differences between men and women, though they also attribute special advantages to women in politics. Still others refuse to give in to any limitations they believe belong to the female sex.

Arlene Pringle and Betty Mason first sound the theme of "times have changed." Pringle says, "Isn't that ridiculous? I've never even thought about that. I've been a woman so long, I don't know. I've seen a lot of changes, of course, in attitudes, and not so much [that] women are more capable now. It's just that they probably are more visible. . . . I think there are more opportunities." But Pringle also echoes the claim of the "Ladies" that "being a woman" is related to family, not politics, when she says, "I enjoy being a woman. I don't know. It certainly has nothing to do with politics. It's family, I suppose. Yes, family and community and I like the things I do." Mason, on the other hand, echoes the "Ladies with Best of Both Worlds" when she says, "I think there's nothing as a woman I could want to do that I could not do. And yet, by the same token, and being in business, being in politics, I still like being female. I enjoy the distinction between male and female. I still like the doors opened and my cigarette lighted, the amenities that are shown." Then comes the theme that women are better than men in some ways. Pringle doesn't think she "would want to do some of the things that the men do. Maybe I can do better than they can when it doesn't take strength." "Being feminine" is a negative for all these women, whether it is lacking physical stamina or being "flighty" or a "clinging vine." Rather, whether "being a woman" or "being feminine," the important thing is to be, as Mason says, "a total human being, a caring person, keeping good values. Being a woman, I still feel that I am not intimidated by a man, men. I don't feel that I need ERA to make people [treat me as a person]."

Dulcie LaFontaine, rather than defining "being a woman" as being a non–gender-specified "person," refers to typically gender-contrasted qualities that she says are admirable in women as well as in men. She also hints that this is a result of times having changed:

> Well, it means someone having strength and caring, which to me are also admirable qualities of men. I heard an adage one time that in every man, every good man, there's a woman. In every good woman there are little qualities of man. And I do feel that way. And I don't consider a woman as somebody real flighty and feminine. To me a woman is someone who is very caring but very strong and very honest. Hardworking with determination and aggressiveness. It's kind of difficult for me to differentiate qualities of men and women because I think in today's world they're very similar. It's a very hard question.

LaFontaine embeds her ideas about "being feminine" in her ideas about "being a woman." Her previous answer indicates that "being feminine" is being flighty, which she perceives as negative and in no way setting boundaries on her definition of being a woman.

Elizabeth Latimer, like LaFontaine, defines "being a woman" in terms that explicitly do not distinguish women from men when she says, "I don't really isolate a lot of problems as being just problems that men solve and problems that women solve. It seems like we have a lot of mutual problems, and we can't just leave it to the men to solve all the weighty issues." At the same time, she does suggest that women are superior to men in some things: "I don't think [women] have as much of an ego involved in it as men in office. I think that if you can generalize, women are more courageous in the sense of really having the courage to be the person you have to be in the situation that you're in. I've seen men lack courage because of the good old boy peer group."

In their individuality these women vary in their responses to the questions on sex and race discrimination. Two seem to believe there no longer are problems, if there ever were. Pringle, for example, answers an incredulous "no" to each question. In this she also echoes the "Ladies," but her meaning differs in that those who are "somebody" believe that they encounter neither discriminating nor privileging treatment; they simply are who they are. Sex and race do not become issues for "persons." Two others recognize one or another aspect of sex discrimination. Latimer says that she personally has not experienced sex discrimination but that women in the legislature do receive negative treatment on account of their sex: "We should have had a woman committee chairman by now. And they don't hold any key jobs on that, so women have been [treated negatively]. As long as you will play the game of being a lady and being liked and don't challenge them too much, then I think sex discrimination will come into play sometimes." It is as if she is chiding the "Ladies with Best of Both Worlds" for playing into the hands of the "gentlemen" by not being aware of what their behavior does for the status of women specifically in the legislature and generally in the society at large. LaFontaine also acknowledges the possibility of racial privilege when she says, "I've never really thought about it. I'm sure that happens in our society. It probably happens to you and to me. But I've never been aware of any situation in which I was given preferential treatment because I was white."

Only Maryanne Thayer responds "yes" on all parts of the question. She says that she has experienced sexism in her political party work: the women stuff envelopes while the men are chairmen or, like her husband, "would be invited to the cocktail party downtown for the fundraiser, because he was the wage earner in the family." Positive treatment on account of sex she remembers vaguely as letting girls go first in lines at school. Concerning negative treatment on account of her race, she has come to understand that as being an outsider in situations where Black people outnumber white people: "I would have problems if I went back to teaching in the city of Atlanta. And I might have felt at times when I was talking with nurses at the nursing home, most of them are Black, I've noticed maybe that I was not part of them or something like that. That's the only negative thing." She also has been aware of positive or special treatment on account of her race. Not now, but when she was growing up, "I was treated better. You know, if I were in a store or something, they would, the salespeople would wait on me before they would the Blacks." She appears not to have made the connection that her racial privilege contributes to her "outsider" status with the Black teachers and nurses.

The idea that draws this cluster of women together is their understanding of "being feminine." All these women characterize femininity as a negative constraint on being the human being or person that they are; all reject femininity as such a limit on their behavior. In breaking the union between femininity and woman/personhood, these women have passed through the first set of Bartky's contradictions. They have unmasked the victimization of femininity and have emerged as strong "Women Persons."

But the consciousness-raising process stops here. Except for Maryanne Thayer, they have re-centered their identities as "persons" or "human beings," thus giving themselves more freedom as individuals to move within and between the private and public spheres of family life and electoral politics. Some do acknowledge special treatment on account of their race. But because they have emerged as strong "Women Persons," apparently before encountering the other contradiction of racially privileged "guilty victim," their new identity has foreclosed any consciousness-raising about "being a (white) woman." Maryanne Thayer, on the other hand, even though she has become conscious of the negatives of various aspects of sex and race discrimination, has not integrated this awareness with her understanding of being a woman, which is presently positive because "times have changed."

"Women Made, Not Born"

Five women introduce the negative aspects of "being a woman" that they understand to be continuing in their present lives in the United States. It is as if these women take us "through the looking glass" to reflect a version of society in direct contrast to the version, reflected by the "Women Persons," of changing times that have resulted in the individualization and humanization of women. These "Women Made, Not Born," recognize that the negative aspects of "being a woman" still exist alongside some positive aspects. They live in a constant state of contradiction, which they understand to be caused by social expectations that conflict with their own needs and aspirations.

Ella Washburn echoes the positive aspects of womanhood introduced by the "Ladies with Best of Both Worlds" and "Women Persons" before bringing in the negative aspects. She begins with a celebration of motherhood: "Oh, it means a great deal. I have no qualms about being a woman, I guess first and foremost because I harp about how great it is to be a parent. It gave me the opportunity to be a mother, and, of course, by virtue of being a mother, I [was able to] become a grandmother." Then she brings in the negative side: "That's a hard question. It means that I have a little harder time because I am a woman, both in my job, probably, and in my everyday life." "Being feminine," for Washburn, is being dependent on men and something negative that she rejects.

The other four women in this group emphasize the negatives from the very beginnings of their responses. Laconic Edith Hammond, for example, goes straight to the point on "being a woman." It means "inequality. I think that's the major thing. I don't think women have ever been recognized for their ability." For Hammond "being feminine" is relative, and here she has more to say. "What may be feminine to me may not necessarily be feminine to someone else. . . . I think when you're brought up in the southern tradition, being feminine, you were taught that the southern belle was feminine. But being feminine to me is just being yourself. If you're a woman, you can't help but be feminine because that's what you are, a female."

Adrienne Stone, in contrast, gives a long contextual analysis of what "being a woman" means for her, saying, "Well, I think about it a lot. But it depends on which context." She begins with the negatives: "Right now I'm in the process of getting a divorce. It means shit . . . injustice. . . . I feel victimized . . . devalued." She then echoes the "Women Persons," adding the time dimension and waxing eloquent on the positives of being a woman:

> Being a woman is definitely much better today than it was twenty years ago. And, you know, I'm very thankful that it changed, that there was a women's movement, that my kids have the opportunity to grow up in a different environment. . . . I think it's much more exciting to be a woman and I'm thankful that it's OK to be a woman over thirty, that we have something to offer. . . . But I think that even though I am feeling victimized and devalued and all these things, I still also feel that women are definitely coming into their own. I mean it's exciting. . . . I think that women are becoming real people for the first time in our society, and I hope it stays.

She believes, however, that times can change for the worse in the future: "I worry when I see the right-wing movement and I see the attacks that I've had and I see Phyllis Schlafly and I see Jerry Falwell. I worry a lot about that, as a matter of fact, that what we are taking for granted is not going to stay. When I talk to people, that is my message. We cannot assume that the progress we have made is here to stay. We must continue to fight for it."

"Being feminine" is as complex for Stone as is "being a woman." She says she has been struggling with the feeling that her marriage is failing because she has not been feminine enough while at the same time she has been wondering if she is competent enough to run again for office.

> I think that I may be going through some feelings that competence is masculine, you know, that I have probably internalized more than I consciously believe, that my competence and my assertiveness and my feminism [are] masculine, and that I am in the process of a divorce because I was not female enough, and therefore I need to become less confident and more helpless. . . . I really wonder if maybe I haven't identified more [with] a stereotyped gender than I consciously [realized], . . .

that it is my lack of femaleness that is what's causing me great deprivations.

Stone, echoing "Wise Elder Woman" Ann Strong, has given a good description of how "internalized oppression" can work to weaken women.

Most of these women demonstrate increasing levels of understanding of what they believe to be the injustices of sex and race discrimination. Hammond speaks mainly of negative treatment on account of her sex and race, based on her lengthy involvement in election campaigns for both white and Black male candidates. Concerning sex, she says, "I think that any new campaign you walk into, you are separated at the instant they see that you're a woman, and it's that feeling that only women can understand. But once the candidate gets to know you, you're OK, as long as you stand there and fight it out." Concerning race, she says, "There again, you know, some of it is supposition, but some of the people that were closest [to the Black candidate], they had their own little clique. And most of it was Black, and you were the white outsider in some instances, and that kind of stuff, until they really need the help, and then you're accepted."

Stone, on the other hand, notes the special positive treatment she has received on account of her sex and race, though she also tells of sexist treatment she has received in her legislative career because of her feminist advocacy. Regarding the latter, she tells of a man who told her he was warned to be careful around her because of her feminism but that he found her to be "a lamb," easy to work with. Concerning positive treatment on account of her sex, she has become "pragmatic." Has she received such treatment? "Absolutely. I used to be much more principled. Now I figure if that's what they want to do, it's fine with me." Concerning positive treatment on account of her race, she thinks "that the Blacks would say that we received special treatment, and no doubt I have," but she cannot cite specific instances.

Maria Montgomery, Audrey Nelms, and Ella Washburn all give more emphasis to negative than to positive treatment on account of their sex. Montgomery tells of being sexually molested as a child and sexually harassed as a worker. Nelms speaks of observing the unequal community funding that the Girl Scouts received in comparison to the Boy Scouts. Washburn tells of the difficulties she experienced getting the hospital to bill her insurance carrier rather than her husband's for her annual mammogram.

These three women also recount experiences that reveal their consciousness of racial privilege. Though Montgomery speaks of the "resentment" some Black people have expressed toward her whiteness, she understands her racial privilege as the source of such resentment: "Compared to Black people, my life would have been very different if I hadn't been white." Nelms says that growing up in a northern city, she was more aware of ethnic difference than of racial discrimination. She was a Protestant among Catholics. But coming south, she became aware of her racial privilege. She tells a story of befriending a Black mother and her family in a housing project, who, when she had some difficulties with the housing manager, "asked me to help her, and I went with them. First he was antagonistic," but then she sensed that he began to listen to her "because I think *he* had his problems with Black mothers in his housing project," and "because I was a white female." Washburn tells a similar kind of story about getting specialized attention from the police after her house, in a predominantly Black neighborhood, was burglarized. When the police officer finally came to her office and saw who she was, that is, a white woman, "then he wanted to spend the rest of the day with me." Before that, she and her husband had had a difficult time getting the police to work on the case, and she had called her city council representative to complain about poor police service.

The "Women Made, Not Born," are noteworthy for being conscious of some of the contradictions society has created for them. While they do not speak of their privileges due to their middle-class status and their heterosexuality, some have become conscious of their racial privilege. All have become conscious of societal contradictions related to their sex and gender. Like the "Women Persons," they have not let society's version of femininity limit their behaviors; but, unlike the "Women Persons," they are not willing to let society off the hook for placing extra obstacles in their paths. "Women Persons" seem to have resolved the contradiction within themselves by exchanging "being feminine" for being non–gender-differentiated "individuals." But "Women Made, Not Born," are not ready to exchange their now fractured identities as "Woman" for those of "individuals," for the very reason that they know society is responsible for this fracturing, and that this fracturing is the consequence of their refusing to live according to what they consider to be society's unjust requirements for "feminine" women.

Hammond and Stone reintroduce a third term into the discourse, "female," which the "Lady with Best of Both Worlds" Jensen initially introduced. Jensen equated "being a woman" with "being feminine," which meant doing the "female-type" things plus what men do. For Jensen, all three terms are positive. For Hammond and Stone, "female" is used interchangeably with "feminine," and both are negative. "Woman" for them is both negative and positive—negative because of the meanings intruded into that word by "female" and "feminine," but positive because of what women can do when they throw off those negative identities, if only some of the time.

For Hammond, Montgomery, and Stone, "being white" has also begun to intrude on "being a woman." "Being white" has meant receiving perceived "resentment" from Black people or experiencing "outsider" status. But Montgomery, Washburn, and Nelms have gone on to understand the cause of the "outsider" status: the injustice of the racial privilege that has set them apart from and over Black people in the situations they describe.

"Women Spinning Women"

The rest of the women emerge as protagonists for standpoints along what becomes a multi-ply thread. "Spinning," as explained by Mary Daly, seems an appropriate metaphor to describe what these women are doing with their newly emerging meanings of "being a woman." That is, their experiences of everyday life seem to provide grist for their ever-emerging constructions of multiply identified selves in relation to various others in their life spaces. In fact, the remaining women in this chapter could replace "being" as a noun with Mary Daly's verb "be-ing" and "becoming" as words to characterize their ways of being women.[7] While quite conscious of the negative aspects of the social construction of "Woman," all these women are beginning to develop understandings of "be-ing/becoming a woman" that emphasize not only the positive qualities of women on their own terms but also the values of linking up with other women, though some also continue relationships with men. The negativity of "being a woman" begins with the anger of Nancy Harding and the cynicism of Sally Martin and ends with the categorization by several other women of women as an oppressed group. The positivity begins with Harding's and Martin's discoveries that they like women better than men and ends with Susan Murphy's, Barbara Bergen's, and Gretchen Bright's spinning the many interconnections that constitute "be-ing/becoming a woman."

There are certain themes that suggest convergences among some of these women in their spinning. The first three women—Harding, Martin, and Greene—emphasize "women together," after first clearing out the negatives connected with their understandings of "being a woman" and "femininity." Harding has recently begun venting her anger because of separation and impending divorce from her husband. She is not as sure as the "Women Persons" that times have changed. "Being a woman" means to her that "we're at a tremendous disadvantage, and you have to fight for everything, everything. You know, it would be nice to think it's changing, and I guess it is. But I just think it's terrible. You know, I do not want to be one [a woman]. I just think our lot is harder in life." Martin contrasts "being a woman"—"just being me," having "something to do that I respect"— with what she thinks cynically that others consider "feminine" behavior: "I guess it means looking feminine, that is, having a waistline and legs and bosom. And it means a well-modulated voice. And it means trying to look interested even if the subject is not [interesting], especially if the man is speaking, . . . and not minding if in the middle of your sentence everybody is suddenly gone, and you're left there by yourself."

Both women have come to a realization that they enjoy being with other women, perhaps more than being with men. Harding tells about discovering women as friends, thus overcoming the isolation she was feeling with her husband, whom she was raised to think of as her "Prince Charming." Martin says, "I used to think that men were the most important thing in the world. And I must have geared my whole life to that. Somewhere along the line I lost that illusion. And now I like men, but lots of times I like women better than men."

Martin also alludes to something positive about femininity that Kate Greene connects both to "being a woman" and to "being feminine." Martin says femininity is not only about pretending to be interested in what men are saying but also in "being a sustainer and a provider." Greene speaks of how her daughter's suffering has pushed her into advocacy for women: "I'm very proud that I've taken very personally this sex discrimination, and where my older daughter has suffered, I've tried to turn that into not so much just taking it personally but seeing how it fits into everything else. But it's made me very determined to do everything I can to change things for women as long as I am around." "Being feminine" is part of what is to be done: being caring and nurturing, and other "feminine characteristics should be important to every woman."

The "Women Spinning Women Together" are not unlike some of the women who have preceded them in this analysis in that all are aware of discriminatory treatment toward them as women but not all are aware of their racial privilege. Martin labels as sex discrimination the kind of treatment by men in social intercourse she has just described in her discussion of femininity. Harding notes that, in her profession, most teachers are women while most principals are men. Greene reports incidents of sexual harassment while she was working as a secretary after her divorce—"very demeaning remarks, innuendos, and I was really afraid to say or do anything for fear of my job"—and "a lot of sexist remarks and sexist jokes going around" when she was lobbying for the ERA at the state legislature. All have been more or less aware of special treatment toward them as women. Harding considers such behavior a "put down" as if she were not capable of managing for herself, while Greene attributes it to "the southern tradition."

Concerning questions of positive and negative treatment on account of race, Harding answers "no" to both questions. Greene, in speaking of the "southern tradition" of special positive treatment of women, fails to specify that such treatment is reserved for white women. While she believes that she received a better education than Black students because of her race, she does not seem to make the connection between her racial and sexual privilege when she recounts the negative treatment she feels she has received from Black women when she was lobbying for the ERA: "I guess that's been one of the most hurtful things. Working with the ERA, there were some Black women who are convinced that working for something like that is a white middle-class woman's issue. And it's very hard to try to work with them to get an understanding." Only Martin comes close to exhibiting some awareness of how racial discrimination works. She cannot remember specific instances of any positive treatment, but she does recount how her daughter came to dislike her own blond hair when they were living in Arizona near some Navajo people. There her blond daughter stood out as different from the other children, who called her the name for "goat hair." Martin seems to understand how racial bigotry can teach a racial minority self-hate, though it is not clear that the Navajo children in that instance intended a racial slur. Thus, "Women Spinning Women Together" stand out in their move to embrace and draw strength from other women, though their lack of consciousness of their racial privilege makes it difficult if not impossible to come together with any but other white women.

Other women—Hazel Beecroft, Fran Daly, Annie Witt, and Tillie Zadar—spin threads, different ideas about their lives as women that link them to the theme of "Women Spinning." Witt, as the youngest woman in the study, says "it's very exhilarating" to be a woman but also very frustrating. She is particularly concerned that times are changing, but in the wrong direction for her:

> One thing I'm real worried about is just being a woman in society now. You know, I mean there was a time [the 1970s] when women could just come out and say, "Well, fuck you. Here I am." But now, even though there are some women who certainly will still do it, there are other

women who are starting to have second thoughts about where all of this has been taking us. They're now deciding that, whether it's sort of encouraged by their church groups or the men in their lives, they're deciding that it's better that women stay at home and have children and do traditional things. So that's a big setback for a lot of people. And for one who is just now struggling to break out of the shell, that's even harder. . . .

Similarly, Beecroft is concerned that women not be forced into roles not of their own choosing, and she believes further "that we as women have a responsibility to bring out the woman's viewpoint in women's history in everything that we do in women's struggle. That's a major thing in my thinking."

Neither Witt nor Beecroft accord much significance to "being feminine" in their own lives. Beecroft, however, exemplifying how women can make Audre Lorde's "powerful connections" by learning from women different from them, says her socialist-theory study group has been reading Lesbian feminist theory about sexuality, and she likes what they say about women experiencing their sex positively: "You know, the positive experience of feeling good about yourself. And that's what I guess I would define as feminine. Well, you're a woman, so you have to feel good about yourself as a woman . . . because I think that we are filled [by society] with negativeness."

Fran Daly and Tillie Zadar, both self-declared Lesbian feminists, introduce new language into the discussion, speaking of women's oppression in a patriarchal world and suggesting a dual-level understanding of "being a woman." Daly says, "Today I would have to say that . . . on a political level . . . it means an identification with an oppressed class throughout the world. And on a personal kind of level, being a woman means being whoever I am, because since I'm female, I am woman, and whatever I do and however I feel and however I behave is womanly because I'm a woman." With "being a woman" goes a triple meaning of "being feminine," parts of which we have seen expressed by some of the other women. Daly understands "being feminine" in a Lesbian context, in which "butch" and "femme" mock the patriarchal setup of "masculine" and "feminine." She also understands femininity in a more general feminist context, believing that gender is "culturally imposed." She explicitly rejects the idea that women are "naturally more peaceful and more able to nurture the planet," calling the idea "a real fallacy." Finally, she gives a feminist twist to the ideas of "Women with Best of Both Worlds" when she says, "I know that I emanate many of the qualities that people traditionally associate with the feminine but that I also have owned my own business for ten years, and then [I am] raising a child on my own and, you know, [I] make hard decisions and handle money and take trips, [I am] very independent in ways that are traditionally thought to be masculine." Daly, though acting in what she considers to be both "feminine" and "masculine" ways, is far removed from the "Ladies with Best of Both Worlds." Unlike them, she clearly rejects the legitimacy of these terms denoting gender.

Tillie Zadar extends Fran Daly's dual-level notion of "being a woman" to its full manifestation of two worlds vastly different from the two worlds—men's and women's—of the "Ladies with Best of Both Worlds." Whereas the latter revelled in enjoying the "best of both worlds," Zadar defines her worlds as society—men's world, which she rejects, and the Lesbian world, which is "outside" men's world and which she claims. "Being a woman" to her "means being an oppressed person. You're treated in an inferior kind of way, you know, in a lot of subtle little things and the obvious things. I don't feel like I own places, like walking around on the street. Men harass women walking on the streets. So you're a foreigner in your own country." But "being a woman" also means to her being a Lesbian,

a woman outside. You're a woman who is not getting anything from men, which is the ultimate as far as men are concerned. They can't stand it, you know. In our society, you're defined by your dependence on men. And to refuse that, to refuse that dependence is to change the definition of what a woman is. So to me, it's more of being a Lesbian than being a woman. Though I think I share a lot of things with all women, straight women and Lesbians. I admire straight women who put up with all the crap, but I can't do it.

Zadar then places into her "two worlds" the positives and negatives that other women have held in contradiction: "But I'm real glad I'm a woman, and I think there's a lot of real positive traits women have been given in our society. You know, being nurturing and listening and care-taking are all really important. . . . So I guess that I'm glad that our culture has given us those things, those kinds of skills, which I think are real basic and important."

Jokingly, Zadar says that this question about being a woman "makes me think of all those commercials for perfume." I respond that this leads to the next question about "being feminine." She says, "Oh, god! Okay, being feminine means being subservient and taking care of men, buying into that whole thing of being weak, dependent and a sexual object." She understands "the feminine" as "a big negative." She says that she plays [that role], she goes to her job "in drag. You know, I wear a little dress, a success dress, when I go to work for temporary, but then, we have a lot of jokes in our community about being 'butch' and 'femme.' It's not good to be femme but it's okay to be butch." "Being feminine" is both one's external appearance and one's actions in deferring to men, and when she left men's society for her "real" life, she left all that behind. "I guess when I came out, I kind of gave up—that's when you really give up any idea about being feminine." In this, Zadar also agrees with the "Lady with Best of Both Worlds" Lorraine Reilly, though they place contrasting values on not being feminine. For Reilly, not being feminine is negative, being "queer." For Zadar, it is positive, being Lesbian.

"Women Spinning Threads" make a full turn into consciousness of racial privilege combined with sexual victimization. Most give examples of sex discrimination in the workplace. Witt reports that her opinions are not valued by her leftist labor-lawyer employers because of her youth as well as because of her sex and her position as secretary. Zadar reports similar devaluing of female clerical workers by the men she works with in a community radio station. Beecroft recalls how she and other women worked full time for half-time pay while the men had full-paid full-time jobs on an underground newspaper.

Daly says she works with other women and so does not experience sexism in the workplace. Rather, she tells how her women's peace group is perceived when they demonstrate: "There is the real strong possibility of being identified as a bunch of crazies. But it's not just because we are women. It's because there aren't any men with us." By the same token, because all the women are white, Daly is aware of the problems this creates for her group with and from Black women: "Since we are the dominant culture in this society, we don't usually get discriminated against because we are a bunch of white women. And the place that I run into problems with that is that I don't want it to be an all-white group. And in approaching Black women, there are assumptions made about me, because I am a white woman, some of which are true and some of which I would like to call into question and get up front." Daly is also aware that often white women receive positive treatment while Black women receive negative treatment because assumptions are "made about us and about how genteel we may be. But there's also the opposite extreme, which I think happens to Black women as well as white women, for whatever weird reasons are in the minds of various men, who want to manipulate or attack a particular woman, and some of it often has to do with your race." Zadar expands on why she thinks Black people in general distrust whites: "You know, you get so much privilege out of being white that it outweighs any kind of negative treatment. In fact, I think you have to work harder to get Black peoples' trust. And I think that's a legitimate thing. I mean, I make men work harder to get my trust than I do women, and it's the same thing."

Witt gives an example of how she understands so-called positive treatment of her on account of her sex and race to be linked to negative treatment of Black women: "When I was hired at the firm I'm working at now, I was the first person to interview with them. They right away wanted me. I think one reason [was] attractiveness." But then she found out that a Black woman had sent some of her Black friends to inquire about the job, "and I'm sure that they would have hired me before they hired a Black person. You know, the office is strictly white, and, as liberal as they are, I'm sure they would have had problems [with a Black female secretary]."

The last three women—Susan Murphy, Barbara Bergen, and Gretchen Bright—emphasize women spinning networks, women integrating facets of their lives so that they can move fairly easily from one task to another or can call upon friends when in need. For Murphy, "being a woman" means "facing the task and the challenge of integrating a number of different aspects of my life, of being a good mother and a good friend and effective in my work and effective in my relationship with my husband. I think women are real lucky because they have so many facets to their life. It's a difficulty but it's also a very positive thing about women." The challenge for Murphy is that, although "a lot of the barriers to women's participation in work and intellectual life and cultural life have been torn down," women with children still find it difficult to participate fully. "For instance, the society assumes very little responsibility for the caring and rearing of children, and that's still put mainly on the woman in the home to see to that." "Being feminine" is a positive part of "being a woman" for Murphy. It "means being able to relate. I think that's the primary asset women have, the primary difference psychologically and personality-wise between women and men, that women seem to have the capacity to empathize and to relate to the situation of others and to draw other people out. And I think that's a tremendous strength that women have."

Bergen continues the theme of interconnection while also noting some difficulties. She says, "When you ask that, what I do is imagine being a man, you know, and I just feel real lucky! I feel like I have a family and a community, and from being a woman and being around the women that I know, learning to make connections between everything and learning to integrate things, it has just made me real happy." But she gets very angry when she hears "that there is a rapist in the neighborhood. I mean, you always call someone to see if they can come stay with you. To realize that you live with that, to recognize that terror that we live with, it just makes me furious." For Bergen, however, "being feminine" is artificial: "It conjures up dressing to please men."

"Being feminine" is also a negative construct for Bright. In fact, Bright understands femininity to be a political construct designed to keep her from knowing her full powers as a "self-realized woman." She begins by saying, "Well, somehow I feel that I don't have a real sense of the intent of the question. You know, to say 'Politics aside, what is being a woman to you?' It's like this is the lottery ticket that I drew in life and in this incarnation I am a white woman in America. I could have been born a cat, you know, but I was born a woman, so this is the role I have this time around." Going on to the question about "being feminine" brings her back to answering the question about "being a woman":

> Well, with the question about being a woman and being feminine, I have two very different responses. One of them is grounded in my political analysis of what I've been taught about those roles and about those characteristics. And, I mean, what I saw when you said "What it means to be a woman" is basically, I feel, it means—you are going to get your answer—that I'm constantly in opposition to the world around me or the society around me. And that if I am a self, self-realized as a woman, then it means a sense of always swimming against the stream and so forth. So that kind of moves me to my innate sense of being a woman and femininity, which, having declared myself to be a woman and affirming that in a system that does not [affirm it], I am beginning over the past five years to know and become acquainted with what my powers are as a woman and what it means to be female.

Bright is using "female" in a positive sense in contrast to the negative meaning that she believes the dominant culture has given to "femininity": "The femaleness recognizes and celebrates and draws from an interconnection with all living things. It's like to me interconnectedness is the hallmark of being. . . . Femininity, you know—again the cultural things are just so destructive." For Bright, femininity does not affirm her powers as a female; femininity disconnects women, isolates them, and herein lies the source of feminine women's powerlessness.

In coming to self-realization as a woman, as a female, Bright says, "The world that I am introduced to inside myself is magnificent. But those [the world outside and the world inside myself] must be kept very clearly separate, and then, where they meet is like, my consciousness must be always there, you know, paying attention all the time [to] how I view myself and how I am taught to view myself." Bright seems to have located Smith's "line of fault" between the lives that are possible from women's standpoints and "the" life that has been created *for* "Woman" in what Bright elsewhere calls "the patri-archy." Bright is standing in a space, her own space, located at a dynamic intersection of the negative patriarchal world with an emerging new world that she is largely responsible for creating. Through conscious actions, she is continually replacing parts of the negative old "outside" world with new parts of her own making. But it is not of her own individual making. She is able to take part in making a new world because she believes in the importance of con-necting with every other living thing, and that connectedness is a resource that goes with being powerful as female.

"Women Spinning Networks" maintain the full turn to con-sciousness of sexual victimization combined with racial privilege. Murphy, because of taking leadership roles in interracial endeavors, can recount an instance of negative treatment related to both her sex and her race. She recalls an idea that she presented after having "been shot at by the Klan along with some other people," coming home from a demonstration in Mississippi. The idea was to "start a project of education around the Klan, and get it funded and do on-going organizational work. But when one of the Black members of the organization from another state heard that I had presented this and there was some possibility that we would go through with it, his reaction was that he did not think a white woman would be ca-pable of leading a project such as this." At the same time she is conscious of special treatment on account of her race because of racism in the law, in society, in the very culture: "Oh, I'm sure. You know, I could go anywhere I wanted to when I was a child growing up, which Black people at that time in the South couldn't. I grew up when Jim Crow was in force."

Bergen adds the dimension of "disability" to the discussion of sex discrimination; she is never sure whether sex-related treatments are also compounded by her being perceived as "disabled" because of crippling childhood polio. She experiences harassment walking on the streets, "and sometimes it's hard for me to tell if it's because of my disability or because of my sex." By the same token, she is not so sure that special treatment is all that positive:

Again, I don't know if it's sex or disability in that do you call it special treatment or do you call it patronizing? You know, I'll go in to get something fixed on the car and they will not charge me very much. I mean, I'm glad that that happened, but it is patronizing as well. I even had one that was kind enough to say to me not long ago, he checked something and it took him a few seconds. He just checked it right away, and he said, "I think it's this. I'll show you how to fix it if it stops again." He just showed me how to fix it and then he said, "I just want to let you know that I didn't do this because you're handicapped; I just do it for any woman that comes in." So, I just said, "Thank you." You know, I didn't know what to say. . . . That was very sweet in many ways, but it shows that sort of trap.

She shows that she sees through a system that makes her negatively "special" because of her sex and her disability.

Bergen and Bright both note with sadness the negative aspect of their relations with Black people. Both also understand the reasons and take responsibility for the mistrustful distance they often feel. Bergen says, "I know that there is a separation that's there, and that just makes me want to work more in the world to make the separation not there. There are many women that I will never get to be friends with because of that. And that's really horrible. I mean, that happens every day." Bright elaborates: "I feel that my relationships with Black people have suffered because I was white." I ask why she thinks that has been. "Well, because I'm racist, you know." She agrees that there is a basic lack of trust because of our history of being racist. "And, you know, I have a lot of sadness around the intimacies, that because of circumstances—and common experiences I have built with Black people, and to feel over the years the impossibility of real depth of intimacy and trust. And that feels like, I mean, negative treatment because we're racist." She understands racism and the consequent so-called negative treatment to be part of the patriarchal system: "But, you know, I'm a white person in a society that is controlled and designed to give privilege to white people, so. . . ." Bright cannot speak of sex discrimination without also speaking of race and class privilege: "Well, yes, it's like in raising one's consciousness about racism and so forth, to begin to name levels of oppression that I experienced. You know, on the one hand

I'm white and middle class, so that gives me some modicum of privilege, but the fact that I'm, you know, that I have to walk around in fear of physical attack, constantly, to me is discrimination as a woman. You know, it's like that feels real obvious to me."

"Women Spinning Threads" and "Women Spinning Networks" manifest in their everyday language and lives how white women can develop consciousness of a "politics of identity" in a culture characterized by "complex domination." By beginning to recognize their own oppressions due to sex and gender at the same time that they also make connections between their privileges and other women's and men's oppressions due to race and/or class, they demystify the distortions that "complex domination" attempts to impose on all women and men. They discover their own standpoints from which they can reach out to others: to link up with other women and/or men, to share ideas about problems and strategies, to form networks that become the ground for new ways of be-ing/becoming white political women.

Before going on to show in the next chapter how different ways of understanding "being a woman" ground different versions of feminism and antifeminism, it is important to reiterate that these twenty-six white female activists understand "being a woman" in vastly different ways. If anyone still thinks that white women in the United States are all alike, then think again. Certainly I am not claiming that these twenty-six constitute a representative sample of the population of white women in the United States. What I do claim is that these women point to some of the ways of thinking about womanhood that must exist in the larger population of white women.

These women, then, suggest that there is now no monolithic version of white women's reality, if there ever was. That is not to say there has not been a dominant ideological expectation that white women must find their greatest fulfillment in life by conforming to the requirements of "(white, middle-class, heterosexual) femininity." These requirements have included being loving wives and mothers and industrious, though unpaid, housekeepers in "the private sphere" and staying out of the "masculine" world of politics and business in "the public sphere." Even as late as the middle years of the twentieth century, Betty Friedan could write about "the feminine mystique"[8] and be given credit for raising the collective consciousness especially of white middle-class housewives. Many of these women went on to join with other women in forming a contemporary movement for equal rights for women in the United States.

Just as there can be no monolithic version of white women's reality, so there can be no monolithic explanation of white women's oppression. In contrast to Friedan's focus on a psychological component of "the problem," Kate Millett, in *Sexual Politics*, focused on a structural component, "patriarchy," as the source of such women's oppression. Feminists taking this approach went on to form a more radical movement for women's liberation. Their objective was and is to change the very social order, "the patriarchy," that they believe undergirds the system of politics and society in the United States today. From these differences in "reality" and in explanations of "the problem," among even this small group of twenty-six white women, come the multiple versions of feminism and antifeminism that these women present in the next chapter.

Chapter 5

Ways of "Being a Woman" Ground "Feminism" and "Antifeminism"

In the last chapter, I introduced Sandra Bartky's phenomenology of feminist consciousness in order to show how understandings of "being a woman" ground feminist consciousness. Furthermore, the interviews with white women engaged in electoral and movement politics have established that "Woman" as a unitary identity is a figment of the patriarchal imagination. That is not to say that this patriarchal illusion has been ineffective: ideas about "Woman" have been used to hide the actual material privileges while bolstering the oppressions that mark different white women's existences. But we can detect evidence for a vigorous politics of identity as all manner of white women express different meanings of "being a woman," different perceptions of treatment according to various combinations of gender, race, economic class, sexuality, and age. It should not be surprising, then, to find that "feminism" also is not a monolithic concept and that different identities as women ground different forms of feminist as well as antifeminist consciousness.

A unitary definition of "feminism" is elusive because even those who advocate "feminism" may exist in different social locations and therefore experience different problems and devise different strategies to address those problems. We saw earlier that some of these white women deny the legitimacy of problems that other white women perceive as sex and race discrimination. Among the white women who perceive such problems, some understand sex discrimination as a problem for "women" while race discrimination is a problem for "Blacks." Others understand their sex discrimination to coexist with their own racial privilege, which is also linked to others' race discrimination or oppression. A unitary definition of feminism is thus also undesirable because of the possible ideological forms of consciousness that feminism itself can become.

Dorothy Smith distinguishes "ideological" forms of consciousness from what I will call "grounded" forms of consciousness, those forms "grounded" in experiences directly sensed and interpreted by embodied social beings. For Smith, ideological forms of consciousness are those constructed *by* certain actors, in response to their own experiences and needs, *for* others also involved in those experiences through the hierarchical social relations that shape the experiences.[1] "Femininity" can thus be understood as an *ideological* form of consciousness constructed, under the rules of "complex domination," by a certain class of men—white men of property—for a certain class of women—white women "qualified" by their skin color and sex for marriage with such men. "Femininity" requires the submission of such women to such men in exchange for privileges that are supposed to accrue for women who so submit. "Masculinity," the requirement that men exercise supposed autonomy in their own lives and control over "their" women's lives, is the *grounded* form of consciousness for such men; that is, "masculinity" is socially constructed and approved by such men for themselves. But from a feminist perspective, "masculinity" reinforces the dominance and privilege of such men over particular women and in society generally.

Smith calls for women to locate a "line of fault" that demarcates the boundaries of ideological forms of consciousness, such as "femininity" for example, from their *own* experience—"the world *directly* felt, sensed, responded to, prior to its social expression [*by* others *for* women]." It is "that line of fault along which the consciousness of women must emerge."[2] This form of consciousness can emerge for women as a grounded form of consciousness when and as each woman recognizes what I have suggested is her own unique standpoint. It will be a *social* form of consciousness in that it will be constructed by women, each advocating her particular perspective from her unique standpoint, among themselves for themselves.

In the case of "feminism," the question remains, however, of just where the "line of fault" lies for each woman and of just how to distinguish "ideological" from "grounded" consciousness. When is the feminist consciousness of some women grounded for them, inclusive or exclusive of variously combined victimizations and privileges, but perceived as ideological by other women, even other feminist women? The clue to the answer may lie in whether one group of women understands its feminist consciousness to be in oppositional difference to other forms of feminism and tries to impose it on other women or whether women understand their feminist consciousness contextually as one source of empowerment and seek to understand and make powerful connections with women possessing other forms of consciousness—feminist or otherwise.

In this chapter I examine the content of forms of consciousness expressed by the white female political activists as they respond to open-ended questions about the meaning of "feminism" to them and about their feelings regarding the women's movement.[3] Only a few women are entirely negative or entirely positive in response to the questions about "feminism" and the women's movement. The other women shade perceptibly from one form of consciousness to the next, speaking negatively of "feminism" and negatively but somewhat positively of the women's movement or positively of "feminism" and positively but somewhat negatively of the women's movement. In content, these forms of consciousness shade perceptibly from a focus on "the feminine" to "people" to "women's rights" to "oppression" and "patriarchy" to "the feminine." "The feminine" means different things for women in the two polar groupings. For some, "the feminine" is a male-defined concept, though for those women, women's definition on men's terms is not problematic but proper for women. Others understand "the feminine" as a women-centered concept, because they have rejected male-defined femininity and believe it is within their power to be self-defining through social action with other women. Additionally, the only women to integrate race and class considerations into their understandings of "feminism" are those who express "Marxist-Feminism" and "Women-Centered Feminine-ism."

"Male-defined Feminine-ism"

The responses of four women suggest a "Male-defined Feminine-ist" form of antifeminism. All of these women are Republicans. The first three are party workers who are the "Ladies"—Linda Helms, Bridgit Malone, and Lavinia Ravenel. The fourth, Lorraine Reilly, is ambitious for public office and is one of the "Ladies with Best of Both Worlds." All suggest that, for them, feminism *should* be about how women and men *should* act in relation to one another: women as females should be woman-like, feminine, and men as males should be man-like, masculine. To these women, it appears that "feminist" used to mean—before the days of "women's lib"—feminine-ist. Now the term has been corrupted by what they see as "failed women," women who are out of step with their own natures.

Helms sets the stage. Apparently believing that feminism should mean being feminine, Helms says that "feminism has been corrupted. Feminism is being woman-like." She criticizes "those women who are out for so-called women's rights. . . . Most of them are very harsh women who have no interest in being a woman. They want to be a man, . . . they want to be mannish." She thinks it is "sad." Reilly is another that believes feminism has lost its real meaning. "It's being a female." But "when I hear that word feminism, I look at it today, and it never was that way. With that ERA movement I look at it as Lesbians and queers. I'm sorry."

Feminism brings to Malone's mind "women's libbers, rabble rousers, ... what's her face, that wrote the—Gloria Steinem, who looks anything but." I gather that Malone meant to refer to Betty Friedan, author of *The Feminine Mystique,* who looks "anything but" feminine in Malone's eyes. Ravenel, like Malone, is concerned mostly about women's looks. Feminism to her means Betty Friedan and failed women: "Everybody I've ever seen involved in it looks like they had never shampooed their hair. They look like they've never had a date. They look like they didn't like men. They all look like they were anti-everything. I'm *for* things."

All of these women say they want nothing to do with the women's movement or with the ERA. Helms, for example, sees those women as "soreheads . . . who are concerned about making women equal with men." And Reilly says, "I just read that this whole NOW organization is going to turn their attention, once ERA dies, to the housewife. Believe me, I don't want them bothering me. What could they do for me? They can't do a darn thing. Go do something else, but leave the housewife alone."

"Antifeminist People-ism"

An overriding theme for most of the eight women who espouse "Antifeminist People-ism" is a concern about "people" rather than "just women." These women have negative feelings about feminism, and two of them also are negative toward the women's movement. The other six cite both negative and positive aspects of the women's movement. All of these women are Republicans. Three are party workers, and the others are office-oriented, either officeholders or office-seekers. Two are "Ladies with Best of Both Worlds," and of the others, all but one are "Women Persons."

Sybyl Jensen and Dulcie LaFontaine set the negative tone for feminism and the women's movement. Jensen seems particularly solicitous of men's psyches and life spans. She says that feminism is a "degrading" term that "never has meant anything to me." Concerning the women's movement, "they ought to stop just having a women's movement and have a people's movement. I think that we have overshadowed the men at this point. We've intimidated men." She is upset with the "bra-burning bit, . . . and if we aren't careful, the men are going to lose their image of themselves as being dominant personalities. . . . I don't mean that they *must* dominate." Dulcie LaFontaine agrees with the male-defined feminine-ist Reilly that feminism and the women's movement refer to the ERA and that women don't need the ERA. She believes that women are stronger without it. One gets the sense that LaFontaine thinks it is a sign of weakness for women to want equal rights guaranteed by government when women already possess these rights and have but to use them. In other words, it is up to women to be strong individuals and to use the rights they have.

Other women admit to "mixed feelings" about the women's movement, Bess Shumaker because she recognizes the greater opportunities women now have for careers, and Betty Mason, because she
appreciates the strides women have made in gaining public office,
including a seat on the Supreme Court. Audrey Nelms and Arlene
Pringle appreciate the women's movement for its concerns and success with women's equal rights in pay and credit but, similar to
Shumaker, not for its "burning the bra, a hatred of men." Nelms,
the exceptional antifeminist in this cluster of women in that she is
one of the "Women Made, Not Born," has a special conflict regarding
feminism and the women's movement. She tried to advocate her
version of "equal rights" feminism in the early days of the movement, but she did not feel that they would accept her because of her
views about her husband and about "enjoying being a mother and
housewife." She has tried but she does not think feminists really live
by what they say about women. Mason also believes the movement
has focused too narrowly: "I would hope they would get back to the
goals of the country instead of . . . just ERA . . . and abortion." She is
very concerned about the survival of the country and says, "I don't
see that as masculine or feminine. I guess it's why I'm having
trouble with all your questions in the last section here because it is
a way of life that we have got to turn around. And it isn't limited to
male, female, black or white. It's to anyone who is involved in and
cares enough to get involved, to get us turned around and back to
the basics of what made this country great and what it is today."

The last two women in this cluster, Elizabeth Latimer and
Maryanne Thayer, are the least negative toward the women's movement but still reject the label "feminist" for themselves. Latimer
fully supports equal rights, including the ERA, but she thinks in
terms of "human rights, not just women's rights." She seems not to
have any problem with women working together to achieve resolution of their issues, but she thinks it is important to frame the issues in such a way that they will garner the widest support. Without directly criticizing the mass tactics of the more radical arm of
the women's movement as it dealt with the ERA, she seems to want
to change the people involved and the terms of the discussion. She
believes that "mainline" economically independent women and local

housewives are the ones that must be persuaded to take up the leadership on this issue.

Thayer is the most ambivalent in this cluster of women. To her, feminism has come to mean militant bra-burning and women who work (for wages) because they would feel guilty if they did not work; economically they do not need to work. In evaluating the women's movement, she says, "I have mixed emotions about it. It frightens me a little." What frightens her is that she sees many of her friends "frustrated because they feel they have to work, and this has caused some divorces and broken marriages, broken homes. I think that they feel like they *have* to work; they feel *guilty* if they don't." She, on the other hand, feels that she is put on the defensive by women her age who "look at me and say 'Are you working?' and think I'm just nuts because I don't have a paying job. And this bothers me. I feel sometimes apologetic because I am not a wage earner." Thayer states that she is not a feminist, but then she goes on to muse about whether she might qualify as one. After all, she believes in equal pay, she wants her views heard, and she recognizes the choices she could have now, which she did not have as a girl growing up, because of the women's movement. She thinks that, back then, women were achieving things on their own, but the women's movement speeded things up: "they wouldn't have done it nearly as fast if it hadn't been for the women's movement."

"Women's Rights Feminism"

I classify seven women as "Women's Rights Feminists" because they focus mainly on women's unequal status under the law and women's need to have their rights under law recognized. A few of these women express some of the same negativity toward the women's movement that the antifeminists express, but overall, the women's rights feminists do not let these negatives override the positives they see in the movement. The "feminine" thread weaves its way through some of these women's views of feminism, surfacing in ambiguous terms for some and pointing toward the women-defined end of the spectrum for others. All but one of the women are Democrats and either "Women Made, Not Born," or "Women Spinning Women To-gether." One holds public office, three are ambitious for public office, and three are party workers. The other woman is a leftist commu-nity activist and one of the "Women Spinning Threads."

Adrienne Stone seems almost to have been listening in on some of the previous interviews. She directly refutes those women's views of feminism and the women's movement. She is aware that many people understand feminism as something very radical, and she is careful to choose the groups and audiences to which she identifies herself as a feminist. Yet she is also careful not to make "feminism" ideological by trying to impose her version of it on other women. She says, "I don't think that many people understand what the definition [is]. People have their own definition of that. And if I don't feel that I'm in a situation to define what a feminist is, then there's no sense using a term that people interpret differently. And then I'm reluc-tant to say, 'You ladies are feminists. Let me tell you why.' I don't like to do that." Stone defines feminism as supporting women's "having equal status with men legally, socially, being viewed as equal persons both under the law and as people."

Stone's greatest concern for the women's movement, in which she has long been involved, is that since the defeat of the ERA in 1982, legislative sponsors and supporters have had to deal with NOW and ERAmerica leaders and members who disagree on the strategies that worked or failed and the strategies to take for the future. She says she knows she has her own ego problems as do the other women, and they must move beyond those. "Until women learn to support each other more, to work together more, to give other women power, let other women have power, to support it whether they like the person or not—women can't deal with that at all as women. They just can't. They want to take it away. We need more unity. We need to like each other more."

Ella Washburn associates "feminist" with "feminine" but backs away from defining one as the other: "Feminism. I guess the word just 'feminine' still means to me being frilly and a female and all that. But that's not the true definition of it. I think feminism, it means being a woman, but also fighting for women's rights." Edith Hammond, Sally Martin, and Annie Witt all agree that feminism is about fighting for women's rights, and they do understand it to be a battle. Martin, for example, says that feminism "historically has been [concerned with] women's rights . . . so feminism is just going to be militant women's movement." She sees the militants as "those people on the edges" who move everyone toward their goals, though those in the middle, like herself, may be uncomfortable with the militancy. Still, the militancy is good and necessary. She says that she is "probably just as militant, but I have my ways of hiding it a little bit. But sure I have strong feelings about the fact that a person who has the skills ought to be recognized not just with a thank you." She dislikes that part of the movement that expresses "resentment of men." Though that is not part of the goals, "it just may be that a lot of people who have been unhappy or have a resentment are drawn to it, and you can't really blame that on the women's movement. But it *is* there. . . . But I have seen the same hatred for women in men too."

Martin also introduces an aspect of feminism that Kate Greene and Nancy Harding take up; significantly, these three women are the "Women Spinning Women Together." That aspect is the value women have come to place on themselves as women: "Women are more satisfied being women, more proud of themselves, and I believe that it has helped us some." To Harding feminism means "being proud of being a woman, being aware of what that is. And I still don't have any great answers. But I think most women aren't conscious of being put down at all and they're not proud of being women, and they have no urge to identify with women and to be with them." Thus, she says, "I think every bit of change and consciousness-raising that I can do helps the women's movement. And I do a lot of it. I really make a serious effort to challenge women to examine their lives and their . . . you know, that may not always be the best thing to do either."

Kate Greene's definition of feminism presents a women-centered notion that will emerge full-blown among the "Women-centered Feminine-ists." Greene defines feminism as caring "very deeply about women's needs, wants, and concerns." She is proud to call herself a feminist and is proud of others who call themselves feminists. She also feels "very good about the women's movement," though, like Stone, she sees a need to "regroup" after the defeat of the ERA. The anger from that defeat can either shatter or galvanize women's energies. She wants to channel the anger in a positive way. She says, "In fact, I've been doing a lot of speaking around the state about not deciding, 'Well, we're going to throw this guy out who voted against the ERA.' But rather say, 'We're going to work with this guy who voted for the ERA, and we're going to make sure that he gets rewarded before we punish someone else.' Now that's the way we build a political struggle."

Because of her young age, Annie Witt says, her views of the women's movement and feminism come more from reading and talking with women who have been involved than from her own actual involvement in the "big movement" of the 1960s and 1970s. She gives a "women's rights" view of feminism, but, as the leftist "Woman Spinning Threads" in this cluster of women, she points to the "Marxist-Feminism" expressed by the next cluster when she goes on to include the idea that institutional barriers must be removed if women's rights are to be gained. The one thing she does not like about the movement "was that early separatism that came out of a lot of radical feminist theory." But she sees the women's movement now as more concerned with integrating the different groups of women and with linking up with other movements.

"Marxist-Feminism"

Three women develop the "Marxist-Feminist" theme, introduced by Annie Witt, of the need to break down the institutions of society and to link movements for change. All are leftist, Marxist, community activists—Susan Murphy, Maria Montgomery, and Hazel Beecroft. The hyphen in "Marxist-Feminist" indicates the tension that arises when Marxist women begin to attempt to integrate Marxism with feminist theory and practice. Heidi Hartmann has described the attempt as an "unhappy marriage,"[4] and Rosalind Petchesky has reported on the efforts of Marxist-Feminist theorists/activists directed toward "Dissolving the Hyphen."[5] The "Marxist-Feminists" presented here express these tensions. Murphy, one of the "Women

Spinning Networks," Montgomery, one of the "Women Made, Not Born," and Beecroft, one of the "Women Spinning Threads," consciously distinguish their views of feminism from nineteenth-century "bourgeois feminism," and thereby for the most part from the "Women's Rights Feminists." Only one of the "Marxist-Feminists," Murphy, mentions women's rights, and she is just becoming conscious of the importance of an autonomous women's movement for her own life. The other two view the women's movement from the historical perspectives that they have learned are so important to Marxist analysis.

Murphy defines feminism as "a bourgeois movement back in the nineteenth century" and "an ideology that espouses the role of women in history and puts forward solutions to the problems of the oppression of women." She notes that that movement was lead by and for bourgeois women, "although it had positive benefits for the working-class women, too." She has never thought of herself as a feminist, because "feminism to me in some ways has a negative connotation . . . anti-male or anti-man." But she does see herself "as an activist for women's rights and concerned with women's rights."

Murphy's assessment of the present women's movement, however, is basically positive, though she believes that it, too, has been too white and middle class. "That's been its shortcoming. I hope the women's movement will grow and mature and [that] more and more it can be bi-racial. And that working-class women will feel that they have a place in it, that the women's movement is concerned with their issues. And that trade union women can feel that they're a part of the women's movement. That the women's movement becomes very broad and more than just a movement for gains for professional women or middle-class women." Montgomery, in contrast, is more negative about the contemporary women's movement, seeing its "ideology as reactionary, inside a section of the women's movement, . . . 'let's get careers, let's get women in the chairman of the board, let's get women in the Supreme Court.' And that men are the enemy." She considers herself a feminist—"someone who is aware of women's repression and is trying to struggle against it"—but she seems to be inclined to want to organize women within a leftist multinational party "to fight the New Right with its militarism and its pro-family stuff."

Beecroft, like Murphy, refers to nineteenth-century feminists as "women who were only concerned with women and not concerned with questions of class and race. . . . That's the criticism of feminists that has been made, that they somehow think that there can be this unity among women from different classes. And I really don't share that." In fact, Beecroft understands the contemporary women's movement to have "had an incredible impact on America, and I think the shock waves are going to be felt for years and years and years." The impact has been in terms of "consciousness" because of the history of the contemporary movement. Unlike Murphy and Montgomery, she understands that "it came out of the civil rights movement with Black women from the very beginning, and then it came out of the Left, and then it was taken over by liberal women to a certain extent, [since] those are the people who now have the institutional forms." Even her assessment of the "liberal" feminists is positive to the extent that she believes they have learned something valuable about and from the political process surrounding the defeat of the ERA.

Beecroft considers herself to be a "socialist feminist." Her study group has been reading radical Lesbian feminist theory in addition to Marxist theory. According to Alison Jaggar's analysis, socialist feminism is attempting to integrate the best aspects of radical feminism and Marxism,[6] so Beecroft may be well on her way to eradicating the hyphen in "Marxist-Feminist."

"Women-centered Feminine-ism"

Four women—Barbara Bergen, Fran Daly, Tillie Zadar, and Gretchen Bright—all women's community activists and either "Women Spinning Threads" or "Women Spinning Networks," believe that women, whether identifying themselves as Lesbians or not, should be self-defining by drawing on their feminine qualities of creativity and affirmation of life. For them, men per se are not the enemy. Rather, patriarchy—a system of domination by gender, race, and economic class—is the enemy, and men, especially white men, are the chief agents of patriarchy.

Bergen sets the stage with her holistic vision of feminism: "a way of looking at the world that is a holistic way, an integrated way." She contrasts feminism with a view of the world that separates out and dominates, beginning with the domination of women by men and manifesting itself in the domination of nature by men and in American militarism in Nicaragua. Suggesting that she has located her own standpoint, she says feminism "gives me a place to stand." She takes a very long historical view of the women's movement: "I'm going to continue in it for my whole life. I don't think that it's ever been out of existence. I think it's been more active within the white middle class, it's more media-oriented, at different times during history. I think that the witches were the women's movement, and I think that it has always been that way, and I think it always will be." She believes the women's movement has all the problems of the larger white racist, classist society, but it is the only place where she has any sense of being.

The other three women add the idea of "Women-centered Feminine-ism" to their understanding of feminism. Daly says that "feminism is a worldview, and I guess I see it as a conscious point of view of a woman-identified woman. That doesn't mean a Lesbian. It means a woman who identifies with herself, . . . [who] sees the relation between herself and the planet, so that feminism affects ecology, affects rearing children, affects how you cook; . . . it has to do with life to me, some sort of affirmation of life and a wholeness." Daly understands feminism in the context of patriarchy, which she defines as "the dominance of the white male system, and that's not necessarily always identified with every white man, but the white man's system that has had power on this planet. The patriarchy refers to the fathers, but what that means to me is that system of behavior and thought and domination of people and of the planet and governments and children, you know, everyone." As for Bergen, so for Daly the women's movement, and patriarchy, go back a long way into history, and the women's movement will need to continue a long way into the future.

Zadar continues the patriarchal thread initiated by Daly and goes on to tie "the feminine" explicitly to feminism: "My feminism is a view of Western patriarchy and how it functions and affects all our lives and everything we do, from national policy down to who washes the dishes. I don't think that's what it means to most people. I know people who have even rejected the idea, the label 'feminine,' because they feel it's too narrow. It does have that label, being women-related, but I don't know, I like it." She, like Daly, "definitely" sees the women's movement as continuing, even though "the media are always heralding the end of all these things." She says she has been "real inspired lately, like with the women's marathon [in the 1984 Summer Olympics] . . . and Geraldine [1984 Democratic vice-presidential candidate Ferraro]. I'm feeling like we are making some progress." But taking the long view, "I don't see that we are going to have any kind of revolution. I see us as plodding along in this manner and kind of socking away, just slowly but surely."

If there is any problem with the movement, from where she stands, it is with the radical feminists that are going in the direction of "this more spiritual kind of 'mushy' politics, which I don't like." She thinks they do not have a well-developed analysis, and though "I can see on a personal level people get a lot out of spirituality, I don't think it has much political impact." She gives a long critical analysis of feminist spirituality, touching positively on processing thoughts and feelings while sitting in circles and negatively on changing names, performing rituals to the Goddess, and going into witchcraft, "putting hexes on men. I think it's a cop-out. It's just fake power that they think [they have], you know, they don't have any real power, and they get into this imagined power, and it's just as imagined as if they wore high heels and felt like they have men wrapped around their little finger. It's the same thing, just a different manifestation." Unlike the "Male-defined Feminine-ists," Zadar does not put all feminists into one box labeled "man-hating bra-burners" and brush them aside. She finds within just one part of the larger women's movement a complex phenomenon that she can describe and evaluate at length both negatively and positively.

Bright presents an understanding of feminism that "reclaims the feminine" but also results in a profoundly political "Women-centered

Feminine-ism." She makes a direct connection between "being a woman" and developing a multidimensional feminist consciousness. In defining feminism, she says:

> Feminism to me is a politics of transformation. It is viewing the world with a vision for possibility, for inner-connectedness, and for a valuing of diversity. You know, when we were talking about "what does it mean to be a woman and what does it mean to be feminine?" it is from that emerging appreciation and understanding and cultivation of myself as a woman and female and feminine that empowers my feminist politics. It is not a reactionary stance for me, but it is an initiating vision, you know, that transforms as it goes. It is not a worldview that is saying "all right, we're going to work for this revolution, and then we are going to have this revolution, and when we overthrow the white male pig, then we will start the new world." You know, for me feminism is something that transforms my world constantly. And it is in living out that transformative view that I have my greatest impact.

In discussing the women's movement, Bright develops the theme of diversity. She sees the women's movement "in a stage of learning how to effectively use the diversity that is there, to see that diversity as a resource rather than divisive. I feel like there is a lot of work to be done to learn how to use our strength of numbers and to find the common differences that we have." But, echoing Annie Witt's concerns, she says, "I fear that there are many of us who are getting tired. I feel like the generation of women that are in college right now are not going to join the women's movement in large numbers. It's more of an Eisenhower generation." Now she believes that, through the various media, young women are being encouraged "to get married and have babies, get back in the box . . . to be the superwoman of having job and family." They read stories about women questioning the choices they *have* made: "like 'I made the choice to follow my career, and I'm thirty-five and I'm not married and I want a child, so what do I do?' or it's like 'the lonely woman at the top' thing: 'I'm up here and making a million dollars a year, and I can't find any men to relate to.' You know, those kinds of things. It's like saying to the younger women, 'Well, you know, you see what happened to them, so watch out.' " Bright would be pleased to know that college students Annie Witt and Tillie Zadar are speaking out against this kind of "patriarchal" conditioning, as Zadar would call it, and are joining in the transformational politics that Bright calls for.

How "Being a Woman" Grounds Consciousness of "Feminism" and "Antifeminism"

In the previous chapter, I introduced the idea from Sandra Bartky's phenomenology of feminist consciousness that the way women understand "being a woman" grounds their feminist consciousness. These white middle-class female activists not only do not agree on a meaning of "being a woman," they do not agree on what feminism is about or whom feminism is for. The reasons have to do with whether each woman takes Alfred Schutz's "natural attitude" toward life in the world, not doubting that things are as they seem, or whether she takes Dorothy Smith's critical inquiring approach to life in the world, questioning both the structure of that world and others' interpretations of it. Some women are questioning what others may be taking for granted, whether it be their place in the world itself or a form of consciousness. Some believe it is the world that is problematic. They say that "feminism" is a creative way of life and that life in the world as it is presently structured must be transformed so that this creativity can be more fully manifested. Other women believe it is a form of consciousness that is problematic. They say that "feminism" is a perversion of "Woman's" true nature and that "feminism" must be returned to its true meaning before their lives in the world are ruined. A recapping of these women's forms of consciousness as "feminist" or "antifeminist" in relation to the ways they understand "being a woman" will demonstrate just how closely their personal and political lives are connected. Table 2 summarizes these relationships.

Four women in my study, the three "Ladies" and one "Lady with Best of Both Worlds," associate "feminism" with bra-burning, Betty Friedan and Gloria Steinem, the ERA, and/or Lesbianism. They reject this meaning of feminism for themselves and say rather that feminism should mean being female and woman-like, liking men. In other words, ideally feminism should encompass their own direct experiences of life in which they enjoy being women who like men. Their talk of failed women suggests that they equate their ideal form of feminism with what is traditionally understood in the dominant culture as being feminine. Indeed, it is more than *being* women who like men. It is, as Linda Helms informed us, *acting* "the Lady" in order to get in return the "special treatment" reserved by "Gentlemen" for "Ladies" who do not push beyond those boundaries set by men, and who do not make issue of any "put downs" they *do* receive as women. Only "Lady with Best of Both Worlds" Lorraine Reilly differs from her "Lady" sisters on this point. She will challenge the men in the political party who disagree with her on conventional "public sphere" political matters. But she will put up with her husband's presumably typical masculine behavior in the "private sphere" of the household: remember her saying, "Sometimes I'll get angry with my husband, and I tell him 'You ought to be happy that I'm not pushing for ERA, or boy, you'd really be in trouble *in this house*'" (emphasis added).

An interpretation of this form of "being feminine" offered from outside the standpoints of these three "Ladies" and a "Lady with Best of Both Worlds," and in opposition to their interpretation, is that of Dorothy Smith. She sees "being feminine" as a social form of consciousness that has become ideological because it is defined in relation to what pleases men or at least does not question what men seem to want done. Men appear to be the controlling factor, even if these women believe they choose their actions in relation to men. Thus, I have designated this form of femininity as male-defined and this form of consciousness as "Male-defined Feminine-ism." By male-defined, I mean that some men, as controlling actors in a system characterized as "complex domination," are understood to have developed and others, including women, to have sustained the principle that there are two sexes with differences between them significant enough to determine power relations in society. Such men, and women, have defined the qualities and behaviors that should distinguish men from women and that can be and have been used to place men in power over women.

Table 2. Relationship between "Being a Woman" and Antifeminist or Feminist Consciousness

	"Being a Woman"	*Antifeminist or Feminist Consciousness*
Ladies		
	Linda Helms	Male-defined Feminine-ism
	Bridgit Malone	Male-defined Feminine-ism
	Lavinia Ravenel	Male-defined Feminine-ism
Ladies with Best of Both Worlds		
	Lorraine Reilly	Male-defined Feminine-ism
	Bess Shumaker	Antifeminist People-ism
	Sybyl Jensen	Antifeminist People-ism
Women Persons		
	Dulcie LaFontaine	Antifeminist People-ism
	Elizabeth Latimer	Antifeminist People-ism
	Betty Mason	Antifeminist People-ism
	Arlene Pringle	Antifeminist People-ism
	Maryanne Thayer	Antifeminist People-ism
Women Made, Not Born		
	Audrey Nelms	Antifeminist People-ism
	Adrienne Stone	Women's Rights Feminism
	Edith Hammond	Women's Rights Feminism
	Ella Washburn	Women's Rights Feminism
	Maria Montgomery	Marxist-Feminism
Women Spinning Women Together		
	Kate Greene	Women's Rights Feminism
	Nancy Harding	Women's Rights Feminism
	Sally Martin	Women's Rights Feminism
Women Spinning Threads		
	Annie Witt	Women's Rights Feminism
	Hazel Beecroft	Marxist-Feminism
	Fran Daly	Women-defined Feminine-ism
	Tillie Zadar	Women-defined Feminine-ism
Women Spinning Networks		
	Susan Murphy	Marxist-Feminism
	Barbara Bergen	Women-defined Feminine-ism
	Gretchen Bright	Women-defined Feminine-ism

From outside the perspective of "Male-defined Feminine-ism," other "feminists" may judge that such consciousness is ideological. But from inside that same perspective, the women standing there cannot be stripped of their agency. To do this, in the words of bell hooks, "mystifies women's role . . . in the maintenance of systems of domination." hooks's point is that women as social beings are inherently "political beings": "In keeping with the tenets of sexist ideology, women are talked about in these discussions as objects rather than subjects. We are depicted not as workers and activists, who, like men, make political choices, but as passive observers who have taken no responsibility for actively maintaining the value system of this society."[7]

Virginia Woolf made a similar point more than fifty years ago.[8] She suggested—speaking, she said, from the standpoint of daughters of educated Englishmen—that women could help prevent war by acting on their differences from their educated brothers and fathers. Rather than contributing to the honor and glory that such men seemed to derive from militarism by worshiping the exploits of these presumably great warriors, women could stop paying any attention, positive or negative, to them, could stop making bandages for their wounds, could stop nursing them. This, Woolf said, was the kind of behavior that "Outsiders" could engage in as part of a strategy to transform the patriarchy. But Woolf also understood the dangers in being an overt Outsider. If the Outsider pushed her father or brother too far, especially in public where he could be observed by other educated Englishmen, he could become exceedingly angry and punish her economically or psychologically or even physically. Fear was and is a rational feeling in such situations, and secrecy was and is a rational defense.

I cannot say for certain whether these "Male-defined Feminine-ists" are motivated more by desire for privilege or by fear of retribution, but in the face of my questions, these women held their ground. For some, their body language suggested that they moved into a defensive position. But confronted with the opportunity, or challenge, to talk about "feminism" and "the women's movement," they chose to share their thoughts and feelings with me.

"Male-defined Feminine-ists" appear to have no problem in identifying with other women they consider to be feminine. They imply "we" when they speak of "they," referring to the problematic women they consider to be unfeminine—the "bra burners," the Betty Friedans, the Gloria Steinems, the Lesbians. "We" are prepared to fight any changes "they" want to bring about *for* us. Again, as the "Lady with Best of Both Worlds" Reilly said, "I just read that this whole NOW organization is going to turn their attention, once ERA dies, to the housewife. Believe me, I don't want them bothering me. What could they do for me? They can't do a darn thing. Go do something else, but leave the housewife alone."

Indeed, on the other end of the spectrum live four "Women-centered Feminine-ists," three of whom *are* self-declared Lesbians. Two of these women I characterized earlier as "Women Spinning Threads," two as "Women Spinning Networks." They also speak of feminism in terms of being feminine. Their differences from the first four women are mainly two: they explicitly understand *this* form of feminine-ism as an ever-emergent way of life in the here and now, and they understand it as women-defined and women-centered. That is, as women grounded in their own direct experiences of everyday life, *they* socially construct *themselves* together with other women as creative, life-giving, and life-sustaining. Fran Daly says feminism is "a worldview . . . a conscious point of view of a woman-identified woman . . . [who] sees the relation between herself and the planet, so that feminism affects ecology, affects rearing children, affects how you cook, . . . it has to do with life to me, some sort of affirmation of life and a wholeness."

Though other women in this study, and not just the "Male-defined Feminine-ists," believe that "feminists" are "man-haters," these "Women-centered Feminine-ists" do not think of themselves necessarily in contrast or in relation to men, as do the "Male-defined Feminine-ists." Tillie Zadar says of "be-ing a woman" that "being a Lesbian, you're a woman outside . . . not getting anything from men, which is the ultimate as far as men are concerned. They can't stand it. . . . To refuse that dependence [on men] is to change the definition of what a woman is." These "Women-centered Feminine-ists," however, in order to remain on their side of the line of fault between their own direct experiences and male-defined femininity, also are conscious of having to resist daily what they term the "patriarchal" institutions and values that structure the larger world within which they live. Fran Daly speaks of having continuously to be aware that her unconscious tells her "what it is to be a good girl. And those are things that are traditionally feminine that I do battle with in my personal life and my inner life." Barbara Bergen indicates that feminism includes taking a stand against the domination of nature by men and American militarism in Nicaragua. Feminism "gives me a place to stand." Their direct experiences demand more ground than "patriarchal" men, and women, grant them, and they are prepared to challenge those limits. Thus, they recognize that they live at one and the same time both in and against the "patriarchal" world.[9] Daily living is a process of resistance and affirmation, of "feminist," in the sense of "Women-centered Feminine-ist," transformation of that world. Just as being a "Lady" inextricably grounds "Male-defined Feminine-ism" in a limited space with no legitimate time and attention for self, so "be-ing" "Women Spinning Threads and Networks" inextricably grounds and carves out ever more time and space for "Women-centered Feminine-ists."

Between the "Male-defined" and "Women-centered Feminine-ists" live women who in my study express three other forms of consciousness of "feminism" or "antifeminism." I have designated these forms "Antifeminist People-ism," "Women's Rights Feminism," and "Marxist-Feminism." The same time dimension that separates "Women Persons" from "Women Made, Not Born," appears to separate "Antifeminist People-ism" and "Women's Rights Feminism." The women who espouse "Antifeminist People-ism" are for the most part those I characterized as "Women Persons," though the other two "Ladies with Best of Both Worlds" express this form of consciousness, as does the "Woman Made, Not Born," Audrey Nelms. Thus, these women, with the exception of the "Ladies with Best of Both Worlds," have rejected "being feminine" as a positive value so that femininity no longer constricts their horizons. Moreover, they believe that any problems that women have faced under the law have been solved and that, therefore, women can live, like men, as "just people." In other words, these women reject feminism because they believe they already possess the rights of individuals for which the "Women's Rights Feminists" are still fighting, and they believe they possess the personhood needed to exercise those rights.

The women who espouse "Women's Rights Feminism" identify as "Women Made, Not Born," or "Women Spinning Women Together." Both groups of these women believe there is still much work to do for women's rights in the area of legal reform because they feel the strictures of law as well as custom in their daily lives, despite their beliefs that they are capable of doing much more than society allows or recognizes. While the "Women Made, Not Born," also stress the negative ways that the requirements of femininity restrict their opportunities, the "Women Spinning Women Together" have begun to reclaim the positive aspects of femininity for women to use among themselves as a resource in their fight for women's rights.

It is noteworthy that most of the women who have come to identify themselves as "white women," that is, women simultaneously conscious of their racial privilege and their sexual oppression, are for the most part "Women Spinning Threads and Networks," who have inscribed their "Marxist-Feminism" or their "Women-centered Feminine-ism" with a concern for the diverse needs and desires of women. They want the women's movement to address their own needs as well as the needs of women in social locations different from theirs. It could be said that they believe "feminists" should work to transform the institutionalized value systems of "complex domination" that confer on them illegitimate race and class privilege along with sexual oppression.

It is the "Marxist-Feminists" who, because of their knowledge of Marxist theory, point out the ideological possibilities for "feminism" and "antifeminism." They speak here of the ideology of "bourgeois feminism," which they understand as privileging one economic class of women over another. Their insight brings me to the problem of the fineness of the lines of fault between different women's experiences, the lines along which different forms of "feminism" and "antifeminism" emerge.

Even among the white women in my study there are differences in age, economic class, and sexuality. Most are married, but some are not and intend to stay that way; a few are divorced. Most are wives and mothers; some are grandmothers. All these women, while not doubting that they are in direct touch with their own experiences, nevertheless do doubt and question what they perceive others to believe about the place of women in society. Some consider themselves "feminists"; others reject that label. If pushed to defend her particular form of consciousness, each would probably argue that hers is "grounded" in her own experience directly sensed and interpreted. Many, however, would characterize other women's forms of consciousness as "ideological," if they were to use the language of theoretical discourse. To take the most contrasting examples, "Male-defined Feminine-ists" reject "feminism" as a form of consciousness and a political movement that *other* women have constructed and have tried to put over on them; hence, the false, ideological nature of "feminism," which would be oppressive to "Male-defined Feminine-ists." "Women-centered Feminine-ists," in contrast, reject "Male-defined Feminine-ism" as false, ideological, and oppressive because it has been constructed *by* men *for* women.

What these women collectively suggest, therefore, is that different forms of "feminism" and "antifeminism" emerge out of different ways of understanding "being a woman." Thus, what is consciously constructed as "grounded" by some is consciously judged as "ideological" from other women's standpoints. Furthermore, none of these women engages "feminism" or "antifeminism" in any form in the "natural attitude." All these women bring fully engaged critical perspectives to bear on other women—and men—in their everyday lives, thus transforming Alfred Schutz's notion of life lived in the "natural attitude" into Dorothy Smith's notion that women can theorize and socially construct their lives with others in their everyday worlds.

Chapter 6

Patterns of Politicization Guide
Paths to Political Engagement

We have seen how structures of affective relationships in the child-hood family, understood in their particular historical, political, and socioeconomic contexts, appear to have laid a basis in the sub-conscious realm for daughters to become identified as women who either would as "feminists" or would not as "antifeminists" challenge the dominant culture's construction and valuing of women as male-identified. Turning now to the role/action dimension of politicization, we will discover that particular family members loom large as role models from whom these women consciously or unconsciously took cues on whether and, if so, how to connect to the political appara-tus, conventional or otherwise. By political apparatus I mean the organizations and institutional roles and processes of conventional politics and governance—the two major political parties, the elec-toral process, and government itself—or the organizations and net-works of communication that constitute political movements.

The process of perceiving opportunities to connect with the con-ventional political apparatus or to create other political apparatus is multidimensional. On the one hand is the flow of given opportuni-ties for political engagement. On the other hand is the process of learning how to utilize existing opportunities or to reject those and to create new opportunities. The women in my study suggest that role- and action-oriented politicization can be likened to an ongoing political drama buzzing with opportunities for connection to exist-ing political structures or creation of different channels to political action. Just as Joseph Schlesinger has found that constitutionally based governments of elected representatives generate an opportunity structure for officeholding,[1] so it now appears from these women's reports that regularly scheduled elections generate opportunities for people to get involved in campaigns at predictable intervals. Political parties and other organizations generate ongoing opportunities to get involved in activities designed to influence public policy. Even movements and the organizations that create them likewise generate opportunity structures through which people can channel actions that otherwise would find no place to go. But movements by their nature are not predictable because they are not structured into the institutional processes of conventional government and politics. Rather, people who make radical critiques of the established "system" must find one another and make movements happen.

There appears to be no set way in which these women made their connections to the political apparatus that they found waiting for them or that they created.[2] Some made their connections straightforwardly, following the examples of their mothers or fathers or other family members. In such cases, the role model does little more than provide an initial cue or model that may later receive reinforcement from a husband or friend or political election or candidate. Some, having observed the ways of childhood family members, took the initial cue or model and developed in a way and along a path unique to themselves and their friends or co-workers. Some received no cues from childhood family members and waited for cues from marriage families or from others in the community before making the connections. Some were taught or later learned to be critical of that dominant conventional political apparatus, and they turned from it to other apparatuses that appeared at particular times in particular places or that they themselves created—movements critical of the substance and form of "politics as usual." In this section, the women interviewed explicate the various ways in which they have become the types of political actors they are.

Mothers and Politicization

Six women tell stories pointing to mothers as prime models of patterns of activity that initiated or shaped the course of their daughters' politicization, regardless of which political arena the daughters entered as adults. Republican officeholder Sybyl Jensen, Democratic party worker Ella Washburn, and Lesbian feminist Fran Daly are women who in their adult years used as a model their mothers' patterns of community involvement. Washburn is particularly conscious of having done so and of her reasons for those actions. She describes her own partisan activism as community service, and her party work as only part of a larger involvement: "I was quite involved all during the time I was a homemaker. I was involved in a civic club out there, and the PTA and the Girl and Boy Scouts, all those things that most mothers are involved in, and mine went a little further in that I was very involved in the political scene. I was very, very interested in that. As soon as my children were large enough that I could be away from home more and more, I got more and more involved in it." Washburn indicated earlier in her interview that she is very much like her mother, and the likeness is apparent in her response to why she thinks her mother was such a joiner: "Well, I don't really know, because like most people her age she was never able to get very much education. But she was very interested in the children and what they had and didn't have, and from the day I can remember, she was active in PTA. . . . And then, from that, she got interested in, you know, other community things." The mother's and daughter's motivation for political involvement are also apparent in this exchange: whatever is good for the children.[3] Washburn says, "Her main interest was her six children and what was best for them." In a similar vein, Washburn followed her mother's lead: "And that was really how I got started. Whatever is best for my children, that's what I'll do—your work, your church activity, everything you do. And most of the times along in that phase of your life it's what is best for your children and your family."

Washburn also shows how husbands and presidential candidates can figure in the process of politicization: husbands can give support and direction to wives' political activism,[4] while presidential campaigns can serve as a magnet for activism at the national level of politics. She tells how her husband changed positions, going from management to being a union representative. From there, he became heavily involved in the labor movement and recruited her to work with him in John Kennedy's presidential campaign.

Sybyl Jensen is another case of a woman who seems to have used as a model her mother's community political involvements, but unlike Washburn's, Jensen's involvement became the basis for her deciding to seek public office. Her husband also seems to have played a significant role in her deciding to run for office. She had long been active in her local community on school and zoning issues and had worked for several candidates in state and local races. She had lobbied at the state legislature and was generally well known as someone who could get things done. When a state legislator resigned, people began to suggest that she run for the office. Her husband gave her the final push, and they went right to work organizing the campaign. She won.

Fran Daly shows how conventional community involvement can put one on the road to radicalism and how complex the journey can be. Daly began her community involvement much as did her mother, who was active in social programs sponsored by her Baptist church to provide food and clothing for poor people. Daly first became involved during high school in Young Life, an interdenominational Christian youth organization. Her first job was with Young Life, where at summer camp she was introduced to "feminist theology, and that really turned me around." Later, when she went to a seminary for a short period, teachers there stressed taking a critical approach, even to the Scriptures, and learning to question received knowledge. Looking back, she understands now that "my involvement with the church was part of what I considered being a 'Radical Christian,' . . . a way of believing as over against the government kind of thing. We believed in changing the world, . . . using that forum for contact with people as a way of raising consciousness and living in a loving and transformative way of life."

During this same period she also came into contact with women from Pittsburgh and New York who had come down to Atlanta as part of the Young Life staff. "And these women had been, were wives of Young Life people [men], who were going to save the world. You know the types. They had been having babies and adopting children and living in poverty and doing all those things. And they [women] were real tired and real ready to talk about those things. And when they started talking I can remember being simpatico with them and saying, 'Let's do a women's group,' just very innocently. Little did we know what we were getting into."

What they had gotten into became a feminist consciousness-raising group. "That was what keeping in touch with your feelings was called back in the early seventies, when you would sit around and talk with other women and hear that they were happy or unhappy with their marriages and why, and how their fathers and mothers treated them when they were children." In other words, consciousness-raising was a form of political theorizing in the contemporary women's movement.[5] The process evolved as women thrown together in particular situations would form small groups and begin to talk about what they thought were their "personal" problems but which came to be understood as problems caused by societal structures.[6] The "personal" came to be understood as political. Daly says that, for the women in Young Life and "Radical Christianity," the language of Christian rhetoric about oppression "got translated for me into feminism afterwards."

In summing up her process of politicization, she describes a process of emerging through layer after layer of consciousness. She began with connecting with successive organizations and communities and

> caring about what happens to the planet through Christianity. [But when I realized that] Christianity is a patriarchal destructive institution, then I had to move into another realm. But my burgeoning feminism coincided with that. It didn't really follow that completely, though the Radical Christianity in part preceded that. There was a long period where those things overlapped and were real in harmony for me. And then [there was] the departure from the institutional expression of that and Christianity into more radical feminism and also becoming a Les-

bian. Those things were all overlapping. And of course, my community changed as I grew. The people that I spent time with talked a different language and lived in different ways. But as I look at my peace work now and the values of the women's community, we work for peace and the values that I had as an early Christian trying to express a hopefulness for the world. They are very similar, but they are spoken in a different language and done by people who look and behave in a different fashion. But they seem real related to me.

And her process will not stop there. Her intent and the intent of her women's community is to transform the patriarchal world into a world at peace and in harmony with the natural forces of the planet.

Republican party worker Betty Mason is another whose politics can be traced back to her religious upbringing, but whereas Fran Daly has left the institutionalized church, Mason has brought her church's religious beliefs to bear on her political beliefs. In explaining her partisan involvement, she says "I did not like the way I saw the country going. I did not like the way I saw morals [being ignored]. And I think it begins with church, and it begins with politics. Too many people criticize but don't get involved." She attributes great influence in this to her mother, who instilled in her "a moralistic way with very strong ties, very strong family ties as well as religious ties." Since her mother had divorced her father, the immediate family consisted of Mason and her younger brother and her mother, who saw to it that the family spent the evening meal together. "Regardless of what else transpired, the evening meal was the family, and we discussed everything that was going on. We discussed world affairs. We would get into healthy discussions as to world circumstances, and, as you well know, no one can be more vocal than some sixteen- or seventeen-year old." Such discussions were "thought-provoking" and made her "search for answers."

Mason provides another case of a presidential candidate's influence on a young woman's politicization, but it was the woman herself, not a husband, who initiated her actions. Barry Goldwater, the Republican presidential candidate in 1964, was the immediate cause for her getting involved in politics. She was an avid reader—she mentions Ayn Rand as a favorite author—and was not happy with the way things were going on the national scene. But "the more I read, the more I heard him, it embraced so much of what I thought and felt, and he had a way of putting into words what I thought and felt that I could not articulate." She telephoned the local Republican party headquarters to find out "when the precinct caucus was going to be. I went into the precinct caucus by myself, without knowing a soul or knowing a bit about politics or what even transpired in a precinct caucus. And with politics, it's like church work, club work, or anything else. All you have to do is let somebody know you're interested and willing to work. And then it's just a matter of how much when." She has been a committed party worker ever since, especially in presidential and gubernatorial campaigns.

Feminist women's community activist Gretchen Bright presents a case similar to that of Betty Mason in that Bright's mother supported a talent that her daughter possessed and would later translate into political action. Bright's talent was, and is, writing, and she knew from an early age that she wanted to be a writer. Her mother supported her in this, though her father would have preferred that she turn her artistic talent to the stage through acting or dancing. Becoming political, for Bright, "is a thread that goes back real early in my life that is based around being an artist and being [a] writer. There were certain aims that I had and certain obstacles to the way that I wanted to live." In other words, her "politics" consisted of finding ways around the obstacles to her self-actualization.

She describes how she tried to find work that would support or use her writing. For a period,

> in my teens and in my twenties, I was fascinated by the existing political system, electoral politics.... I believe that my experiences working in city government and being quite involved in the behind-the-scenes role of electoral politics taught me a whole lot.... I mean writing speeches for politicians is a pretty surreal experience. I think that I realized the corruption that is necessary of an individual's integrity in order to obtain an elective office. That was real painful [to reconcile with] my idealism of my earlier years, but I also felt liberated from that.

During this period she also read Mary Daly's *Gyn/Ecology*, and "it definitely changed me. It affirmed much of what I had been growing toward politically and experiencing. She recognized and described the way I felt and explained a lot about the overall system of patriarchy that gave me a toehold on creating a vision for myself. And while I have grown to put her in context, I will forever be indebted for her clarity. I wish her style was more accessible."

Reading Mary Daly seemed to cement her liberation from conventional electoral politics, though paradoxically she still votes. She continues describing her journey out of "the system": "So when I got a view of the personal kind of destruction that I think happens in that system [the personal compromises that politicians make in order to get elected], marrying that to my overall growing perspective of the patriarchy and what the system is really designed for, I don't feel a need or that it is really necessary to work in the system." Now she feels that everything she does in her daily living is political. Her political goal is "to continue to develop myself as a whole person. I believe that doing that . . . enables me to manifest the activities and resistance and visionary things in my exterior life. The intent of the patriarchy is to diminish my wholeness and to prohibit my wholeness. Without a political commitment to healing myself and then developing, nurturing and encouraging my wholeness, my efforts in that in the outside world will be turned against me."

Finally, Lesbian feminist Tillie Zadar represents a case of a woman who has combined her mother's electoral politics and a boyfriend's radical politics into an amalgam that is cemented with her own contribution of coming out as a Lesbian. In tracing her political history she goes back as far as her high-school years: "In high school I had been politically involved in a bunch of different things. My mother was always involved in electoral politics, so I would do a lot of phone calls, stuff like that. And then I had a boyfriend at the time who was very radical, and would do things that—my mother is pretty radical." She breaks off in mid-sentence on "radical" in describing her boyfriend. She has described her mother as having been involved in electoral politics, but speaking of her radical boyfriend reminds her that her mother has changed, has become more radical, working for an environmental defense fund and for a center that helped displaced homemakers find jobs. Now Zadar says her mother is "kind of semi-counterculture." When Zadar's sister married recently, their mother came to the wedding. The day after the wedding, Zadar says, "me and mom went down to a demonstration. Reagan was in town the day after, and we went together to this big demonstration. It was great! You know, we took the bus."

Returning to her boyfriend, Zadar says that in high school, in the late 1970s, she had a thirty-year-old radical leftist boyfriend, of whom both her parents disapproved. He seems to have inspired some of her more radical political activities in high school: running a campaign *against* prom queen, for which she "nearly got beat up"; raising a "red flag of revolution over our high school." She also refused to participate in Girls State, to which she was invited, because of their rules. "You had to wear white gloves to dinner, . . . you can't be engaged or married, and if you have a boyfriend you cannot even call him. . . . You had to sign this thing saying that you would stand for the pledge of allegiance. . . . Obviously they had trouble before, so I refused to go to that."

It was when Zadar entered college that she reached what she considered a pivotal point in her life. She joined the staff of the newspaper, which was run as a radical feminist collective. "That was really a learning experience for me, because I was more of a liberal feminist at that time, and having all that exposure with the radical feminists was like 'Whooo!' The hostility on campus particularly that quarter was just palpable." The hostility was verbal, not physical, and was directed by some of the male students at the radical feminists, who were Lesbian separatists. It was during this period, Zadar says, that she began to think about becoming Lesbian herself. During another quarter she did a work-study project in New York with the Democratic Socialist Organizing Committee, which is now the Democratic Socialists of America. She went to New York with a reputation as a feminist and returned to her campus having come out as a Lesbian. Her last quarter in college she again worked on the student newspaper, which again formed a radical Lesbian feminist collective.

When Zadar came to Atlanta, she joined a Lesbian feminist group that has made a difference in how she thinks about her political world. In college she worked with Lesbian feminists, but in Atlanta she actually lives in the Lesbian community. "There is a community, and to be part of that is real important. . . . That's the lifestyle thing, . . . another way of living. . . . I remember when I first came here, I hadn't really known very many older Lesbians. All the Lesbians I knew were young and it was just really affirming to see all these women who were out there doing all kinds of things, you know, that were in their thirties and forties and fifties and older and to know that there was a history then." Zadar says that she "always had this outside kind of view of our culture, . . . and being a Lesbian has furthered [making an outside political analysis] because I think you are even more outside. Not only are you [further from] a capitalist society but you are away from a heterosexual society, too. That fosters being able to look from the outside at interactions." Hence Zadar's compartmentalized conception of the political world as "inside" and "outside." She sometimes wants to work "inside," meaning inside electoral politics, as when during the 1984 presidential campaign she considered doing some volunteer work for Geraldine Ferraro; and she still votes. But mainly she works "outside," that is, inside her Lesbian community.

Fathers and Politicization

Eight women tell stories of their politicization that point to fathers as prime models or initiators of their daughters' approaches to politics. Republican party worker Arlene Pringle describes her father as someone who "was pretty opinionated" and "had some talents in writing." Pringle was not close to her father; in fact, she says she feared him because "he was so big, and then I didn't have a chance to get that close to him with him gone so much" in connection with his work. Yet, as we shall see shortly, he seems to have provided a distant model for the form her politics took in her adult life—writing letters and doing publicity for her Republican county party organization.

Pringle distinguishes being "active" from being *"personally* active." When her children were little, she says she was active in the PTA, "and if you don't think PTA is politically involved, think again. They're not partisan, but they are political." Then when her husband was asked to get active in the local Republican party and did not want to be that public for business reasons, she took his place and became a precinct leader. But she says she got "personally active" when Ronald Reagan began to pursue his presidential aspirations, because she liked the man and what he stood for. It is as if much of her political work had been done for others or at the behest of others until she became "personally active" for something she herself cared about strongly. During this period of "personal" activity, she also carried on letter-writing campaigns to the U.S. Congress in connection with her memberships in Stop-ERA and Citizen's Choice, a taxpayer lobbying group.

Republican party workers Linda Helms, Audrey Nelms, and Maryanne Thayer and leftist Hazel Beecroft all attribute their interest in politics to their fathers. In all these cases, the fathers were more interested than directly active in politics. For Helms, the influence appears to be indirect. She says that her father never discussed politics with her when she was growing up, though he read widely and kept up with the world of politics, but he would always be able to answer any questions she put to him about political matters. Helms did not get actively involved in politics until after Barry Goldwater's presidential campaign, but she says, "Although I was not interested in politics until after the Goldwater years, I think it was [father's] background that finally brought it into focus for me." She got involved in the local Republican party as a result of Goldwater's loss in 1964. "Before 1964 I couldn't have told you the name of a governor probably. I was totally disinterested in politics and paid little or no attention to it. I did vote, but that was about all. But I didn't know who I was voting for. And I'd read the paper, and if they recommended Joe Blow, I'd vote for Joe Blow. But in 1964 I was awakened by Goldwater's campaign as to the direction this country was taking, and it disgusted me." That year she made a contribution of twenty-five dollars to his campaign, but because she had had a new baby that year, she did not get further involved. After the election, the Republican Women's Club contacted her and invited her to a meeting, and from that time on she got actively involved in all the political campaigns that came along, be they congressional, gubernatorial, presidential, or local.

Audrey Nelms's and Maryanne Thayer's fathers were more actively interested in politics, reading and discussing with their daughters and, in Nelms's case, going to meetings. In Nelms's home state, there was a very competitive three-party system, which greatly enhanced her father's and her own interest in what was going on politically. She remembers wearing a Hoover button to school as a young girl. When she came to Georgia and found virtually a one-party system, she and her husband joined the local Republican effort to develop a two-party system for the state. Thayer's father, a minister, kept his politics separate from his ministry, but he and his own father seem to have had a great interest in Franklin Roosevelt's four administrations, though they disagreed with more and more of Roosevelt's policies. Thayer remembers the excitement of the Eisenhower campaign for herself. In college she joined the Young Republicans to make social contacts. She was getting married when Goldwater was running for president so did not get involved in his campaign, but after that she got progressively more involved in her local Republican party, working much harder in political campaigns than her husband, but with his approval.

Hazel Beecroft's father taught his children to be critical of the political system. For example, he used the case of the internment of Japanese Americans during World War II to illustrate the inconsistencies between U.S. political theory and practice, "between what we say and what we believe [about equality]." He was sympathetic with the leftists, the anticapitalists, but he "was very anti-politics. [He believed] 'you can't change anything in the world.'" Beyond her father, Beecroft had a cousin who was a beatnik poet, and through him and friends of her older sister's, she was exposed to the beatnik culture of the late 1950s and early 1960s. But it was her husband, whom she met shortly before they moved to Atlanta, that got her directly involved in political movements. As she notes, it was an easy "leap from that kind of consciousness [critical, beatnik] into politics. I already had the kind of mind set and consciousness." But, whereas her father had been defeatist in his "anti-political" thinking, her husband was positive that change could be made. They first helped organize the antiwar movement on a local college campus, and then when her husband got sick and had to leave graduate school, they worked with a group to start an underground newspaper. From that, she and the other women on the newspaper staff organized a women's liberation group, and she also later joined groups formed in solidarity with various Latin American liberation movements.

In contrast to the preceding women, Republican party worker Lavinia Ravenel, Democratic office-seeker Nancy Harding, and leftist Annie Witt all had fathers for whom politics was intimately related to their occupations. Lavinia Ravenel's father, who was a big landowner and railroad executive, and a "Republican back when his vote didn't even count . . . was very active in local politics. He was always interested in who was going to be mayor of our town." She thinks she "got it [politics] from Daddy," because as the youngest child, she was the only one left at home after her brothers and sisters "were out and gone, pursuing their own interests." She went places with her father and generally became his companion in things political. She maintained her political interest "when I was still single." After she married, in Atlanta, she was recruited by a neighbor, a corporate executive, to type and do telephoning for the local Republican party. Her baby was still "in the crib," but "they could bring things to me and I'd do them, and I'd make telephone calls and things like that." After that, she joined the county Republican Women's Club and served as its president. She got active in Atlanta long before the Goldwater campaign. "This area was Republican before Goldwater. As a matter of fact, Goldwater carried the place."

Nancy Harding's father was a political reporter; his grandfather had been a lieutenant governor of the state, and his father had owned a large newspaper. So Harding came from a very political family on her father's side. Like her father, she earned a degree in political science, and while he became a journalist, she became a high-school teacher. It is no wonder that she attributes her earliest interest in politics to her father. She came of political age during his reporting of the civil rights movement, and she was "devastated" by the assassination of President Kennedy. She says she became more conservative as the "counterculture—drugs and hippies" unrolled, but she maintained her path as a very issues-oriented political person. Her family members all participated in raucous political discussions frequently. She actually got involved in Atlanta Democratic politics during a Taft Institute for high-school social science teachers. The institute, sponsored by a local college, brought local political figures together with teachers in a continuing-education program for the teachers. At an institute dinner she met and was recruited as a campaign worker for a local county politico. From there she became involved in the county Democratic Women's organization and in numerous political campaigns. She became increasingly disillusioned with party politics because of the sexism she encountered from some of the candidates she worked for and because of what she considered the pattern of all talk and no action: "we had meetings every month, hour after hour after hour debating these ridiculous resolutions stating positions on whatever the issues were at the time. And once these resolutions—people would battle and cry and get involved and fight, and then the resolution is passed, or it fails. And if it's passed, they mail it to the newspaper, and that's the end of it." She has withdrawn from party politics, but she says that when her preschoolers get a little older, "I might be more interested in a group with a cause," a feminist cause such as abortion rights.

Annie Witt attributes her rebellious political style to the intolerance of her father, though she believes she must take responsibility for herself also being intolerant with him. She says she has always had trouble dealing with authority figures. "My father and I fought constantly . . . and I'm sure that he had everything to do with it. . . . I can remember times just being screamed at for doing something, and he just didn't have the patience to understand that was just a growing pain or something. I couldn't understand, but I was just like him. I mean I was intolerant of his intolerance." She is especially rebellious in relation to her father's stand on nuclear power, which she connects to his work with nuclear submarines.

> Maybe that's part of my rebellion too, that he's really influenced by his perspective on nuclear power. I remember we used to get in arguments

about nuclear power when I didn't even know anything. I didn't know how to argue with him, and he used to just show me designs of nuclear submarines and how they operate and everything. And when I look back at it, he really had an interest in arguing for it. I mean his whole life was wrapped up in it, so I really respect him for that. He couldn't have been happier doing what he was doing.

More recently, she says she has begun to use as a model some of her mother's brother's ideas. Now a thirty-year-old law student and looked on "unfairly" by the rest of the family, her uncle has "gone through a lot of false starts in his life and was really involved in the brick-throwing and tear gas and everything in the sixties. And he just, you know, has these ideas which appeal to me." She has picked up other ideas from reading leftist newspapers and journals, after she says she learned in high school that "*Newsweek* and *Time* were the same thing . . . and discovering that I wasn't getting the truth."

Her first actual involvement with things political came as a result of her job at her university's radio station. "My earliest effort to make some kind of contact with people was when I did this interview with a representative from the American Friends Service Committee on the draft. . . . I just did an overall kind of examination of the issue." Most recently she has gotten involved in the Women's Committee on campus because of her interest in women's issues, and they asked her to chair the committee. She is also getting involved in Nine to Five, an organization of clerical workers, as a result of the sexism and racism she has experienced or observed in the law office where she works as a secretary. Thus, she seems to have transformed her earlier rebellion against her father's politics into contemporary political action against sexism and racism.

Parents and Grandparents and Politicization

Seven women tell stories of their politicization that suggest multiple sources of their interest in and approaches to politics. Republican officeholder Dulcie LaFontaine and Republican office-seeker Bess Shumaker are rather self-directed women with strong political roots in their childhood families. LaFontaine traces her interest in party politics back to childhood, when she "listened to all the party conventions on my little radio even when I was in the third and fourth grades. I was a debater even in the fifth grade. So I've always been very political." She attributes her political involvement to the example of her maternal grandmother, who "was a political activist" and to discussing politics with her father. That LaFontaine's grandmother had a mind of her own is evident in this story: "A lot of people used to tell me that 'Mama' had a chinaberry tree in her yard and that if she liked the candidate, she would sit under that chinaberry tree in the afternoon and she would tell everybody that came by to support this candidate. Back in those days people would tell my grandfather, 'You know, you should keep Marguerite at home. She's too nosey.' And my grandfather would say, 'Well, I'll let you tell Marguerite that.'" LaFontaine's father encouraged her to debate politics with him. "Daddy and I could just really get into heated arguments. But it'd be all right. And I think he kind of encouraged it. I think he liked to bring the fire out in us, because I think not having any sons, he liked the idea that we were aggressive and what he calls winners."

LaFontaine says she and her husband were raised in families that were Democrats, but when they voted for the first time at age twenty-one, they voted for Eisenhower for president. Her husband's family "almost put us on the black list." They got involved in Republican party work in Texas, "through friends, and we walked door to door for Republican candidates." When they moved to Atlanta, they continued their Republican party involvement. She also begin to monitor the General Assembly during legislative sessions, and it was as a result of this work that she "got so excited about it that I decided I would run for office." She says she had a lot of ideas about things that needed doing that the incumbent was not doing. Even though he was Republican and had been in office for eight years and she had helped get him elected, she felt that he was taking her serious concerns too lightly. She began to ask people, "Would you support me if I ran for the House?" They would respond, "Well, who's the incumbent?" She would tell them, and they would say, "'Oh, you'd better believe I would!' And then it just sort of snowballed, and before I knew it, I had made a definite commitment, and I told everybody I was going to run, and I announced. And I shocked the incumbent to death. In fact, he told people he had no opposition. A woman was running against him. And, of course, that just spurred me on. And I just went about it in a very low key." She ran the classic kind of grass-roots campaign that women candidates have become known for making in small districts.[7] She won the primary and then the general election.

Bess Shumaker remembers enough of her father, though he died when she was four, to know that he "dabbled in politics. . . . He worked on a lot of different campaigns and all. Of course, you know, politics back then wasn't what politics is now." Her mother she describes as someone who was always ready and willing to take on challenges, which she *had* to do as a young widow with five children at the beginning of World War II. She refused to go on welfare, for which she could have qualified, because she was unwilling to let the welfare agency know how she spent her money. Shumaker says, "She was a very intelligent woman, very opinionated. Of course, there again, to raise five kids under the circumstances she had to be. . . . She just basically was a 'paddle your own canoe'–type person, . . . a 'take charge' person. It's got to be done, so you do it. And that is my attitude."

There seem to be clear links between Shumaker, the political office-seeker, and her politically involved father and "take charge" mother. For Shumaker, life seems to have been a series of challenges, which she learned she could meet as she was growing up. Her father and mother provide the starting point. A cousin who was the local sheriff asked her to distribute campaign literature for his elections. A teacher of "American Problems" reinforced her interest in politics. Being drum major in high school showed her "you *can* accomplish. You *can* do the things. You *have* an equal opportunity." Her mother and music teachers may have also contributed indirectly to her political future by encouraging her voice training. When she graduated from high school, both her parents now dead, she turned down college scholarships and took a professional singing job on a

weekly television show. She notes that her singing abilities and per-
formance experience have made it easy for her to take the micro-
phone at large gatherings and communicate with people. On the
basis of her media experience, and because she was upset about
Watergate, in 1974 she reentered the political arena, after taking
time out to marry and raise her own family. She worked for Republican candidates, at both national and state levels, while also running her own campaign for the state house, attempting but just
failing to oust a "dangerous" liberal incumbent "who spends tax-
payers' money like a drunken sailor."

Democratic party worker Edith Hammond and Republican party
worker Bridgit Malone both trace their earliest political memories to strongly Democratic parents, and Hammond to strongly
Democratic grandparents also. Not only was Hammond's family pro-
Democrat, it was anti-Republican. She says, "I was brought up to
believe the Democrats are the only party and that you never wanted
to make a mistake—my grandfather told me, 'Don't ever make the
mistake, child, of voting for a Republican,' and he was right. Absolutely. I'm convinced of that more every day in my life." Her grandmother always said that a Republican man that lived across
the road was "no good." And her mother always voted Democrat.
Hammond herself first became active in politics when she went to
work and joined a union. As president of her local, she also began to
raise campaign money for Democratic candidates. She has since
worked in numerous Democratic congressional and mayoral campaigns.

Bridgit Malone's mother and father were strong Democratic supporters, but Malone early became a strong anti-Democratic pro-Re-
publican Catholic activist. She tells how her father took her with
him on many of his Democratic social outings. "He was a shop
steward for the union, and he belonged to the Democratic Club, as
lots of friends did. He enjoyed playing cards. . . . He took me to Irish
football games. That's the game where I met Mayor Jimmy Walker
at the time, came out to one of the games. Oh, he took me here,
there, every place. I know when he went into a bar and grill to have
a beer, he took me in. I can still see myself sitting up on a stool eat-

ing a pretzel or two." Both her parents were strong Franklin Roosevelt supporters, but "I couldn't stand Roosevelt. Never liked him. Never liked him. And I'll never forget, at the time when Roosevelt died, and my mother called me in. She said—oh, she adored Roosevelt—she said, 'He's dead,' and I said, 'Oh, thank God.' Well, he was getting senile. He was giving everything away, Yalta, ... and she didn't speak to me for a week." Why didn't she like Roosevelt? "I never trusted him. . . . I can still hear him say, 'Oh, I'll never send your boys overseas.' My husband went. And I still swear, don't forget that got him out of the depression. We were not out of the depression at the time. . . . I didn't like Eleanor Roosevelt because, well, don't forget, I was Catholic. She was entertaining the Red Loyalists at tea in the White House when they were killing nuns and priests in Spain. That was another gripe I had."

If Malone's mother and father laid the groundwork for her political involvement, the Catholic church provided the direction. She used to picket for the Paulist Fathers, who published anti-Communist pamphlets, when Communist meetings were in session. She had a boyfriend who ran a program on politics at the university radio station, and she says he had a great influence on her. Bishop Fulton Sheen was her "idol." When she married and moved to Atlanta with her husband, the Republican party provided the direction and opportunity to get active in party politics. Her husband got her involved in a campaign for a Republican candidate in whom his business associates were interested. Then she dropped out for a while to raise her children. Eventually she got involved in another electoral campaign and then into the party organization proper, serving in various capacities at the precinct, district, and county levels.

Republican officeholder Elizabeth Latimer, Democratic officeseeker Kate Greene, and leftist Maria Montgomery all cite multiple sources of their politicization, beginning with family members, but they also add another dimension to the process. Each one speaks of certain principles that enter into motivations for political action. Latimer says she grew up "during the depression and after the depression years, so my parents were probably somewhat political. They were Republicans in their philosophy. They didn't approve of welfare and prided themselves that they went through the depression without taking any welfare. You know, they were not Roosevelt's admirers." Her father had run away from home to join the Marines, so "we were taught patriotism before anything else." She also was taught the work ethic—"that you could accomplish what you wanted to if you wanted to work hard," and the Christian ethic —which she contrasts to "just a Christian home" in which people are loved unconditionally: "we had to meet certain standards of conduct and behavior to be acceptable."

In probing for the source of her interest in politics, she speculates that she was raised with all these values "that I thought everybody knew, which you don't realize until you kind of get out in the world. But not everybody was brought up that way." Part of her motivation seems to come from seeing the need to right wrongs in the larger world. This is confirmed in her next observation. After college she read *The Diary of Anne Frank*, "and I felt that that should never happen again and that all of us felt guilty because it happened in our lifetime. And I think the lack of participation—my parents really couldn't participate in a lot of things because they were busy surviving, and so I think that I feel the responsibility people have to carry on and you can't leave it for somebody else to do."

Latimer says she first got active in politics in Atlanta "when I went to a Republican meeting and basically found people who were involved in the Republican party who I didn't consider were Republican." Elsewhere in her interview she refers to these people as "mad Democrats," meaning Democrats who had left their party because they disagreed with the national Democratic party's liberal stand on racial equality. Rather than get involved in this group's "in-house fight," she "just spent [her] time in issue-oriented organizations." Education was a particular concern for her, and she got very involved in trying to improve the educational system in her county. Eventually, given her interest in educational policy and given that the state house incumbent in her district had a "high absentee record, I decided that someone needed [to challenge him]. I tried to get other people to challenge him. And so I decided I would, and I had some people encourage me to do that, too." She says that basically she ran against the local Republican party in the Republican primary, since the "party stalwarts" did not support her. She won the nomination and went on to win the general election.

Kate Greene's mother and father agreed on one thing: white supremacy and racial segregation. Her mother was a fundamentalist Baptist, and her father was a Klansman. Greene seems to have modeled herself upon both parents in having strong views of right and wrong, but Greene's turned out to be in direct contradiction to her parents' views. She says of her mother: "She really just had very strong ideas about how we should act, not just her children, but the world in general." She says her father's Klan activity "is a source of shame for me, but it also I think has gotten me where I am today." She tells of being taken to a cross-burning when she was seven years old and of feeling very scared. "And I remember even then at seven something inside of me saying there's something wrong. Something basic is very wrong."

Greene also appears not only to have used as a model her father's partisan and movement politics and her mother's moral concerns but, as already noted, to have replaced the content of their politics and morals with her own. Greene is concerned with racial justice, and whereas her parents were Dixiecrats, she is a "real" Democrat. "John Kennedy was when I started politics. That was my first presidential election, and I was just so impressed by him. . . . I just thought he stood for everything that was right, good, and decent. And I knew he was a Democrat. And I thought, 'Well, he's a Democrat; that's what I need to be, too.' So I decided I was a Democrat." At the time, she was living in a small town in the Deep South, and the civil rights movement was beginning. Her interest in John Kennedy led her to be involved in the civil rights movement and "discovering Bobby Kennedy, and feeling almost as strongly about him, and later on even being stronger for Bobby than for John. And Martin Luther King being so close, it just sort of all seemed to come together right. See, I have real strong ideas about what's right and wrong, too." She did not participate in any civil rights marches because "I have to tell you, I'm ashamed of it, I was afraid of marching." But when the antiwar movement started, she did participate in some of those marches. When the women's movement emerged, she joined the ranks of those working for the ERA.

Unlike any of the other Democratic and Republican women in my study, Kate Greene moved from movement politics to party politics. An older woman in the local Democratic party urged her to get involved and to run for a spot on the county executive committee. Though she initially failed to win the position, she persisted and eventually gained office in the county party. She is now ambitious for public office, though she does not yet perceive that the opportunity is right for her to run. She cites a woman in the state legislature who sponsored the resolution to ratify the ERA as a role model. This woman probably provides a direct inspiration for Greene's political ambition, and she certainly confirms for Greene the effort involved and the courage required if one takes on unpopular causes in electoral politics.

Maria Montgomery argued politics with her father and debated "God, life, politics, and men and women" with her mother. She says her mother told her that women were superior to men. Montgomery also cites her grandmother as a great influence because her grandmother "was a real independent woman, and she worked very hard." Her grandfather "is a real old chauvinist. But my grandmother just goes around him." Her parents taught her notions of justice, especially racial justice. "My parents said, you know, human beings are equal. You can't say the word 'nigger.' You have to treat people right. They were pretty strong about that. An honest day's work, whether you're a janitor or a professor—that people were basically good and if you worked hard, you deserved a decent living and a good life for yourself."

Yet Montgomery observed situations that did not match up to these principles. One involved Black people: she grew up in a racially segregated town. "I was always aware of it ['colored town'], and it was always uncomfortable for me." The other involved poor white people:

> I went on vacation with my grandparents to my grandfather's hometown. And we visited the remaining members of his sixteen brothers and sisters, the ones that survived. And that was the turning point in my life

because they were all terribly poor and terribly ignorant and good people. I mean that was my impression. And what I kept thinking the whole time—sharecroppers, you know how they live, well that's where we visited—these people who are so good. . . . They're not dumb. They're hard working. And yet look how they live. What's wrong with this country. That's what I kept thinking. The system isn't working. And I put that together with 'colored town' and realized that the platitudes of this country and what really happens—there's something wrong. So that was a real turning point, because those were white people, too.

Whereas Latimer and Greene keyed on racial injustice as the wrong to be righted—ultimately through partisan electoral politics—Montgomery keyed on class and racial injustice as the wrong to be righted. It is little surprise, then, that she found Marxist theory and eventually the Communist party to be relevant to her ensuing politics.

Montgomery began to realize that her ideas and opinions "were in the minority" when she began to read the morning paper and discuss the editorials with her father. But she also saw that there was much to be done. In high school she sought and gained office in student government, but she was frustrated by the other students' lack of interest in her political issues, such as the death penalty and women's rights. She started calling herself a Marxist, "even though I didn't know anything about it, because I knew that it was radical, and I knew that they had a lot of views on the reforms that I had views on. But I didn't know really what it was about except that it was class conflict. So I wanted to find out, I had a burning desire to find out what it was about." In college, in the early 1970s, she took some courses in Marxism and began to go to campus demonstrations. She was already married to her first husband by this time, but he did not share her political activism. Then she began to attend events sponsored by the "free university" on campus—revolutionary films, discussions. "And then I met people in leftist parties. And I didn't know that there were any leftist groups at that time. I had no knowledge whatsoever of the CP [Communist Party U.S.A.] and the other parties, any of them. And so when I found out that there were all these organizations, all these networks, I just jumped right in. I was so glad to find other people with my views, even though we had differences, that I found the one I liked best and joined up."

She joined the Communist Youth Organization of the CPUSA and began to work on a series of issues that would occupy her time until she graduated from college and moved to Atlanta to enter graduate school. "The first thing I organized was for International Women's Day. We had a week of activities. And I organized three different viewpoints—the Communist party viewpoint, which I consider middle-of-the-road, the Marxist/Leninist Maoist viewpoint, and the Lesbian/feminist viewpoint." This was actually organized through a collective of women in the Women's Center. After that she and her second husband were instrumental in organizing an anti-Klan rally, and then they organized around campus issues such as divestiture in South Africa, budget cuts, and tuition increases. When they moved to Atlanta, they continued their campus-based organizing, now with a newly formed Communist Party–Marxist/Leninist (CPML), and they also organized around issues in the larger community having to do with racism, sexism, and nondemocratic tactics of some local union leaders.

Adult Politicization

Five women tell stories of their politicization suggesting that their childhood families were basically apolitical and that they developed their political interest and involvement after they left their childhood families.

Republican office-seeker Lorraine Reilly, like Democratic party worker Ann Strong, grew up in a city that was governed by a political machine, and according to Reilly, this political environment held out no opportunity for her to get involved. She and her husband had one chance to vote there before they moved to Atlanta, and she describes the polling place as dark and offering only paper ballots. Before she was old enough to vote, she had already decided that elections were not for her, "because I tell you when I was a kid, you had Roosevelt as president," and a man for governor and a man for mayor. "And for sixteen years, I mean really, there wasn't anyone else. . . . I mean, I thought this was it. I mean there wasn't a change at all. To me it was ridiculous. You had three high positions and the same people every election. . . . At the time I figured why even have an election." But when she and her husband had been in Atlanta for a while, they saw an opportunity for change. The Goldwater presidential campaign mobilized them. "We finally started getting interested in the Republican party down here in 1964 when Goldwater ran. Up until that time it was a shoo-in for almost any Democrat that ran." After the Goldwater campaign, she began to go to Republican precinct meetings and decided then that "I was going to go all out and get involved in it. I didn't know if I would have that much time, and then it all worked together. I mean I could go off to any meeting I wanted just as long as dinner was going to be served [at home]." She has worked in numerous Republican campaigns for local, state, and national office, and she also has gotten involved in the local homeowners' association. She is very concerned about how development is changing her residential area. Given her reputation, which has grown out of her long involvement in the area, she says she is thinking of running for the state legislature. She has been dissatisfied with the Republican candidates who have challenged the Democratic incumbent in the state house, and she is biding her time until she perceives that the incumbent becomes vulnerable and capable of being beaten.

Democratic office-seeker Sally Martin appears to be a case of what Arlene Pringle defined as someone active but not "personally active." She first became interested in politics as an adult "because somebody took me by the hand and said, 'I want you to join the League of Women Voters.'" That was a neighbor, who also got her involved in a Great Books discussion group and then in a Great Decisions discussion group. "And then once I was there, then the other people would ask you to do this and this. . . . But I really didn't seek it. It was sort of grafted onto me." She says, "I never *was* interested in politics. I think my own cultural background would say stay out of politics, and my church would say that. And so, it never occurred to me." If anything, Martin is a good example of how some white women have been socialized to stay out of politics. Martin would appear to be an unlikely candidate for public office, but again people were asking her to run, and she consented, though she lost. Martin appears to have become "personally active" since she became involved in a nutrition advocacy program for young mothers-to-be. She says her other political work has not been important to her; she has only done it when asked. But she seems to speak with more fervor of trying to represent the concerns of those who, she believes, otherwise would go unrepresented, "people who don't know how to get into the system on their own."

Democratic officeholder Adrienne Stone is another who was recruited to run for office, but that experience has made her very "personally active" in her political arena. Stone indicates that her family was not particularly politically interested or involved. She says she was "somewhat involved in national campaigns like with Kennedy. . . . I can't quite explain that, it always kept my interest, even though I was always removed from it." But it was not until after she had married and had young children that a friend recruited her to run against an incumbent Republican in the state house. She says she heard another woman say recently that "I've always been the kind of person that just likes to do things that I'm not expected to do." Stone says, "And that sort of clicked with me. There's always been a streak in me to want to be relatively unique." Certainly running for the state legislature would be very different from the kind of life she had been living. Her husband's work kept him away from the house for long hours, she "didn't really have a job that I liked," and the most important task she had seemed to be car pooling. The woman who recruited her was a personal friend who also "was very active in the [local] Democratic party. . . . She said, 'I will run your primary. You can do it, Adrienne. It's no big deal. You're in for forty days, and you know, you'll get blah, blah, blah. And we'll get rid of this guy.' . . . She simplified it a bit. I'll tell you if I knew what I know now, I probably wouldn't have run." Stone was not heavily involved in any community organizations. She was following the emerging women's movement, though she was not active in it. "But I would watch these things on television and read them. And I was there. I didn't quite know where to make my mark, but I was there. And I was outspoken as an individual. . . . So I really had things to say. I didn't channel them. But being in the legislature made me less angry because I had places to channel that."

Leftist Susan Murphy says her parents were "not at all political." She did not get interested in politics until after she had attended a fundamentalist religious college, married and divorced, and returned to finish her college education in a women's college in the Deep South. "I belonged to the Young Democrats, which was the most radical organization on that campus, believe it or not. And we brought the first Black speaker to the campus. The speaker was a young Black woman, Marian Wright Edelman, who was a lawyer at that time for the Legal Defense Fund in Mississippi. And she had a tremendous impact on me. It was very influential in my making up my mind to go to law school."

Upon graduation from college, Murphy embarked on a series of actions that would bring her to her engagement in the Communist Party–Marxist/Leninist. Before returning to college, she says she lived on the Texas-Mexico border and became aware of the plight of the Mexicans who came across the border to work. "I wasn't real active. I think that was the dawning of consciousness for me though." She earned a law degree, and while in law school became active in a radical organization of Black and white lawyers who had been active "in the civil rights cases that sprang up across the South." The purpose of the organization was to give law students experience in civil rights work. The time was the late 1960s and early 1970s, and her belief during this period was that "the law" could be used "for the benefit of people who were trying to organize trade unions, trying to organize for freedom and democracy, and still in the civil rights movement. . . . The main thing that I'd try to do was to convince people that even though things had slowed down, the need was still there, and the social movements were smaller, but they were still there, and that there was a role for lawyers to play."

During the late 1970s, Murphy says, "I became very frustrated with what I was able to accomplish with legal work and decided that I wanted to organize full time." It was at this point that she "became openly a Communist. I had been sympathetic to Communist ideas and Communist politics for three or four years. I had been drawn to Marxism as an ideology." She had first come into contact with October League members during a worker's strike at a local manufacturing plant. "And there was an older white woman who had been in the CPUSA in Atlanta and was in the October League and was involved in that strike. And her life and her work and her beliefs were very—my experience with her and my friendship with her had a big impact on me." Murphy did full-time community and union organizing until her child was born, but then she found herself having to cut back on the work she was doing in order to take care of her child. The CPML was also falling apart. Now she and some of the others are stepping back and assessing where they went wrong on strategies and tactics, but she has not given up on Marxism "as a worldview." She will continue to work to build organizations and bring about social change for "the little people."

Lesbian feminist Barbara Bergen says her "entry point into any political arena at all was through feminism and coming out as a Lesbian, and I've certainly expanded, I've incorporated that into a much wider range." She means that she has incorporated politics into all the ways she lives her life. "It *is* my life. I mean that also sounds like all I do is go to meetings and stuff. But it's more incorporating, the same way I try to incorporate a sense of the spiritual and the political in everything that I do, and just to pay attention to all of those aspects in everything I do."

She explains her journey into the political arena as a series of points of changed consciousness. "I knew I loved women a lot, and I think it was through that love that I guess I came to love myself enough to be able to be confident and feel like I could make a change in the world and that I could be effective and to work in groups that were empowering." When she came to Atlanta, like Tillie Zadar, the first place she went was a local Lesbian feminist group. She went to work on the "Boogie Woman" committee, which planned parties and social stuff. "And I learned a lot about being able to process and work in groups and just get things done, plan things within that context [of feminist process]. And it was a real political context, even though what we were doing was planning parties basically." I asked her to repeat the name of the committee. She replied, "Boogie Woman Committee, usually called the Program Committee, but that was *so* boring. Have you ever read Audre Lorde's 'The Uses of the Erotic'? You know that speaks a lot about wanting to live fully, and that everything I do, I want to feel that sense of living fully. It seems such a waste to do anything differently."

How did she gain this consciousness? First, as a child she read all the time, especially science fiction. "And really, science fiction began to be real feminist—a lot of women writers, a lot of real strong characters, and I was reading everything in science fiction that came out." After graduating from high school, she went to college to become a physician's assistant, "and it was terribly woman hating, you know. And the whole way of training you is the medical model, so that they exhaust you, sort of like the Marines. And that was a real—I was coming out during that time as well. I was realizing how woman-hating the system I was working in was, and then, right between finishing school and getting my first job, I read *Gyn/Ecology*, and she just *blows* the medical establishment apart." But though Bergen read the book and agreed with Mary Daly's analysis,

> I really felt it, but I didn't have a community that I could talk to about that in, so I just sort of let it sit there. And over the next three years, I began to hate what I did more and more, and I got sicker and sicker, and finally I left it. But I think over those three years what enabled me to do that was having a larger and larger community of women to find validation that said "It's stupid to work sixty hours a week" and also finding I was a different me at work than I was when I was off work, and that sort of dichotomy was horrible.

Again, like Tillie Zadar, finding a community of women made it possible for Bergen to continue her journey out of her daily pedestrian work life and into the world of Lesbian women's community. Finally, finding the women's bookstore gave her the opportunity she needed to connect "into the general range of feminist reading. I mean I went there and just gobbled up the books there." The bookstore continues to sustain her as she continues her daily political life.

Connecting Patterns of Politicization
with Arenas of Political Engagement

In the ongoing political drama of politicization as played out in the
lives of the women in this study, no relationships emerge to suggest
that different childhood family members initiate different paths of
political development in their daughters. If parents have been political actors, then mothers are as likely as fathers to have provided
early models of political action for their daughters. Close female
friends are as likely as husbands or boyfriends to have encouraged
some of these women to enter the political arenas they have chosen.
Political campaigns, especially those of presidential candidates,
have served to activate a good number of these women. No matter
what type of political engagement has been the end result of the
process of politicization for any of these women, however, there have
been any number of paths forged from early beginnings to present
arenas of action for any number of reasons.

Several patterns emerge, however, to distinguish certain aspects
of the process. In most cases, political interest develops sometime
during childhood and paves the way to later political action during
adulthood, though some of these women engaged in political acts
during their elementary- or secondary-school years. Republican
party worker Audrey Nelms tells of wearing her Herbert Hoover
button, and Republican officeholder Dulcie LaFontaine tells of listening to the national party conventions, both during their grade-
school days. Marxist organizer Maria Montgomery and Lesbian
feminist Tillie Zadar both brought their political beliefs to bear in
high-school activism.

But there is also a minor pattern of political engagement preceding political interest. Republican Arlene Pringle announces this
pattern when she distinguishes her previous political campaign activity at others' instigation from the political letter-writing activity
she initiated when she became "personally active." Democrat Sally
Martin is another one who indicates that she did her campaign
work and even ran for public office because others asked her to do

so, but only recently does she seem to have developed a "personal" political engagement in a government program to assist young mothers-to-be. And Lesbian feminist Barbara Bergen attributes her politicization to coming out as a Lesbian. She recognized for some time that she was a Lesbian, but it was when she committed the political act of *coming out* as a Lesbian that she says her politicization began.

Continuing the distinction between interest and engagement, these women's stories of politicization also reveal that different parts of the political drama play different roles in the process of politicization. "Significant others"—one or both parents or grandparents, or teachers, friends, husbands, or candidates—are likely to fuel the women's political interest. Organizations such as political parties, campaign organizations, or ad hoc mobilization organizations, along with institutionalized elections or created movements, provide the actual opportunities for action.

Bridging initial interest and political action, in whichever order they occur, is some form of political belief system or some form of consciousness-raising that appears to be decisive in channeling political actors to one political arena rather than another. Not all women give evidence of this aspect of politicization, though it may be present for most or all of them. Those for whom it is most obvious are those whose politics seem to be driven by some form of political principle that they are attempting to actualize in political arenas chosen as a result of their political analysis. A key aspect of this political analysis appears to be where these women place the blame for what they believe is wrong and needs correcting. Some focus on *people* as individuals; others focus on a *system*. Thus, two women as different as Lesbian feminist Fran Daly and Republican party worker Betty Mason both had mothers who demonstrated religious involvement and taught moral principles, which very heavily influenced the motivations these women bring to their forms of political engagement. Whereas Mason blames people for veering off the path of morality and stresses teaching people the "right" values and getting the "right" people elected, Daly blames a system of values and stresses changing the "patriarchal" system that cultivates "oppressive" values. And two women as different as Marxist organizer Maria Montgomery and Republican officeholder Elizabeth Latimer both were taught the Christian work ethic by their parents, only to lead them to two very different conclusions about why they should become political activists. Latimer recognized that others did not follow that ethic, and she became active in order to convince others that it was a good principle to follow. Montgomery recognized that others did follow that ethic, but without the rewards they were supposed to reap from their actions, and she became active in order to change the political economic system that she believed was responsible for such a miscarriage of justice.

These differences in analyzing their political worlds, however defined by each women, go to the heart of differences in politicization that I introduced in the first chapter as political socialization and consciousness-raising. Contrasting those who have chosen movement politics with those who have chosen electoral politics, it appears that the politicization of most party activists is more nearly a process of socialization, in that women in such a process are learning how to connect as individual role-players supportively to the ongoing political apparatus provided by the dominant culture of the conventional political system. Some choice is provided as to whether one goes Democratic or Republican, for these are the major organizations and philosophies that structure this political arena. And some choice is given as to whether one develops more liberal or conservative stances toward the role of government and law in society. Thus, there are those socialized to this system of government who exercise their belief systems as to whether government is taking society along the right or wrong path. Very conservative women in this study, to be found among the Republicans, believe government before the Reagan presidency has taken the United States down "immoral" or "socialist" paths. Very liberal women, to be found among the Democrats, believe the Reagan presidency is undoing whatever good previous administrations have wrought. But virtually none of these women suggests that the two-party presidential *form* of government should be brought down or changed or abandoned. All such women, Democrats and Republicans, can be said to have been *so-*

cialized into the ongoing political system. Once socialized, they have for the most part maintained their activism through the regular ongoing opportunities of electoral politics and policy-making provided by that political system.

Not so the leftist and women's community activists. Some of them actually started out being socialized into conventional electoral politics. But somewhere along the way, critical consciousness-raising began, and the women moved slowly but surely into stances of critique and resistance against what they call "capitalist" or "patriarchal" systems. Their movement has been unpredictable as to where it is leading, except in a very general direction—"outside" the dominant conventional political apparatus. Their movements have proceeded in fits and starts, depending for the leftists on which large issues of policy they decide to contest, be the issues class-determined or racist or sexist in nature, and which tactics they determine are best for mobilizing and organizing new adherents to their cause. Movement "outside" for the women's community activists has depended on how they have decided to act to resolve contradiction after contradiction in their personal lives and then in the newly created life spaces of their women's communities. Both sets of movement activists are especially adept at articulating the emergent Marxist or feminist theories that have provided the frameworks for their changes in consciousness, changes which seem to be unending.

It is also the case that some of the Republican and Democratic women have been very adept at articulating their political philosophies. It is in this articulation that we hear some of the reasons these women have become political—to serve the needs of their children and to get people to be more "moral" and family-oriented. These concerns, which affect peoples' rather "personal" lives in the so-called "private sphere," in addition to concerns for a two-party system or electoral victories in the so-called "public sphere," only serve to strengthen a point enunciated by some of the women's community activists, that "the personal is political."

Chapter 7

Definitions of "the Problem"
Shape Understandings of "the Political"

In the last chapter, some of the women's stories suggested that they
came to be the political women they are, engaged in their chosen
arenas of electoral or movement politics, because their beliefs about
causes of problems and ways to solve those problems called for certain forms of politics. In this chapter, the women elaborate upon
those forms of politics in ways that further illuminate both the
shape of their political worlds and their reasons for engaging those
worlds in the ways they do. Their elaborations come in response to
my interview questions: "Moving into a somewhat philosophical
realm, could you say how you define 'the political'?" and, "To you,
what is 'the political'?" My analysis here is an expanded and revised
version of an earlier essay,[1] which addressed the question of how
white female activists' conceptions of "the political" compared to the
conventional definition provided by the discipline of political science.
My conclusion at that time was that white female activists' conceptions included but extended beyond the conventional notion of "the
political" as those behaviors associated with legitimate governance
by elected public officials and their constituents. I used the terms
"intrinsic" and "extrinsic" to place each activist in relation to her
conception. The intrinsic conception places the person herself in
some form of "the political" as an active agent, while the extrinsic
conception places the person outside some form of "the political,"
which "happens to" her.[2]

   In this chapter, I expand the earlier analysis to show that some
women conceptualize "the political" extrinsically, some intrinsically,
and some compartmentally so that they are extrinsic to one aspect

but intrinsic to another. The result is an accordion-like construction of "the political" that bridges one arena to another in the grand theater of politics. That is to say, moving from the arenas of party workers and office-oriented activists in electoral politics to the arenas of leftist and women's community activists in movement politics, one hears "the political" given different form and substance depending on each woman's particular standpoint within her chosen arena.

Exclusively Extrinsic Conceptions

In two cases women understand "the political" extrinsically. Audrey Nelms, erstwhile office-seeker, sees "the political" holistically as government encroaching on individual freedom. At the same time, she would like to think that people could take care of themselves and help one another through interpersonal relations in the community:

> It affects our everyday life more than we realize ... because over the years I would call it almost an encroachment by the federal government in our day-to-day lives ... and regulation, and sometimes you just feel *helpless* because of the restrictions, of control.... I guess down deep I would be almost a true libertarian ... [with] the fewest restrictions as possible.... I would like to have more of *my* money in *my* pocket to take care of the community needs than having somebody do it for me. I would like that decision and I guess I have, maybe it's a naive faith, but I think people would take care of each other.

Her understanding of "the political" splits into the actual and the ideal. On the one hand, she sees government in actuality as out of control and encroaching on our lives totally. On the other hand, she envisions a polity in which people could live in freedom and community with as little government as possible. Thus, she places herself outside the actualized "political" as government because of her libertarian ideals. But she also finds herself outside the ideal of "the political" as freedom-in-community because real government prevents the ideal from being realized.

Maryanne Thayer, erstwhile party worker, also sees "the political" holistically as involving different philosophies—liberalism and conservatism—and different "types of governments, socialism, communism, capitalism. . . . It touches everything," especially the economic—recessions and depressions. "The political" also conjures up "the dirty work, the pressure politics, and how government is run." She has "very strong opinions on certain things" but also gets "disillusioned very easily." Still she "keep[s] up with what's going on in government probably more than the average person." Like Audrey Nelms, she is concerned about "big government, government spending, actually just the fact that government can't seem to put it all together, Democrats or Republicans. I worry about what is happening to this country. [But] I don't know a solution." Unlike Nelms, she has no ideal conception of how it could be. She places herself outside a government that can do little to solve problems, and she herself is confined to expressing strong opinions and feeling disillusioned. "The political" is powerless government and powerless self.

Although Nelms and Thayer still work periodically in election campaigns for particular candidates, they have disengaged themselves from "the political" as they see it: encroaching but ineffective government. They do not include the political parties as positive parts of "the political," and Nelms for employment-related reasons and Thayer for family-related reasons no longer hold party office. They appear to be alienated and disillusioned, totally extrinsic to their negative view of "the political," except for Nelms's ideal but unrealized vision of political community.

Extrinsic to Organization but Intrinsic to Linking "Private and Public Spheres"

Four women understand "the political" in ways that emphasize linking the so-called "private sphere" and "public sphere." They speak of themselves as linking public officeholders with people in families, in communities, or "behind the scenes." Three of these women—Arlene Pringle, Nancy Harding, and Edith Hammond—also speak of "the political" in ways that suggest they are extrinsic to officeholding or political party organization. Only Lorraine Reilly has continued her active involvement in her political party organization, though this involvement is only implicit in her conceptualization of "the political."

The first woman, Arlene Pringle, erstwhile party worker, draws a "fine line between politics and statesmanship." For her, "the political" involves public officeholding, and ideally officeholding as service, but she places herself outside that. She says she is political to the extent that she stays aware of what is going on in government by reading "the newspaper cover to cover and a number of magazines." She keeps files, and when any of her grandchildren in high school need help on that kind of homework they "always call Mamaw because if anybody has it, she does. The other day I got a call from a friend of mine, . . . and one of her children was having to name the cabinet officers. So she called me to find out who they were." Unlike Maryanne Thayer, who also "keeps up with what's going on in government" but is disillusioned by it all, Pringle stays informed about government so that she can pass information on to grandchildren and friends' children, and she is aware that she is known in her community for that.

The second woman, Nancy Harding, who may yet run for the county school board, has dropped out of her party for the present because she is disgusted with the sexist behavior of the party activists and elected officials for whom she has been working. For her "the political" is definitely not what she was taught as a political science major:

> Do you mean as a process, or the issues? What a question. That is a hard one. My degree is in political science . . . and I know what it's supposed to be, and I don't think it's that at all. I'm very cynical about it. . . . I had illusions of democracy, and anybody can get involved. I think that part is true . . . that if you're willing to work hard enough and stick it out, you'll get involved. That's the only democracy I see in it. I think a few people make the decisions for everybody based on, usually, what's best for them . . . for the person making the decision.

In other words, using Dorothy Smith's terminology, Harding believes "democracy," as practiced in her experience, is ideological. She believes "the political" "is a payoff for what you're actually doing. . . . Power corrupts, not necessarily in the sense of money . . . but in terms of principles." She even admits that, if she were in that position, "I'd do the same thing if I had the power. So I can't even necessarily condemn these people for their kinds of decisions."

At the same time that she can place herself in the shoes of politicians wielding power and corrupting themselves, she also can see the value of her own position outside all that. She believes she has a better idea of what is desirable and possible from an average citizen's standpoint. She gives two examples of local officials who were certain that their "pet bills" would pass, but who were "slaughtered" in the final votes. She knew the bills had no chance, but the politicians would not listen to her. "I'm in this community, and I talk to people all the time, and I was real interested in it. And you hear what the average person thinks. And you don't get the tunnel vision of professional politicians who spend their whole life with politicians. You know, they're very isolated." She is a bridge between the people in the community and the politicians, if the politicians will only listen. She is outside the ranks of the politicians but inside the community of opinion and an agent for ordinary citizens. In the future she may move off the bridge and become more intrinsic to office-seeking, officeholding, and governance.

The third woman, Lorraine Reilly, who is still waiting for the right opportunity to run for a seat in the state legislature, approaches the extrinsic part of her understanding of "the political" obliquely. Does she consider herself political? "Not really. I mean just ordinary, really. Of course, my interest has always been in politics, even when I was a teenager. But . . . growing up . . . you only had one mayor, one president, and one governor. And they were in from the time I was a small child until I became almost an adult." She explains "the political" to which she is intrinsic as follows:

> There's so much going on, and people are not aware of what is happening. . . . If somebody doesn't do it or try to inform other people, I'm afraid we're going to lose the little bit of freedom that we have unless people really get interested in it. [So "the political" is] getting other people involved, and I want a better world for my kids . . . even with my own chil-

dren, well, you have to start with that they talk with their own friends. And the next thing, you've got families [of her children's friends]. Their parents voted Democrat. They're turning around now and voting Republican. And then I have taken some of them to some of the parties and introduced them to the elected officials. And they find that they're not villains or people off in space some place, that they're common people that they can speak to. And this, I believe, has really helped.

In other words, "the political" in her past was the party machine, which was impermeable. Today she sees herself as an "ordinary" mother-citizen gathering in her political flock of neighborhood (precinct) friends and bringing them into contact with the elected officials of her own party.

The last woman in this group views "the political" holistically as "everything." Edith Hammond, erstwhile party worker now holding appointive office, is similar to Audrey Nelms and Maryanne Thayer in her initial approach to "the political" as a controlling and regulating force in all our lives, whether we realize it or not: "I think politics controls your whole life, even while you're sleeping, because some person is setting how much you're paying for the lights, the gas, the telephone, whether or not you're buying milk with so much cream in it. [People have got to be involved] to find out what does control your life, how you can go about correcting the situation. It's just a matter of survival." She is also similar to Thayer when she says that she is political only to the extent that she is aware, but she is different from Thayer in that she has not become disengaged from "the political." She is still trying to influence what goes on from behind the scenes. "There are people that move out front; there are people that play in the background. And I would be one basically that would rather play in the background."

Extrinsic to Office and Power but Intrinsic to Working for the "Right" Candidates

Four women voice what has long been considered "the political" for women in the United States: working for candidates for public office.[3] One party worker, Bridgit Malone, states it quite succinctly:

As far as I'm concerned, it would be trying to elect somebody and work for the election of somebody who I thought was a good, upstanding person, honest person, and basically, would think politically the way I do. Which I think is the name of the game, really. Because if you don't think like, say, your elected official that represents you at the time, it is so very frustrating every time you look at a vote, and everything they do, . . . and the only comeback you have is to work to get them out.

The other two, erstwhile office-seeker Lavinia Ravenel and party worker Linda Helms, add the idea of the two-party system. Helms explains in more detail than Ravenel:

Oh my goodness. Politics. Well, politics runs this country. We have a two-party system which is a beautiful system. Other countries have many parties, and it's chaos. We have two parties in the system, the Democratic party and the Republican party. The Democratic party and the Republican party have changed positions over the last hundred years. The Republican party now stands for freedom of the individual in a free-enterprise system and less government and more personal responsibility. The Democratic party stands for, they have become a party of socialism over the years. They now believe in strong government control, strong government regulation. They do not believe in personal responsibility. They believe that people are the victims of their environment. Therefore, if somebody's poor, he should be supported by the government. The Republican party believes that if a man is able to work, he should support himself, and he is not entitled to the taxpayer's money, which is what I believe.

Helms goes on to elaborate on party government and power, thus linking herself to those in power through her campaign work:

Politics is a way of governing, and politics is power. And many get in it for power. Many get in it for a way of running a country, a philosophy of government. But politics, whoever has the political power runs the country and makes the appointments that determine how the country is run. . . . The idea is to get your party in power so that the country is run the way you feel it ought to be run. And many get in it for the power that it gives them . . . for themselves, and because they see a way of gaining control over other people, which is, I don't deny, is part of politics. But then there are many people in political office and many people who work behind the scenes of politics. That's where I fall. I have no ambition to be in political office myself, but to elect those people who believe as I do.

The fourth woman, party worker Betty Mason, adds a religious dimension to her rather holistic conception of "the political." She, too, links herself to the system of power in the sense that she sees herself as having a hand in determining the direction of political life. She also echoes the earlier group of women who understand "the political" as linking people to or educating people about the politicians who run for office.

> From a religious standpoint, I think it is a commitment to a way of life. It is determining the direction that we would like to see life go in, other than religiously. And I don't really think you can separate the two. A lot of people think the two ought to be separated. I don't. I think part of the reason we're in the trouble that we're in today is there has been a separation. I don't think it should be intertwined to the point that one tells the other what to do, but I think those who have a moral commitment should stand up for what is going on in the world that's right and wrong . . . through the caliber of persons that we put in office. . . . [We need to be] constantly educating people, making people more aware of who and what they're voting for. . . . I think we have in every aspect become a very immoral decadent society. And I don't think that the church alone can turn it around. I think it's going to take what we do in the legislature.

These four women play what could be considered peripheral roles in electoral politics. Most campaign volunteers do not have a chance to share in the powers and prestige of office. But these women see "the political" *as* electoral politics, and they positively assert an intrinsic view of themselves working in their conception of "the political." As Schlesinger's "benefit seekers,"[4] these women find their payoff in their connection to political power through the election of "right thinking" candidates.

Extrinsic to Office but Intrinsic to Advocacy

Two women—in addition to Ann Strong, whom we heard in chapter 2—conceptualize the extrinsic aspect of "the political" as holding office and the intrinsic aspect as some form of fight for a cause. One of the women has run for office in the past and lost and now rejects office as a viable means of achieving her ends. The other rejects office on general principles.

Ella Washburn, erstwhile party worker, begins by defining "the political" as "everything, just about everything in your life is affected by politics. [Examples?] . . . There's so many rules and regulations about everything anymore that your home life's affected by politics. What you have and don't have is affected by politics. And a lot of things you are *totally* against were brought about by politics—the present administration [Reagan], that sort of thing." She sees herself as very political, which involves "my strong support of and work for ERA. That's the main thing in my life lately." Holding public office is not appealing to her, she says, because she could not do the things required to stay in office—swapping favors and trading off on her beliefs. But working for the ERA, she does not have to compromise. She ends with a description of and explanation for her kind of politics: "For the first time in my life I demonstrated. And it was for ERA." She has also participated in the AFL-CIO Solidarity Days in Washington, D.C., and in Georgia, and in numerous other demonstrations for the ERA.

> I'm afraid I've become very biased. If somebody's running and they don't vote for ERA, I'm afraid I have to say I can't vote for him. . . . But I decided a long time ago the only way to get anything is just to be very very adamant about it. And the labor movement probably sets the best example. If they want anything, they strike for it, or they go out and fight for it. And of course that's the way we did with the Woman Suffrage, isn't it? That's what we had to do way back then. . . . You have to almost get obnoxious about it.

Sally Martin *has* run for office but with no expectations of winning, and now her definition of "the political" excludes running for office. She defines "the political" in part as "the art of getting along with people, so that in a broad category, politics is involved with everything." But she sees herself as "unpolitical" according to this definition:

> I think I'm pretty unpolitical. I'd like to be a little more politic than I am. That is, I'd like to be able to speak more circumspectly and not go dashing out and making very wild statements. But I don't want to be

more of a politician. I don't have any aspirations to run for a public office, not that kind of politics I don't. . . . I wouldn't mind serving, but I don't want to run and stay elected. [Why not?] Because it's a terrible thing always to have to be pleasing this group and that group because people won't ever stay pleased. . . . I'd rather do my own thing and not have my job depend on it.

But Martin thinks of "politics also in two other ways. One would be party, which is political and specifically defined. Then there's also issue politics." Issue politics is her "thing" now, being an "advocate" for the unrepresented, the "people who I feel don't have enough voice, and maybe who don't know *how* to get into the act, who need a representative." Presently she is working with a program designed to get teenage mothers-to-be to learn about their own and the prenatal nutritional needs through county health departments. She also works to get state health block-grant funds allocated to this particular program.

These women, then, focus on a concept of "the political" that is intrinsically cause oriented and advocacy based. Their advocacy contains an element that has emerged in other women's understandings of "the political": that of educating others about political ideas. Their view of "the political" acknowledges officeholders, compromise, and policy-making—but only in the extrinsic sense that those people and their process are the causes of the problem at issue and the targets of their advocacy.

Intrinsic to Governing and Power within Government

Six women, four of whom were state legislators when interviewed, understand "the political" in terms of governing; and three of these additionally speak of power and power structures within government. The three women who think of "the political" only as governing focus on different aspects of governing, the first of which has emerged before: educating constituents, taking care of the peoples' business, and building a two-party system in order to reform the legislature.

The first woman, office-seeker Bess Shumaker, begins by saying that "everything in this *life* is political" and goes on to say, "That means difference of opinion. . . . It's easier for me to talk about the difference and not necessarily in terms of Republican and Democrat. I think it basically comes down to liberal and conservative. And then you have these cats who say they're middle of the road. As far as I'm concerned, they have no opinion." She also gives rather lengthy discussions of the political as "selfish motives," "greed," and "human nature." Her disgust with this latter sort of politics is apparent, and she is also disgusted with people who do not understand "the seriousness of government." Her example of a businessman dumbfounds her; he wanted her to sign a petition against a tax assessment, but he did not even know his commissioner's name. She told him, " 'You should've gotten concerned when you went to the ballot box the last two years.' I said, 'Has anyone in the neighborhood called Bob Jones?' He said, 'Who?' Bob Jones is his commissioner. So, what do you *do* with people like that? But what concerns me is when people *don't know* who is making the rules and laws." Though *she* sees "the political" intrinsically as inherent to life and human nature, she recognizes that others are not as attuned as she to how government is set up. Thus, she tries to educate those less aware to what government is about.

Another woman, officeholder Sybyl Jensen, speaks of "the political" as "an individual who works with a group to take care of the business of the people." Sometimes the group is her colleagues in the legislature. Sometimes it is particular constituencies, such as a neighborhood experiencing a problem with an expressway. "We are the designated or the elected people to look after the business of everybody else. . . . You say politics, but let's call it government, the process of governing." For this woman who calls herself a "political animal," there are no ifs, ands, or buts. The political is governing, and she is political to the core.

Still another woman, officeholder Elizabeth Latimer, sees "the political" as building her party so that the state will have two-party politics and as a result the electorate and the legislature will be faced with important issues. "Basically I ran for the first time . . . on the Republican ticket because I felt strongly we needed to have a two-party system and that the two-party system in Georgia certainly was not effective at that point, but has become more so, and will become more so. And it's essential that it does. But I did not want the Republican party to be made up of people who were just the mad Democrats." She explains that "mad Democrats" "were really former Democrats who didn't have a very broad approach to life [meaning they disagreed with the racial-justice policies of the Kennedy and Johnson administrations].... They came in during the Goldwater days." She was interested in attracting people into the Republican party who were former Republicans that had moved into the area from other parts of the country. "And I think that it's important for us to address some of the issues. We have to educate the people before we get the legislators to address the issues. The Republican party will have to challenge, and I think we have two good gubernatorial candidates, and the issues will be raised this time. Regardless of who's elected, it will make a difference on what happens." In other words, she is another political educator. Her purpose in two-party politics is to raise issues in order to educate the people and the officeholders.

Since Latimer has been in the legislature, she has come to see "the political" also as involving reform efforts inside the legislature. She believes that, through two-party politics, the minority party eventually will gain enough seats in the legislature to effect reform of the dominant party's leadership, which is entrenched and not receptive to questions raised from within that party.

> When I first went down there, I didn't consider myself just political [party-affiliated]. I was willing to work with anybody whom I basically identified as working for the good of the cause, and I still will do that. But I will say *now* that I do, will become more political because I see the people in the Democratic party whom I've identified as working for the good of the cause say "We cannot reform the legislature from within. The Republicans are going to have to do it." There is no way that they can get rid of [the leadership]. And it's a long haul for us to do this. But the Republicans will make a change in the state faster now than they did in the past.... The population shift has been to the suburbs, 17 percent growth, and we created about ten new seats around Atlanta that will go to the Republicans.

[Does that mean the constituencies are changing?]

The leadership doesn't know it. They're still back in the Dark Ages. But that'll come. . . . I'm patient. See, I think women have learned patience because we have had to. In the first place, we have dealt with children, and you don't raise children unless you learn patience. And you learn you just have to inch along.

Elizabeth Latimer takes the long view, a developmental view, of "the political," of which she has been an integral part. She does not speak explicitly of power, but she is quite aware that there is a legislative leadership entrenched in power. On one level she continues to work with whomever she identifies as supporting her issues, but on a more recently added level, she has taken up the challenge of reform, which will come out of ever more successful Republican party-building.

Two other women in the legislature echo her understanding, but both go on to talk about power explicitly. Dulcie LaFontaine says:

What I see as politics is a proliferation of ideas. And everyone in this House has an idea from their own background of what they think bills should be and what ideas should be. We have people in here who are pro-labor, who are anti-labor. We have some that are in the middle. Conservatives in both parties, liberals in both parties. But I would say that the political process—you know, put the campaigns behind you and everything else—is the coming together and working together and hopefully coming up with laws or lack of laws that will protect the people of the state, that will serve the best interest of the people of this state, and also future generations. Because that's what politics evolves down to—the laws that are voted on, the reds and greens on the [electric tote] board up there that become part of the permanent journal, that affect the daily lives of the people in this state. . . . So politics boils down to power and how you use it or misuse it. And hopefully, most of us use it positively rather than negatively. I guess that's it. Positive or negative use of power is what politics is all about.

Adrienne Stone says that "the political" is "power—getting and using power." She is aware that she is outside the legislative power structure because of the negative treatment she received while working for certain pieces of women's rights legislation. Thus she is a living example of what her Republican colleague noted: Democrats who go against the leadership get nowhere on reform. Since she does not consider her party to be a vehicle for reform, she is working quietly with other women of both parties in the legislature to form a women's caucus that can coordinate priorities and rally support for bills addressing a variety of women's concerns.

The last woman in this group, office-seeker Kate Greene, touches on governance and power in her understanding of "the political," but she also gives a particularly feminist version of power as the ability to accomplish certain goals.[5] She says:

> Well, gee, there's so many facets of it. I think most people have the mistaken impression that it's nothing but a power struggle. And in some ways, it is. It is a power struggle, but it's that because there are people who feel that they see things that need to be done, and they're willing to go through those struggles in order to get in a position to do those things. . . . I really see it as people who think that they can administer the government in the best way, and they're willing to go through all the hardships to get to that place to be able to do it, because it's really not easy at all.
>
> [Do you consider yourself a political person?]
>
> I'm probably much more one now than I was in 1977 because I've learned that politics is the art of the possible. You really have to become a realist. You have to see what *can* be done, and "I'm going to see it done." It's that "This is what I think ought to be done, and here's the piece of it that I can get done." And that's politics. You have to learn to mediate, to spend time with the people that you really don't like at all, and try to see their point of view. And I think that that's what it's all about. It's very psychological.

These six women aspire to reach or have reached the inner sanctum of conventional politics—public office. They are intrinsic to a conception of "the political" to which the women preceding are extrinsic. Given that their political world revolves around government, it is not surprising that three of them make power an explicit core concept in their understandings of "the political." Through government they develop and use power both to take care of "the people's" business and to bring about reform as they understand it from the perspectives of their Democratic or Republican affiliations and their liberal, conservative, or moderate stances. Some of the women who follow will return to discussions of power, but they will be more concerned to dislodge power from government into the lives of people directly.

Intrinsic to Life–as–Political-Action to Change "the World"

Three women echo some of the women in electoral politics who said that everything is political, but these three place themselves inside some form of revolutionary politics for changing the present political system in the United States. They speak not of armed struggle to overthrow government but focus rather on bringing change through the very lives they lead—what they do every day and why they do what they do. They explicitly discuss a principle that other interviewees have implied: "The personal is political."

Tillie Zadar is one of two activists who are still in their early twenties. As we shall see, Zadar and Annie Witt are still in the process of "making sense" of and trying to integrate the various aspects of their lives. From Zadar's standpoint, there are two worlds—that of "the mainstream," which includes traditional electoral politics, and that of the Lesbian community. She lives in the Lesbian community but makes forays into the conventional world, which she mainly sees as "outside" her world, though she also speaks of herself as an "outsider." Zadar thinks about "the political" on two levels:

> Well, it's many things. On one level "the political" is action which is directly aimed at changing society in some way, be it electoral politics, which is very traditional or, you know, demonstrations, which are less traditional. That kind of actual—you know, I always think of it as going to meetings and stuff like that. That's sort of my initial view of what is political, but I also have the more philosophical perspective that, you know, the personal is political, that whatever I do in everyday life is political. And I think that being gay a lot of times, just walking around . . . I mean everything, everything has a political side to it. And you can be political and fostering political change in real small ways, like just by

insisting that people not use sexist language, and being "out' [as a Lesbian] in class, which I'm very strong about. So there's sort of that kind of living this way, living—you know, that we shop at [a food collective] and that we keep our money in [a neighborhood credit union] so that people can't send it to South Africa. You know, just living that way, that's living in a political way.

I ask her to elaborate some more on why her whole life is political, and she adds the dimension of conscious intentionality: "Well, I think everyone is logical. It's a matter [of] making conscious decisions . . . I guess I made a real conscious decision, I have a real vision of the future, and I guess I try to live towards that."

She goes on to divide the political in yet another way between "the mainstream" and her own world. She sees herself sometimes as "inside" her world and "outside" the mainstream, but other times she seems to be speaking from inside her world when she sees the mainstream as "the outside." She sees her life as a political statement that "I'm not going to buy into whatever it is on the television," or "I'm not going to buy into the mainstream culture, I'm going to live outside it." She says she knows people who really live outside, making their money "under the table and not paying taxes. . . . I'm not so, you know, I kind of do it in a half-assed kind of way." As a student of anthropology she sees a link between "culture and politics." She says, "I think that I'm always reminded of being counterculture when I'm in the outside world. You know, I think of it that way, I think of it as the mainstream world, and like right now I'm working temporary to make extra money, and when I'm out there I feel it's like being in another country or something."

I make the observation that her work for the Geraldine Ferraro campaign means that she goes back and forth between the two worlds.

Yeah, I go back and forth a lot. Part of it is, I have a real, you know, from my family, a real traditional strong Democratic background. Like I watched the convention and I was just, you know, I was caught up in it. . . . I was really in there because I have this Democratic—it's an emotional tie, you know. And I believe in electoral politics. I don't think they're the answer to everything, but I have a lot of friends who don't, and I just feel like well it's, you know, voting is the cheapest thing that

you can do. . . . And I really respect people who work inside politics, like
DSA [Democratic Socialists of America], they work totally inside mainstream politics with the Democratic Party, and I really respect that, and
I think they can get a long way doing that. And then I also respect the
people who say "No way" and "Stay out of that," who want to just work
in other ways.

By dividing her political world into two parts, Zadar makes it possible to retain some of the conventional politics that she came to
value growing up in her family while she also makes a place for her
newer more revolutionary politics.

Annie Witt, who as a student activist finds herself pulled by both
leftist and women's communities, is wrestling with how "the political" fits with the various parts of her life,[6] which is becoming more
and more politicized. As a student activist, she was instructed by
the school administration "specifically not to be political." She thinks
that instruction meant to be noncontroversial, especially not to address issues that women should decide for themselves, "like abortion
and everything that stems from that, . . . lesbianism, . . . hair under
my arms . . ." or not to attack a sexist poster put out by a fraternity.
At work, as a secretary,

I think about being active at work because I work with people who consider themselves communist or, in some cases, just very, very, very liberal people. So there's a lot of political discussion and stuff going on and
dealing specifically with labor. So I'm constantly exposed to that. I can't
get away from it. Sometimes it's a drag. And I think that that can be a
burnout for my political activism at school. And I think at this point I
am going through that period where I'm getting frustrated with having
to deal with this politics or that, sometimes it's like hypocrisy. But in my
work place, like these guys are real pro-labor, but they have this really
funny idea about their secretaries. I mean, my consciousness has just
really been raised about what I am to the office. So my political view has
really expanded to include the whole economic sphere. . . . I go through
phases where I feel like I really despise politics. But I could never, I know
that I could never lose that interest that I have in it. Whenever I read
something that ticks me off, I get really angry, and I feel like I want to
go out and do something. Sometimes I get really overenthusiastic. I do it
to myself like, I burn out fast. But I think what I'm doing now is just
trying to find out where it does fit into my life. How can I be political
without losing myself in it or something.

And finally as a musician:

> I was talking to a friend who said that I don't have to separate my other
> life from being political, that being political doesn't mean that you have
> to separate the two. So, I see fusing my music with issues and ideas and
> things. I'm not going to produce music in a vacuum.

And so how would she sum up her definition of "the political"?

> That's really hard, because I'm not quite sure of it, you know. I want to
> say that "the political" is being active with, working with other people. I
> mean, other people have to be there because you can't be political on your
> own to make any kind of dent. I see being incorporated in the idea of
> political making specific advances or developments or changes in society,
> in the political system. . . . I've been told I have this strange idea about
> what it means to be political. So getting back to that idea about separat-
> ing the two, I am trying now to work to the point where I can really feel
> very comfortable and very natural with incorporating in my life politics
> and all of these other things and to understand that they are in fact in-
> separable. And I've found that notion of the personal being political and
> political being personal, that they are interpenetrating. . . . I think that
> working with other women and working on projects dealing specifically
> with women's issues to me is more essential to what it means to me. I
> think that just working with other women who are struggling with the
> same kind of crap that I'm putting up with in my office is one step to
> building a stronger base for some definite changes in how clerical work-
> ers are viewed by men and by the women themselves. . . . Then there's
> all these other issues, you know, nuclear power is a very pressing is-
> sue. . . . I was just thinking how the word political is really tossed around
> now. It has grown to mean so many things. And, you know, it makes me
> wonder now if there really is any kind of all-inclusive definition for po-
> litical.

I quote her at length because she vividly portrays her thought processes as her political consciousness is raised first by one experience
and then by another until it encompasses her life.

Fran Daly has made the full transition into life–as–political-action. She understands "the political" on two levels: one she calls
"direct political involvement," which means working in this or that
group; and the other she calls "a view to affecting the world," which
is her version of "the personal is political." She gives an example of
the second level, showing that this conceptualization of political in-

volves critical and intentional action: "So, whether that is affecting the system or an institution, an institution like racism, it is to say that, therefore, [the way I raise my child] is part of working against racism. Well, it is, but not just because I *did* that, but because I *believe* in that . . . and see it that way and I try to use it for that, so that *I* give it the political implications."

Daly's definition of "the political" comes at the end of a long section of the interview in which I have asked her to describe her "women's community politics." As we saw earlier, her politics is life encompassing, from her household arrangements and status as a Lesbian mother to her work arrangement, which is a women's collective business. She has described linking women to the resources they need, encouraging women to love and value themselves as women, and creating a "transformative work experience," which involves nonhierarchical decision-making and sharing all work functions from typing to deciding what orders to place. In other words, her life–as–political-action is directed at transforming "the system," and this action encompasses both envisioning the future and materializing the vision in the present.

All three of these women include two common ideas about "the political." One is that "the political" involves working with others to engage in direct political actions, whether this occurs through ad hoc groups or formal organizations. The other is that "the personal is political," meaning the very ways they think about and live their daily lives constitute "the political." Both forms of political action are directed at changing not only their own personal lives but also society as a whole. They believe that every change they effect in their own life space contributes to a larger systemic change.

Additionally, these women present two different modes of organizing their political worlds. Daly seems to have arrived at what Witt is seeking: a way to integrate "the political" with all aspects of her life at home and at work in her community. Zadar takes a different approach, dividing her political life world into "Lesbian community" and "mainstream society." She seems to have become adept at moving back and forth, inside and outside these two spaces. Taken together, without using the word "power," these women's definitions of "the political" presume power and suggest that these women have become empowered through living their lives as political action.

Intrinsic to Developing Power for Change

The other five women in revolutionary movement politics also approach "the political" holistically, but they focus on a power dimension to which they give different meanings depending on their arena within movement politics. The women in the leftist community speak partly in the oppositional language of Marxist analysis, though they have begun to apply this analysis to women's oppression.

Hazel Beecroft focuses on change through consciousness-raising, confronting and resolving contradictions. She begins by saying, "I really have embraced the idea that it's our responsibility to create a better world, and it's through Marxism as one of the guideposts to do that. . . . Everything in your life is related to a certain political way you have of looking at the world, and you have to think about what you're doing in trying to help." She then gives an example, without stating the principle, that illustrates "the personal is political":

> It comes up in raising kids all the time, what kind of consciousness you want to teach them. Regular people do it, too. It's just that the Left made it so conscious from the beginning. Everything was so talked out that you had to change—your ideas about women, about relationships, about power structures, about Black people—the kind of consciousness changes that you were forced to go through as you went through different processes [trying to mesh how you act politically with how you believe theoretically]. You have to be open when people say, "Hey, that's a contradiction when you *do* this and you *say* this."

She gives two classic examples of contradictions in the old Left, how they talked about equality while "totally oppressing women . . . and totally oppressing Black people. And the new Left really attacked those and really dealt a lot with peoples' consciousness."

Maria Montgomery understands "the political" by focusing on

power struggles of groups. She says, "Well, I think it has to do with power, struggles for power. But at the same time, I think that it can't be removed from the economic sphere of society. Struggles for power occur in the marriage, in the bedroom, in communities, in City Hall, in the Capitol, all those places." I ask what she means by struggles for power. She replies,

> I think it means the ability to mold your interests, to see that your interests are met. And I think of it not in terms of individuals but in terms of groups. Like when I think of it in the bedroom, I think of it as women versus men. And when I think of it in the community [it's] struggling for power as a poor person, as a tenant, as a Black, as a woman, as a worker, as a teacher, as a student—your role in a grouping in society. You're struggling for recognition of your interests and for the actualization of your interests.

Montgomery, too, implicitly brings in the principle of "the personal is political" when she refers to power struggles in the bedroom, in the classroom, and in the community.

Susan Murphy expands upon the idea of empowering people through revolutionary organization and movements. What is "the political"? She responds, "The political quest for me is to be part of creating institutions and organizations and movements that affect the balance of power in this country. When that's important to you, politics permeates everything, really, everything." Then she, too, gives an example that draws on the principle of "the personal is political":

> Like, for instance, I noticed the fact this year that the school where I have my four-year-old, and I chose it very carefully, didn't do a program on Martin Luther King's birthday. Now that's a small thing. But, you know, we're a generation down from where I was when I grew up, and we're in Atlanta, Georgia, and I expect, just like I expect my child to learn to read and do math, I expect him to have some knowledge of Afro-American history and some respect for Afro-American culture. And I expect the school that I send him to, for that to be an integral part of their program.

She has more to say on "creating institutions and organizations and movements." She is as political to the core as the state legislators we heard earlier, but she is acting from an entirely different perspective outside the bounds of their "political"—outside but not disengaged from their world. In her past, she says, her "politics of social change" has included "Ralph Nader–like actions, . . . monitoring and trying to get the capitalists to behave themselves." But mostly she has been involved in more "radical" politics: "I've been involved in trying to build organizations where people have power, and through their organizations they assert their power and assert their influence and attempt to bring about change for themselves and their families but also gain through organizations and movements a sense of what they can do and a sense of the importance of being organized and being involved in a movement."

In the future, after reflecting on the lessons she has learned from past struggles:

> I'm still very much interested in figuring out a way for myself to work for the rest of my life among the people, to build organizations and institutions that can give the people in this country more control over their own lives. I have many more ideas about what those organizations ought to look like. I think that, for example, one organization that's desperately needed in this country is a third political electoral party that is an alternative to the Democrats and the Republicans. I hope that in my lifetime I will see that built in this country. I don't think it's the only institution that's needed, but I think it's one, that there is a tremendous need for it so that people can go to the ballot box and vote for something that has the capacity to deliver to them and have a program that they can genuinely believe in and which I think neither the Democrats nor the Republicans have right now. And the right kind of candidates. Yes, I think it's an important tool because this is a country where the right to vote is ingrained in our culture. . . . I hate to say something that sounds so simplistic and rhetorical, but the small people need their own party, their own organization, their own voice. They need a vehicle, an electoral vehicle to fight through. I still think they need other organizations, too. I mean I think they need radical women's organizations and farmer's organizations and the trade unions. But I think there is a need for this political party. I also think they need their army. They need an organization of trained leaders with a revolutionary strategy. I haven't given that up yet. But I do think this electoral thing is one thing that needs to be built in this country.

And so we hear again that "the political" involves party building, this one to empower the "small people."

Barbara Bergen, women's community activist, begins her discussion of "the political" explicitly with the principle of life–as–political-action: "Well, there's the feminist adage, you know, 'the personal is political,' and that's real true to me in a real deep sense. To me, the political is my everyday life and to be aware of my effect on the world in my everyday life."

Next comes "the spiritual" as an aspect of her understanding of "the political." "The spiritual" concerns how she acts within women-only groups:

> I really can't disconnect [the spiritual] from "the political" at all to myself. And that comes from me wanting . . . to work within women-only groups and as much as possible I like working with a lot of Lesbians. And that's because "the spiritual,"—I can be more vulnerable and more open in those groups. I can be more creative, and I think that has a lot to do with "the spiritual," being able to combine the two aspects of not having to shut down and be on guard. I really can't work for long in a group where I have to be on guard. It's too draining. I can be much more effective— and it's not to say that the work that group is doing is not good—but I can be much more effective if I don't have to use that energy fighting for things that are real simple to me, like nonhierarchical structures. Having to be on guard, or calling someone always wanting to be boss, or something of the type, you know, I don't want to waste my time doing that.

For Bergen, whatever she is doing is political because she tries to do it in accord with the principles of what she calls "feminist process," which is also a feminist interpretation of power: "a nonhierarchical process where each woman is encouraged to find her own power and not have to jockey and manipulate for it, not to seek power in a scarcity model but to see that there is a whole bunch of it. You don't have to think that there is just a little bit of it so you have to grab for it." She goes on to explain that, though the "feminist process" may require a particular meeting to go on for a long time, over the long run the "feminist process" is "the most efficient way of doing things. . . . It seems that if you do that work, although it seems to take a long time, everything else just falls into place. . . . You don't end up with people hurt, unsaid feelings that are going to sabotage you later on, you try to avoid that. . . . You're taking care of every-thing step by step. You don't have to back up, you haven't run over anyone on your way to the goal. Everyone has been paid attention to."

Gretchen Bright, women's community activist, gives a very de-tailed and integrated explanation of "the political" as it revolves around power. "The political: I think to me it would be the way I interpret power and the way power is used in society, and so my political views would be my interpretation of that, my response to it, and my vision." I then ask her to define power. She gives a very long response that explains why and how she moved across the threshold from one world to another but still retains her self-grounding while living in these two worlds that seem to be super-imposed one upon the other, as if the world has a "double identity." She begins by defining power in the "white male supremacist world" and her resistance to it:

> I mean my observation is that in the society that I am in, the organiza-tions and the people that are *in* power, that is, who [have] control over the resources that we need to live and to grow, the choices and the values that the political system right now embodies are—I'm in opposition to—so as I examine that, what does it look like, what does it, you know, who are these people and what are their values? It became clear to me that it was a white male supremacist system that we are working in. I think the shock of that once I allowed myself just to look at it, ask the ques-tions, look at it and see it, I know sent me for a couple of years, as with many women, into a phase of life where I had to deal with constant anger at—you know, it was like finding a place to stand politically. It also pushed me into this threshold of, "I see, know, I'm in resistance around me, and how do I go on with my life?"

She found the "place to stand politically" in the women's collective business of which she became a part. That changed the way she ex-pressed herself as a writer and as a teacher:

> The essence of my classes is helping people begin to self-reflect, look at their patterns, how they operate within the society, and encouraging them to ask questions. And to me that's a threshold point for them to begin to see the larger picture. So for me, my work has given me a daily structure to resist and to envision my politics. I feel very much like what

the entity [the collective business] that we've created, particularly in the past three years, is an actual physical manifestation of a vision that explores what could happen in society if these values could be brought [into being], and having that actual experience is extremely empowering to me. It in a very direct way manifests hope where I still have to deal with a sense of futility and despair when I look at the effect of the politics we're in right now.

In comparison to Susan Murphy, who is engaged in a power struggle with the capitalists and envisions creating organizations that *will* empower the "small people," whom she terms "they," Bright is now involved with others, whom she calls "we," empowering herself and the others through their own "physical manifestations" of an alternative way of living.

There is both an anticapitalist dimension and a feminist dimension to Bright's understanding of "the political." I ask her to describe in more detail just how the women's collective is a "physical manifestation" of their "vision." Here she begins to explain the "double identity" of "the political" as occurring in a "capitalist patriarchy" and in a collective that materializes a feminist vision:

I feel in many ways that we have a double identity in a sense in that we made a decision to be a straightforward absolutely on-the-books clear incorporated-for-profit entity, so that we are a part of the capitalist system. . . . We have all the rights of property owners and business owners in the capitalist system. So having that as our outer—almost like an armor, that is how the patriarchy negotiates with us. That is, we have claimed our rights by their rules and by their system. Within that we have a right of privacy and a kind of privilege because of playing that game that allows us to create inside that boundary whatever we want. So part of our vision and part of our mission is to reinterpret the capitalist system in a feminist way.

But Bright notes the "privilege" that goes with that capitalist system, and she notes the danger of their position that puts their feet in two camps, so to speak: "Now, I feel this is a dangerous position, there is no safety inside that, and there is no way that we can beat them at their own game. However, as a working experience and as an experience with a proprietorship, by keeping our feminist views always in the forefront, we have been able to create an em-

powering experience in a system that is designed to disempower."
She goes on to give examples. On the resistance side, they have declared themselves to be enemies of "the patriarchy," and that makes
them a target of the patriarchy. On the empowerment side, they
have done things that make them, however, not "financially successful" by capitalist standards: They have declared a thirty-two–
hour work week; they pay themselves subsistence salaries and their
part-time hourly workers "quite a bit more than minimum wage."
They see this as spreading their resources around. In order to avoid
burnout they have "very clear stress prevention benefits": encourage
liberal vacations not at the expense of the business and encourage
each person "to have lives and activities outside of the store." In
contrast to "business as usual," they have made decisions that "affirm the whole person, and to me that is, you know, one of the core
parts of the feminist vision." Alluding again to the feminist world in
contrast to the capitalist world, Bright says that, by affirming these
women as whole persons and supporting and encouraging such a
way of life for each of them, "the store acts as a grounding place and
as a support for that kind of work." Dorothy Smith would be pleased
but probably not surprised that this feminist is describing what she,
Smith, believes can happen when women step over "the line of fault"
into a space where they can construct a new "reality."

Education and Power as Themes
in Understandings of "the Political"

These white women tell us that "the political" encompasses specific
kinds of actions or "everything." Two women who understand "the
political" holistically, and especially in relation to economics, also
understand "the political" as either so powerful that it shuts them
out or so powerless that it cannot resolve the problems of society.
They have withdrawn from "the political." The other twenty-four
women understand several varieties of political action of which they
are a part: *linking* private citizens together or with public officials;
linking themselves to the "right" candidates and hence to the power

to bring about a better way of life; *advocating* constitutional changes, programs for unrepresented mothers-to-be, more support for public education; *governing* and *using power* in government; *developing power* for political *change*; and *living* politics *as* a total way of life *for* a better way of life.

There are some relationships between political arena and understanding of "the political." These are displayed in table 3. Office-oriented activists, especially officeholders, but also some office-seekers, both Democrats and Republicans, are the only type intrinsic to governing. Movement activists, both leftist and women's community, are intrinsic either to developing power for political change or to living–as–political-action. Erstwhile Democratic party workers *and* office-seekers have turned to advocating; "erstwhile" seems to

---

Table 3. Women in the Study, by Understanding of "the Political" and Arena of Political Engagement

Exclusively Extrinsic
  Audrey Nelms, erstwhile Republican office-seeker
  Maryanne Thayer, erstwhile Republican party worker
Extrinsic to Organization but Intrinsic to Linking "Private and Public Spheres"
  Arlene Pringle, erstwhile Republican party worker
  Nancy Harding, Democratic office-seeker
  Edith Hammond, erstwhile Democratic party worker
  Lorraine Reilly, Republican office-seeker
Extrinsic to Office and Power but Intrinsic to Working for the "Right" Candidate
  Bridgit Malone, Republican party worker
  Lavinia Ravenel, Republican party worker
  Linda Helms, Republican party worker
  Betty Mason, Republican party worker
Extrinsic to Office but Intrinsic to Advocacy
  Ann Strong, Democratic party worker
  Ella Washburn, Democratic party worker
  Sally Martin, erstwhile Democratic office-seeker

be the key here. Given what some of the other women have said about the resistance of the Georgia Democratic leadership to reform, it should not be surprising that these Democratic women have disengaged from their party organizations but have gone on to other forms of political engagement. Rather than drop out and stay out, they have turned from electoral politics to advocacy politics. The Republican party activists who work for the "right" candidates, on the other hand, seem to be more in step with their state and local party organizations. The women who understand "the political" as linking "private" citizens and "public" officials are not confined to one party or one form of political engagement in electoral politics. These women have suggested a form of politics that involves educating, and this idea joins them to a political tradition with a long history, a tradition not often noted in contemporary studies of political behavior.

By "educating," these and other of the electoral activists refer not

---

Table 3, continued

Intrinsic to Governing and Power within Government
  Bess Shumaker, Republican office-seeker
  Sybyl Jensen, Republican officeholder
  Elizabeth Latimer, Republican officeholder
  Dulcie LaFontaine, Republican officeholder
  Adrienne Stone, Democratic officeholder
  Kate Greene, Democratic office-seeker
Intrinsic to Life–as–Political-Action to Change "the World"
  Tillie Zadar, women's community activist
  Annie Witt, leftist community activist
  Fran Daly, women's community activist
Intrinsic to Developing Power for Change
  Hazel Beecroft, leftist community activist
  Maria Montgomery, leftist community activist
  Susan Murphy, leftist community activist
  Barbara Bergen, women's community activist
  Gretchen Bright, women's community activist

to formal institutionalized educating, though that too certainly is political, but to the efforts of citizens, voters, party workers, and officials to "educate" others on whom to elect or on what needs to be done politically to solve this or that problem. The idea can be traced back to the works on education and ruling of John Locke and Jean-Jacques Rousseau, who in turn developed a theme that can be traced back to Plato in *The Republic*.[7] Jay Fliegelman notes that both Locke and Rousseau emphasized the importance of education for governing; in fact, the concept of governing "took on in the eighteenth [century] more of its root sense: 'to steer,' 'guide,' 'direct,' and 'regulate.' It carried with it, that is, all the force of its other sense: 'to educate.' For a 'governor' in the seventeenth and eighteenth centuries referred to a tutor in charge of a young man's education as much as it did to an officer of the state."[8] Fliegelman focuses his attention for the most part on the antipatriarchal politics of revolutionary America in the sense of the move toward egalitarian father-son relations, the age dimension of patriarchy for men. Regardless of Fliegelman's lack of attention to women's problems in patriarchy and women's possibilities beyond patriarchy, women now, as then, have been attuned to the significant identification of educating and governing. Just as Virginia Sapiro has noted the political nature of women's citizen educational efforts,[9] so the female electoral activists in my study continue this long tradition of understanding the education of citizens, voters, and officials as "political."

What "educating" is for the electoral activists becomes "consciousness-raising" for the movement activists. Leftist Hazel Beecroft in particular notes the distinction when she says, "It comes up in raising kids all the time, what kind of consciousness you want to teach them. Regular people do it, too. It's just that the Left made it so conscious from the beginning." And she explains the process, whether it is between parents and children or between activists and those they are trying to move or among women in a consciousness-raising group: the key is recognizing contradictions and taking time to talk through them. "Everything was so talked out that you had to change—your ideas about women, about relationships, about power structures, about Black people—the kind of consciousness changes that you were forced to go through as you went through different processes [trying to mesh how you act politically with how you believe theoretically]. You have to be open when people say, 'Hey, that's a contradiction when you *do* this and you *say* this.' "

There is a difference between "educating" and "consciousness-raising" in that educating can imply a hierarchical relationship between "teacher" and "student," while consciousness-raising is supposed to occur between subjects as presumed equals. But there are also similarities in that those doing the "teaching" or "moving" presume to know some "truth" that will also become self-evident to others if only they will receive the information and rationale or recognize the contradiction. The teachers and movers present what only others have the power to receive and act on.

There is, then, a subtle difference between these women's forms of teaching and moving to effect change and the more conventional form of policy-making in which groups organize in order to exert influence on the authorities, who in turn, by reason of office, possess the power to make policy. In the conventional mode, groups in and out of government are thought to exercise countervailing power, are expected to bargain and compromise, and thereby make policy. Both sides are assumed to be powerful, and when in conflict each must give up something in order to resolve the conflict. Educating and consciousness-raising, on the other hand, imply a model in which those with knowledge but no or little power, at least in governmental terms, approach those with no or little presumed knowledge but the power to act or effect change. Those bringing knowledge into the equation emerge with some degree of increased power if a successful exchange of knowledge and action is made.

If educating and consciousness-raising run as one theme through these women's conceptions of "the political," then power is another major theme. In fact, power takes different forms in relation to different types of political engagement. For the electoral activists, power appears to reside in government, and they align themselves with power in various ways. Those who are almost entirely extrinsic to "the political" appear to be powerless; those who work for the "right" candidates suggest that they link themselves to this form of power; and those seeking office or holding office talk in terms of themselves exercising this form of power.

For the movement activists, the power that resides in government is "real" but from their perspectives is being misused. And they seem to believe that government power is not the only power. The leftist activists speak of seeking to organize the untapped power of the "small people," but their vision is more comprehensive than the groups that pursue narrower "special interests" through the conventional mode of policy-making. The power of the "small people" organized, it is believed, will strike a balance of power that will slow down the capitalists at a minimum and remove them and their values from government entirely at a maximum. The leftist activists are closer to the electoral activists than to the women's community activists in this regard. The leftists, like the electoral activists, keep their focus on the system of established government in the hopes of changing it in a revolutionary fashion.

The leftists are closer to the women's community activists in another regard. The women's community activists share the leftists' belief that there is more than government power to be developed and exercised. But for the women's community activists, power resides in women's collective lives and has always done so. There have been times in history when women's powers were suppressed; Barbara Bergen referred to the burning of witches in the Middle Ages as an example. Certainly these women would agree that the time in which they live is a time of suppression, sometimes subtle as in the psychological phenomenon of "internalized oppression," sometimes physically violent as in rape and battering. Women's power, according to these activists, must be organized nonhierarchically and according to the nonexclusive principles of feminist process that Bergen also described. While women's power must be used in part to resist further encroachment in women's lives by "the patriarchy," women's power is also to be used as a source of energy to create women's space and time on their own terms, and not only personal space and time but also community, even global, space and time.

Chapter 8

"Politics as Usual" versus "Politics of Reality"

Though the structure of complex domination might be intended to appear static and "usual," Black feminists have been among those leading the challenge to that appearance of inclusive "reality." White political women in this study collectively provide evidence of joining in that challenge. They, too, appear to be breaking out of their consigned social location in complex domination to engage the world from standpoints that exhibit their individuality as well as their sociality. Their various engagements result in a lively contest of "politics as usual" versus "politics of reality." Thus, I set out to learn more of how selected white political women understand their worlds and their places within those worlds. I began by asking, first, why they understand their worlds in different ways, and, second, how those different understandings shape their political engagements. Their answers provide, in response to the first question, insight into the processes of political socialization and consciousness-raising and, in response to the second question, models of white women's political activism.

Complex domination poses a number of problems for white women to address if they are to become political women. These concern questions of identities and values and of actions considered appropriate to realizing those identities and values. Beyond processes of politicization and models of activism, the ways these women have identified as white women are pivotal to understanding the unending debate over sameness and difference that feminists and antifeminists have joined over the centuries and into the current decade. Their identities as white women reveal their assumptions about differences and similarities between women and men as well as among women. Their identities as white women also suggest an outline for a political morality play about the rocky path from privilege to empowerment.

Why Different Understandings of Political Worlds?

The women in this study expand our understanding of the process of politicization involving both values and roles. Specifically, they appear to develop different political values about the place of women in the world and thus enter or create different political arenas in which to act according to those values. While this two-part process is much more interactive than can be conveyed in a necessarily linear written presentation, the process can be summarized in terms of two aspects, one of which seems to be more structured than and thus basic to the other.

The more basic aspect, presented in chapters 3 through 5, involves variously structured childhood families experienced and responded to within historical periods of emergent or submergent feminist movement. From such contextualized childhood family experiences develop white women, of differing identities, espousing differing values with regard to the question of the place of women in the world, that is, espousing differing forms of feminism or antifeminism. This aspect of the developmental process appears to lay the ground for the other, less structured, aspect of politicization, presented in chapters 6 and 7, which involves the women's using as models politically engaged parents or significant others and entering into the larger community of political discourse via reading and discussing "the political" with those parents or others. From such experiences emerge white women with different analyses of causes of "the problem," different understandings of "the political," and thus different stances in support of or in opposition to what I call the political apparatus of institutions and organizations that constitute conventional politics in the United States. The interaction between values and roles or actions taken results in either of the aspects of politicization that I have characterized as political socialization or consciousness-raising. That interaction occurs as each woman interprets, "theorizes," with others, about how and why "the political" operates as it appears to do and thus what should be done about it in which arena.

Models of White Women's Political Activism

The process of integrating values with political engagement results in women who present distinct combinations of: identities as women, identities as feminists or antifeminists, understandings of "the political," and chosen arenas of engagement. Looking first at the women engaged in electoral politics, all three "Ladies" are Republican party workers. All three "Ladies with Best of Both Worlds" are Republican officeholders or office-seekers. All three "Women Spinning Women Together" are Democratic office-seekers. Republican "Women Persons" and Democratic "Women Made, Not Born," on the other hand, distribute themselves in both arenas of electoral politics, both as party workers and as office-oriented party activists.

The explanation for the relationship between way of understanding "being a woman" and arena of political action seems quite straightforward for the "Ladies" and the "Ladies with Best of Both Worlds." The women who identify as "Ladies"—Bridgit Malone, Linda Helms, and Lavinia Ravenel—by definition would feel out of place and improper if they "pushed" to hold office themselves. While they certainly have stepped out of the home setting, in which they feel most comfortable and proper, they have at least taken a role as party worker that can be justified as extending their familial role of service to the larger community. On the other hand, the "Ladies with Best of Both Worlds"—Lorraine Reilly, Sybyl Jensen, and Bess Shumaker—who value "the best of both worlds"—feminine and masculine, "private" domestic and "public" political—feel quite "at home" in public officeholding or office-seeking. Understandings of "the political" held by the "Ladies" and the "Ladies with Best of Both

Worlds" reinforce the choices they have made in regard to arena of political action. The "Ladies" believe that "the political" is working to get the "right" candidates elected. The "Ladies with Best of Both Worlds" include a political educator, Reilly, who seeks to link voters to her party's candidates, one of which she herself hopes to be in the future, and two, Jensen and Shumaker, who define "the political" as governing and using power in government.

Likewise, understandings of "the political" and "feminism" have helped shape the choices for political action made by the "Women Spinning Women Together" as well as by the "Women Persons" and the "Women Made, Not Born." The "Women Spinning Women Together" carry their concerns for women's needs into their versions of politics, from political educating—Nancy Harding—to advocacy— Sally Martin—to governance itself—Kate Greene. Their concerns with individualism and rights direct the "Antifeminist People-ist" "Women Persons"—Dulcie LaFontaine, Elizabeth Latimer, Betty Mason, Arlene Pringle, and Maryanne Thayer—toward the Republican party and most of the "Women's Rights Feminist" "Women Made, Not Born"—Adrienne Stone, Edith Hammond, and Ella Washburn—toward the Democratic party.

Turning to the women engaged in various aspects of leftist and women's community politics aimed at transforming the "capitalist" system or "the patriarchy," all but one understand "being a woman" as "Women Spinning Threads"—Annie Witt, Hazel Beecroft, Fran Daly, and Tillie Zadar—or "Women Spinning Networks,"—Susan Murphy, Barbara Bergen, and Gretchen Bright. These are women continually in the process of becoming. They appear to be locating standpoints from which to transform self and society, to create new political "realities," in order that they and theirs might live their lives to the fullest on their own terms. They presume the togetherness of women claimed by the Democratic office-seeking "Women Spinning Women Together," but their "spinning" has become revolutionary. Their understandings of "the political," which include life–as–political-action to change "the world" and developing power for change, complement their identities as women, requiring as actors women who are confined neither by a patriarchal identity of "Woman" nor by a conventional political identity of "Individual."

Whether from their various roles within the conventional political drama or from their various standpoints in the drama of newly emerging "political realities," the women in this study leave us with questions, and point to future discourse concerning, "the political." What is it, and what should it be if white women, among others, are to move from a social location within complex domination that combines privilege with oppression to empowerment in a transformed world? Some of these women would not agree with my proposition that complex domination poses problems for white women and would opt for a continuation of conventional "politics as usual." They include the antifeminist "Ladies" and "Ladies with Best of Both Worlds" and "Women Persons," who have for the most part won roles for themselves within the ongoing drama played out in the arena of electoral politics as political educators and party campaign workers and office-seekers and officeholders. These women's identities tend to preclude them from acting for women as women or against racism, except in cases where they perceive that ladies' privileges or women's or racial minorities' individual rights are threatened. Though all antifeminists and Republicans, they do not agree among themselves on whether or when they should act on such issues. They do agree that government as constituted, especially under the 1980s leadership of the Reagan administration, is the obvious and legitimate stage for public policy-making. They only need to work to correct what has gone wrong while previous Democratic administrations directed the action.

Perhaps the "Women Made, Not Born," and the "Women Spinning Women Together" would better support my proposition that complex domination poses problems to be addressed by white women, though they also would still opt for conventional "politics as usual." Overwhelmingly Democrats and feminists, their identities make them sensitive to the sexism they and other white women encounter as well as to the racism that Black people encounter, though most have not linked the two problems together. The problem as they see it is one of rights under the law, rights that need to be equalized with those of white men. Again, government as constituted is the obvious and legitimate stage for legal reforms, but the director and actors need to be changed. Democrats, including "women and (possibly) Blacks" need to take over the roles played by Republicans. Even two of the leftist women—"Marxist-Feminists" — and two of the women's community activists—"Women-centered Feminine-ists"—are willing to consider some involvement on this political stage as candidates (the Marxists) or as voters and campaign workers (the women's community activists). This kind of role is clearly a new idea for these Communist Party–Marxist/Leninist organizers (in contrast to long-standing "old Left" and Communist Party U.S.A. strategy) and would focus their efforts on replacing both Democratic and Republican "capitalists" with more "progressive" directors and actors on the main stage.

Electoral roles are clearly marginal for the women's community activists. They spend as much time as possible in creating another political arena from which to undermine and replace bit by bit the structure of complex domination, which they would agree oppresses all women and many men, even while also privileging some of those women and men. Their identities make them sensitive to the interlocking nature of privilege and oppression, which they perceive to reside not simply in the laws but in the whole structure of society, including the most personal and intimate aspects of their daily lives. They are, therefore, most likely to be among those women, and men, moving past the "main stage" of conventional electoral politics and government to make places for themselves in an ongoing effort to transform all aspects of daily life in society, possibly including conventional "politics as usual" if the ripple effects of their concerted actions reach into that arena.

Their movement clearly puts them at odds with the women on the political "main stage," though some of their statements about "mainstream" women are more supportive of those women's efforts than some of those women's statements are of Lesbians and other "Women-centered Feminine-ists." Most women on the political "main stage" would consider these feminist women misguided in thinking they can change society without focusing on legal reform. To these feminist women, however, their movement is profoundly "political" in the sense that they are shaping not only laws and institutions but "reality," that is, creating another "reality," other structures and cultures that include them as legitimate actors.

The Debate over Sameness and Difference

The differences in the ways these women identify as (white) women and as "feminists" or "antifeminists" mirror some of the variations and tensions found in both Nancy Cott's history of feminism in the early twentieth century and contemporary feminist debates in the United States. These tensions have to do with *difference* or *sameness*, both difference or sameness *vis-à-vis men* and difference or sameness *among women*. These tensions around difference and sameness have ripple effects in white women's politics, whether in the conventional arena of electoral politics or in the nonconventional arena of movement politics.

The oldest woman in the study, "Wise Elder Woman" Ann Strong, mirrors the early feminism almost perfectly in her understanding of "being a woman." She was born soon after the turn of the century and was growing up during the 1910s and 1920s, the period covered by Cott's study of early feminism. Strong talks of wanting to be herself and always working to improve herself. She also talks of women's special roles in the home that allow them to become involved in vital so-called "voluntarist" politics. And she talks about the importance of rights for women, but she does so along with the privileges that go with their special roles. She does not think women should be made to feel that they must choose between keeping house and pursuing a career, but she also thinks men should share the responsibilities of housework while women share the responsibilities of politics in the community. In her conception of "feminism," she stresses the emphasis on the continuing need to fight for women's rights. Thus, one part of Strong's identity as a woman links her to the theme of *difference* from men of the "Male-defined Feminine-ism" expressed by the "Ladies." Another part of Strong's identity as a woman links her to the theme of *sameness* with men that is implied in the focus on women's equal rights of the "Women's Rights Feminism" expressed by the "Women Made, Not Born."

If "Wise Elder Woman" Ann Strong resonates with both "feminism" and "antifeminism," then the forms of "feminism" and "antifeminism" that I have named "Women's Rights Feminism" and "Antifeminist People-ism" in turn bring together more than one understanding of "being a woman." "Antifeminist People-ists" are for the most part "Ladies with Best of Both Worlds" and "Women Persons." "Women's Rights Feminists" are for the most part "Women Made, Not Born," and "Women Spinning Women Together." If, as I noted earlier, the major difference between these two forms of consciousness is a difference of time of achievement, with the "Antifeminist People-ists" believing that women's rights have been achieved and the "Women's Rights Feminists" believing that women's rights have yet to be achieved, then a focus on *sameness* unites these two opposing forms of consciousness. Both forms are premised on the belief that women are not and should not be considered different from men in possessing rights. This belief seems to be grounded in different but complementary ways of identifying as women: the "Ladies with Best of Both Worlds" believe nothing should stop them from enjoying the best of the "men's world" along with the best of their own "ladies' world." The "Women Persons" believe they *are* equal with men in personhood. The "Women Made, Not Born," believe they *should* be recognized under the law as equal with men in personhood. All of these women express the idea in one way or another that women should not separate themselves from men or from the world of men. Their resulting politics is over whether the fight for women's rights as individuals has been won and whether the debate should move on to other issues.

But then a *difference among* "Women's Rights Feminists" emerges with the "Women Spinning," who reflect in part the contradictoriness of the early twentieth-century feminism that Cott presents as well as of contemporary feminism. The "Women Spinning Women Together" speak of how much they have come to value their friendships with other women in contrast to friendships with men. Stressing the collective nature of women's experience and en-

deavors, they presume *sameness* among all women, a presumption
that is in tension with their idea of women's individuality, which
premises their "Women's Rights Feminism."

In direct contrast to their "spinning" sisters, some of the "Women
Spinning Threads" and "Networks" express another form of consciousness of feminism that develops the themes of *difference*, not
only from men but also *among women*, into "Women-centered
Feminine-ism." These women are not the "man-haters" that others
believe them to be, though they choose to refuse men access to their
bodies. They choose to live and work with and among women as
much as possible while also recognizing that their racial privilege
and their sexual preference make relations with women of color and/
or heterosexual women more difficult than they like.

Still others of the "Women Spinning Threads" and "Networks"
add to the tension by expressing "Marxist-Feminism," which by its
hyphen indicates a lack of fit with either "Women's Rights Feminism" or "Women-centered Feminine-ism." This lack of fit comes no
doubt from the emphasis in Marxist theory on class, which unites
men and women but divides them together into two opposed classes.
Thus, while the "Marxist-Feminists" can be presumed to believe
there are no differences between the sexes, they are still divided
from today's "Women's Rights Feminists" by their anticapitalism
and their historical analysis that equates this form of consciousness
with the nineteenth-century bourgeois activism of "the woman
movement." They part ways with the "Women-centered Feminine-
ists" by their unwillingness to divide themselves from men as they
perceive Lesbians to do.

As all these women bring their identities as (white) women and
their "feminism" or "antifeminism" together with their understandings of "the political," they likewise bring their conflicting beliefs
concerning *difference* and *sameness* into the world of politics through
their various political engagements. Those who enter into electoral
politics graft their white-women–grounded perspectives onto the
ongoing political party system that developed before white women
gained voting rights. At least among the women in this study, those
advocating "feminism" enter as Democrats; those opposing "femi-

nism" enter as Republicans. It should be noted that the lines are not so clearly drawn for women generally among those involved in party politics in the United States today. Nevertheless, both groups express their beliefs in the political sameness of women with men by engaging in political actions similar to those engaged in by many men. Whether Democrats or Republicans, proponents of "feminism" or "antifeminism," some seek office, hold office, and exercise the power that resides in government. Some, engaging in a form of political action—education—that contemporary political science tends to recognize less among men as such, do all they can to link the different actors in the system together and to "educate" the voters, the candidates, or the officeholders so that government power will be exercised for the "best" ends. Some, all Democrats and proponents of "feminism," engage in advocacy for their causes, most of which they believe will improve the lot of women. Two other women, both Republicans, appear to have dropped away from any form of political action, powerless and alienated but not inclined to give up their beliefs in the equality of women to men in order to join movements to alter, change, or revolutionize the world.

Two small groups of women place themselves at what appears to be an indeterminate boundary between electoral politics and movement politics. One group is composed of three Democratic electoral activists, "Women Spinning Women Together," who espouse "Women's Rights Feminism." The other group is composed of three leftists, a "Woman Made, Not Born," a "Woman Spinning Threads," and a "Woman Spinning Networks," all of whom espouse "Marxist-Feminism." I say the boundary appears indeterminate for these two groups of women because, for all but one of them, their various identities as "Women Spinning," which stress the collective nature of women's lives, make them potential candidates to join the women's community activists, while their understandings of "the political" keep them focused on conventional elections and government and working with or in competition with men.

The three Democrats, all office-seekers, include one who has run for office, lost, and turned to advocacy for the needs of poor pregnant women, and two who plan to run for office when the opportunity opens for them. One of these understands "the political" as using government power, and the other is a political educator who attempts to link officeholders with the pulse of community opinion. All of these women are doing what they can to make government work in response to women's needs and interests. Thus, their reformist orientation keeps them within the arena of electoral politics.

The three leftist activists all understand "the political" as developing power for change, and their revolutionist orientation moves them "outside" but near the margins of electoral politics. One stresses consciousness-raising around power relations and relations between the races and the sexes, another talks of power struggles to get interests realized, and another presents a strategy for organizing the power of the "small people," including women, in order at least to counterbalance the power of "the capitalists," who she believes have made a mockery of government for and by the people. These latter two are willing to organize a third political party and run for office, using the machinery of conventional politics to revolutionize conventional politics.

In effect, in a political system designed to protect the "natural inalienable rights" of "individuals," which at the founding of the nation meant the rights of white men of property, these two groups of women are attempting to bring women as a collective force into the machinery of a government that was designed to accommodate "individuals," and only privileged ones at that. These women appear to be drawing on the power that for them has been suppressed in the *difference* imposed on them because of their sex. From positions of *difference* they are seeking to achieve *sameness*, at least sameness of *place* in the power struggles that constitute "the political."

Two other groups of women, the "Male-defined Feminine-ists" and the "Women-centered Feminine-ists," give full political significance to *difference* from men, but with distinctly different consequences. Coming closest to playing the role in the drama of life assigned to heterosexual white middle-class women under the rules of complex domination, the "Male-defined Feminine-ists" identify as "Ladies" who also understand "the political" as working for the "right" candidates for office. That is, they link themselves to the power of government by making connections with candidates they believe have a good chance of winning office. It is their difference from men and their "proper" behaviors as women that they believe fit them for the privileges they expect to receive as "Ladies" who eschew "man-hating" and "bra-burning" for male-defined femininity. It is also their difference from men in the matter of power to govern that makes it necessary for them to link themselves to the potential power of candidates for office, presumably predominantly male candidates. It is not that they eschew power; they believe they can gain power best through linking themselves into the power that others legitimately possess and will use for them.

On the other side of the stage enter the women's community activists, whose identities as "Women Spinning Threads" and "Networks" form the basis for their "Women-centered Feminine-ism" and their understanding of "the political" as life–as–political-action–for–change. They come the closest to having rejected the role in the drama of life assigned them under the rules of complex domination and are in the process of moving "outside" the conventional political theater to create their own drama. Bit by bit and piece by piece, they are carving out new spaces in which women may create new forms of "reality," forms they intend not to let settle into rigid ideological institutions. Theirs is a world in which women celebrate women's differences from men but are also learning the need to celebrate differences among women.

These activists make it clear in their discussions of "being a woman" and "feminism" and "the political" that they do not believe in inherent biological essences of "Woman" or of the female sex. They believe that "the patriarchy" has been erected as a "white male system," according to one of the women, a system of domination based on dividing men from women by sex/gender and dividing women and men from one another by sexuality, color/race and class. They also believe that "the patriarchy" does not count for all that has been or is or can be in the way of power and resources and creativity. Reaching back in history to periods when women were recognized as powerful members of societies, they claim their power from within the present-day community of women as they materially and consciously engage in living but questioning everything that appears to threaten all life. In other words, these women claim their power standing on their own ground in their own time, each engaging her own standpoint from which to make her unique contributions to an ongoing collective transformation of women's lives.

A Political Morality Play about Privilege and Empowerment

I suggested in chapter 1 that the white women in this study provide a progression of examples of identities, thoughts, and actions that suggest a political morality play about possible moves from privilege to empowerment. In that play we can observe what it might look like and sound like to move from embracing a position of privilege to resisting a system, complex domination, that confers such privilege. The examples begin with women rather firmly anchored in acting out expectations to maintain the femininity and privilege befitting white women under complex domination. Then follow examples of women coming to consciousness of racism in society and of their own racial privilege, of the pain that accompanies such consciousness-raising, and of some actions that might bring these women into alliance with women of color and any others moving toward a "politics of difference" and "coalition politics" to wage a "politics of reality."

The actualities of racism and of white privilege, which is a part of racism, have existed for centuries. The *naming* of "racism" by people of color as a problem that white people have perpetuated through our white power structure is a more recent phenomenon, as is the *naming* of "white privilege" as an aspect of racism. For white people, acknowledging one's participation in racism can be difficult, but coming to consciousness of one's participation in white privilege can be even more difficult. As Minnie Bruce Pratt has written, "It is an exhausting process, this moving from the experience of the 'unknowing majority' (as Maya Angelou called it) into consciousness. It would be a lie to say this process is comforting."[1] But before the pain can be felt, the sheer "naturalness" of the given race/gender setup of complex domination must be questioned. And for the questions to be raised, there must be a recognition somehow that something is wrong with that setup.

The problems with "white privilege" are complex,[2] because they arise within the matrix of complex domination. Within that matrix there is the illusory nature of the "privilege," which, for white women, in actuality is supposed to be "protection." For white women, physical and economic protections are supposed to ensue from being attached to a white man, first father and then husband. If the white man provides economic sustenance and does not sexually or otherwise abuse the woman, then he has fulfilled his part of the bargain. For her part, the white woman owes her father loyalty and obedience and her husband loyalty and obedience along with sexual and other caretaking services; and as long as she performs her duties, her "privilege" is supposed to continue.

Note that a Black woman or other woman of color, even if she were the blood kin of a white man, would not be *due* such care or "protection" even if she submitted to the white man's sexual requirements or otherwise provided caretaking services to him. Herein lies the racial aspect of the white woman's "privilege," which is conferred simultaneously with the Black woman's debasement. At least, those are the meanings that are supposed to attach, respectively, to "being a white woman" and "being a Black woman" under the rules of complex domination.

The "Ladies" in this study best exemplify the condition of denying any mistreatment of them and of expecting privilege in return for acting the lady. Linda Helms explains the terms of this exchange quite explicitly. Lavinia Ravenel contributes illumination to another aspect of the exchange, granting praise to the men in her life—father, husband, son—who have performed their due, taking good care of her.

The "Ladies with Best of Both Worlds" appear to be similarly engaged in the exchange of lady-like behavior for gentlemanly treatment, conscious that they use their "charms," as Bess Shumaker and Sybyl Jensen explain, to get such treatment. But they also value their abilities to act independently of men and express awareness of discriminatory treatment from men. At the same time, they seem unwilling to acknowledge race as an issue for Black people. The thinking seems to be that, if they can act independently in the face of sex discrimination, then Black people can do the same for race discrimination. They appear to be unwilling to grant "preferential treatment" as a remedy for continuing racial discrimination by whites at the same time that they accept "preferential treatment" for their own lady-like behaviors when they do "turn on their charms."

The "Women Persons" have moved beyond behaving in accordance with the expectations of complex domination to the extent that they have discovered their standpoints as "individuals." With this identity, which they recognize to have been long in coming for women in the United States legal system, they expect now to exercise the rights that such a legal status entails. Similarly they believe that, just as sex and gender should no longer be issues for them or for anyone else, so color and race should no longer be issues for them or for anyone else. Like the "Ladies with Best of Both Worlds," they speak of mingling comfortably with Black people in their political party activities. Only one of these women, Maryanne Thayer, expresses the first inkling of discomfort around Black women, these being teachers in the public schools or caretakers in a nursing home. However, she seems not to have made the connection that her feeling of being an "outsider" around them may be related to their being on guard with her. If she has not recognized her racial privilege or expressed her recognition, then these women may not trust her enough to let down their guard with her.

The "Women Made, Not Born," and "Women Spinning Women Together" present another move away from the expectations of complex domination by openly venting their anger about sex discrimination in their and their daughters' lives and in women's lives generally. They also express recognition of racial discrimination by whites and of their own racial privilege, some in more detail than others. Similar to Maryanne Thayer, Adrienne Stone and Kate Greene speak of perceiving Black women's resentment about their efforts on behalf of the ERA, but they seem to be focusing on the Black women's lack of cooperation in the drive for ratification rather than trying to understand why some Black women felt and acted as they did around the way white women worked on this issue.

The "Women Spinning Threads and Networks" present still other moves away from the expectations of complex domination. They have begun to engage in consciousness-raising and to act to change their own and others' values about racial privilege. Many standpoints become apparent as each presents one or another aspect of this process. Tillie Zadar, echoing the concerns of Maryanne Thayer, Adrienne Stone, and Kate Greene about Black peoples' mistrust or resentment toward them, says she has felt this too. But she says she understands those feelings toward her as white because she as Lesbian feels those ways toward men, who she expects to work hard to earn her trust. Gretchen Bright claims responsibility for what being white under the rules of complex domination has meant when she says she understands why Black people mistrust her, "because I'm racist." Barbara Bergen says that, because she feels that separation between the races, she wants to "work more in the world to make the separation not there." That is, she wants to take action against racism and racial privilege in society. And Fran Daly wants to "get up front" not only her recognition of her racism and racial privilege but also some false assumptions that Black women have about her because she is white.

I read in Fran Daly's statement a call to Black women and other women of color to meet her half-way in what Audre Lorde has called a "politics of difference," an exploration of the many differences that have been imposed by the requirements of complex domination and of the even greater number of differences associated with women's standpoints. Along with that politics can be practiced a "coalition politics" as called for by Bernice Johnson Reagon. But if coming to consciousness of racial privilege is slow and painful for white women, engaging in politics of difference and coalition can be even more difficult but also liberating and empowering.[3]

Feminist "coalition politics" is a concept that resonates with coalition-building in conventional "politics as usual," which is still predominantly white-male–dominated. But conventional white political activists, men and women, and no doubt others, could learn something useful from feminists by understanding the origins of Reagon's "coalition politics" in the civil rights movement of the 1960s. In that movement, as in others, and similar to the phenomenon in interest group politics, forming coalitions involves making alliances on common issues among groups that are unequal in resources and status. Reagon brings the concept to the attention of feminists who are practicing a "politics of identity" that promises to become more conflictual as more women, and men, enter into the process of identifying themselves in terms of various combinations of oppressions while not always recognizing the simultaneous privileges they also may enjoy.

Whereas coalition building is used to resolve conflicts around rights and interests, however, feminist coalition politics is intended to resolve conflicts around identities and differences that emerge in the process of struggling to break out of the various confining social locations of complex domination. Though not all the women in this study would agree with the way I have set up the political problem to be solved, they nevertheless have been forthcoming in showing just how different women in the social location labeled "white women" can be. Their life stories suggest that, within this social location defined only by color/race and sex/gender, exist women who identify in a variety of ways as "women," as "white women," and as "white political women." In fact, none of these concepts covers entirely what the life stories of these women suggest may be unique standpoints that can be engaged by each and every woman. It will be the perspective from each one's standpoint that somehow will have to be taken into consideration if "coalition politics" is to become an arena where women of many identities can gather to work out who we are in relation to others and what we can and cannot agree upon for purposes of action. It may well be politics of "reality"— identity, difference, and coalition—that will enable women collectively to emerge empowered from our previous confines of oppression and privilege.

Notes

Chapter 1

1. Cf. Kirkpatrick, *Political Woman*, with Lane, *Political Man*, and Lipset, *Political Man*.

2. Examining the meanings and uses of essentializing "Woman" and universalizing knowledge of "Woman" is beyond the scope of my study, but feminist theorists have begun the examination in detail. See for example Spelman, *Inessential Woman*; Fuss, *Essentially Speaking*; and "The Essential Difference: Another Look at Essentialism," special issue of *Differences: A Journal of Feminist Cultural Studies*.

3. The description of the Combahee River Collective is taken from Eisenstein, ed., *Capitalist Patriarchy*, 392; the "Statement" was first published in the Eisenstein collection and was later published in Hull, Scott, and Smith, eds., *But Some of Us Are Brave*, and in Smith, ed., *Home Girls*. My citations in the following discussion refer to pages in *Home Girls*. The notion of "complex domination" continues to emerge in Black feminist theory as articulated by bell hooks in *Feminist Theory*.

4. Combahee River Collective, "Statement," 272, 273, 275. I would like to thank Nancie Caraway for bringing Black feminists' "politics of identity" into focus for me. I had been focusing solely on the ideas Black feminists generated in me for "complex domination," and Caraway's reading helped me to see the obvious relationship between the structure of complex domination and a politics of identity. See Nancie Caraway, *Segregated Sisterhood*.

5. Ibid., 275, 281.

6. hooks issues this warning in *Feminist Theory*, 27–29.

7. Combahee River Collective, "Statement," 277.

8. Beck makes an excellent case for the need "to rethink our categories" in "The Politics of Jewish Invisibility," esp. 101.

9. Cf. Hartmann, "The Unhappy Marriage of Marxism and Feminism."

10. See Wittig, "One Is Not Born a Woman."

11. Lorde, "The Master's Tools Will Never Dismantle the Master's House," in *Sister Outsider*, 111–12.

12. Ibid., 112.

13. Reagon, "Coalition Politics," 356–57.

14. Ibid., 358.

15. Ibid., 359.

16. Lugones and Spelman, "Have We Got A Theory For You!" See, also, hooks's essay on "Feminist Scholarship: Ethical Issues," in her collection, *Talking Back*.

17. Bourque and Grossholtz, "Politics an Unnatural Practice"; Carroll, "Review Essay: Political Science, Part I"; Elshtain, "Methodological Sophistication and Conceptual Confusion"; Iglitzin, "The Making of the Apolitical Woman"; Sapiro, "Women's Studies and Political Conflict"; Shanley and Schuck, "In Search of Political Woman."

18. See Jaggar, *Feminist Politics and Human Nature*, for a good critical analysis of these unexamined assumptions and the problems they cause for women and women's politics.

19. For the sex/gender system, see esp. Rubin, "The Traffic in Women." On race/gender and class/gender systems, see Eisenstein, *Capitalist Patriarchy*; and Sargent, *Women and Revolution*.

20. This focus in the discipline of political science has been noted by, among others, Elshtain; and Lovenduski, "Toward the Emasculation of Political Science."

21. The early political behavioral literature, which sometimes included discussions of women's lower levels of political participation, as well as the later behavioral literature on women and politics, begins with an assumption that sex-role socialization, or what more properly should be called sex- and gender-role socialization, explains in large part why women have not been as politically active as men. On sex/gender systems generally, see Rubin; and Tresemer, "Assumptions Made About Gender Roles."

The early political behavioral literature includes, for example, Lane, *Political Life*; Campbell, Converse, Miller, and Stokes, *The American Voter*; and Greenstein, *Children and Politics*. The behavioral literature on women and politics includes, for example, Jennings and Thomas, "Men and Women in Party Elites"; Costantini and Craik, "Women as Politicians"; Lee, "Why

Few Women Hold Public Office"; Stoper, "Wife and Politician"; Fowlkes, Perkins, and Tolleson Rinehart, "Gender Roles and Party Roles." More recent book-length treatments include Sapiro, *The Political Integration of Women*, and Klein, *Gender Politics*. A mid-1980s bibliography on women and U.S. politics contains over 1,600 entries; see Nelson, *American Women and Politics*.

The socialization literature in general, of which the literature of political socialization and "sex-role" socialization are parts, stresses the indoctrination into or the learning of the culture and of societal roles by individuals. In general see Clausen, ed., *Socialization and Society*, and Goslin, ed., *Handbook of Socialization Theory and Research*. With reference to political socialization, see for example, Dawson and Prewitt, *Political Socialization*; Easton and Dennis, *Children in the Political System*; Sigel, ed., *Learning About Politics*; Jennings and Niemi, *The Political Character of Adolescence*, and *Generations and Politics*; and Renshon, ed., *Handbook of Political Socialization*. With reference to "sex-role" socialization, see Weitzman, "Sex-role Socialization," for a good review of this literature.

22. The trend began in the mid-1970s; see Johnson and Stanwick, *Profile of Women Holding Office*; and Johnson and Carroll, *Profile of Women Holding Public Office II*.

23. Thus, for example, Kelly and Boutilier hypothesized and found in *The Making of Political Women*, 25–40, that some women have been socialized to what they term a "modern sex-role ideology." Similarly, Susan Carroll reported, in *Women as Candidates in American Politics*, 134, that most women who seek and gain elected office can be characterized as androgynous, that is, not believing they should be constrained by gender roles in their social behaviors.

24. The original work on political opportunity structure is found in Schlesinger, *Ambition and Politics*. Susan Carroll examines the influence of political opportunity structure on women's representation in *Women as Candidates*, 108–12.

25. See for example Dworkin, *Right-wing Women*, and Klatch, *Women of the New Right*.

26. Fowlkes, "Ambitious Political Woman."

27. Fowlkes, "Developing a Theory of Countersocialization," 182.

28. Ibid., 183–84.

29. See for example Freeman, *The Politics of Women's Liberation*; McWilliams, "Contemporary Feminism, Consciousness-Raising, and Changing Views of the Political"; and Klein, *Gender Politics*.

30. Niemi, "Political Socialization," and Renshon, *Handbook*.
31. See esp. Renshon, "Assumptive Frameworks in Political Socialization Theory"; see also Cottrell, "Interpersonal Interaction and the Development of the Self."
32. Noteworthy in this regard is Connell, *The Child's Construction of Politics*. Working out of Piaget's theories of cognitive development, Connell asked children themselves to describe their political worlds.
33. Niemi, "Political Socialization," 128. See also Jennings and Niemi, *Political Character*; and *Generations and Politics*.
34. Niemi, "Political Socialization," 118.
35. The major studies were those by Greenstein, *Children and Politics*; Hess and Torney, *The Development of Political Attitudes in Children*; Easton and Dennis, *Children in the Political System*; Jennings and Niemi, *Political Character*.
36. See esp. Sigel and Hoskin, "Perspectives on Adult Political Socialization—Areas of Research."
37. See esp. Schutz, "On Multiple Realities."
38. Dorothy E. Smith, *The Everyday World as Problematic*, esp. chap. 3.
39. Following Schutz, I have taken this construction from Mead, *Mind, Self and Society*.
40. Note that I reject the classical liberal assumptions, elaborated by Jaggar in *Feminist Politics and Human Nature*, that human beings begin as pre-social atomistic individuals who exist in the dualistic mode of mind independent of body. Rather, following Dorothy Smith, I accept the Marxist conception of consciousness as belonging to embodied persons who are at the same time social beings. See Smith, *Everyday World*, 123.
41. Schutz, "On Multiple Realities."
42. Cf. Smith, *Everyday World*.
43. Schutz, "On Multiple Realities"; and Smith, *Everyday World*, 84–85.
44. Smith, *Everyday World*, 85.
45. Ibid., 49.
46. See for example Allen, *Free Space*, and Cassell, *A Group Called Women*.
47. Smith, *Everyday World*, esp. 105–7.
48. See Hartsock, "The Feminist Standpoint."
49. See Keller and Grontkowski, "The Mind's Eye."
50. Good critical analyses of standpoint theory include Harding, *The Science Question in Feminism*, and Grant, "I Feel Therefore I Am."
51. Smith, *Everyday World*, 78.
52. Ibid., 80.

53. Zillah Eisenstein has called for theorizing "individuality" as opposed to classical liberal atomistic "individualism" in *Feminism and Sexual Equality*.

54. See for example the differences among Black Lesbian feminists revealed in Abdulahad, Rogers, Smith, and Waheed, "Black Lesbian/Feminist Organizing."

55. Schutz, "On Multiple Realities."

56. Ibid.

57. The Atlanta Party Study is described in Fowlkes, Perkins, and Tolleson Rinehart, "Gender Roles and Party Roles."

58. Fowlkes, "Ambitious Political Woman."

59. My questions on "the political," "being a woman," "the feminine," "feminism," the relative merits of holding office versus working through groups, the significance of race and sex in growing up, and self-family relations are original, while the other questions have been taken from studies by other scholars, including Kirkpatrick, *Political Woman* and *The New Presidential Elite*; Irene Diamond, *Sex Roles in the State House*; and Wahlke, Eulau, Buchanan, and Ferguson, *The Legislative System*.

60. Especially useful histories for my purposes have been Giddings, *When and Where I Enter*; Cott, *The Grounding of Modern Feminism*; and Harrison, *On Account of Sex*. I did not collect personal written materials—autobiographies, journals, letters—from the women. On the methodology of life histories and life stories generally, see Dollard, *Criteria for the Life History*; Davies, "Criteria for the Political Life History"; Lasswell, *Psychopathology and Politics*; and Sheridan, "The Life History Method." On intensive qualitative analysis of cases, in addition to Glaser and Strauss, *The Discovery of Grounded Theory*, see Brown, "Intensive Analysis in Political Research," and Herbst, *Behavioural Worlds*.

61. Cf. Glaser and Strauss, *Discovery of Grounded Theory*.

62. Smith, *Everyday World*, 106.

63. Ibid.

64. Ibid., 125.

65. Marilyn Frye introduces a "politics of reality" in *The Politics of Reality*.

Chapter 2

1. Cott, *Grounding*, 20.

2. Ibid., 3.

3. Ibid., 4. Note that Cott capitalizes "Feminism" when speaking of the emergent modern feminism of the particular period she is analyzing.

4. Ibid., 4–5.

5. Ibid., 5.

6. See for example Lewis, "A Liberationist Ideology," and Jaggar, *Feminist Politics and Human Nature*, 149–51.

7. See for example Sapiro, *Political Integration of Women*, 77; and Klein, *Gender Politics*, 3.

8. In order to protect the identities of the women, I give only their approximate dates of birth and define place of birth and growing up in terms of regional divisions of the United States as designated in the population census. See U.S. Dept. of Commerce, Bureau of the Census, *Historical Statistics of the United States, Colonial Times to 1970*, pt. 1, p. 5. The regions, divisions, and related states are: Northeast Region–New England Division: Maine, New Hampshire, Vermont, Massachusetts, Rhode Island, Connecticut; Middle Atlantic Division: New York, New Jersey, Pennsylvania; North Central Region–East North Central Division: Ohio, Indiana, Illinois, Michigan, Wisconsin; West North Central Division: Minnesota, Iowa, Missouri, North Dakota, South Dakota, Nebraska, Kansas; South Region–South Atlantic Division: Delaware, Maryland, District of Columbia, Virginia, West Virginia, North Carolina, South Carolina, Georgia, Florida; East South Central Division: Kentucky, Tennessee, Alabama, Mississippi; West South Central Division: Arkansas, Louisiana, Oklahoma, Texas; West Region–Mountain Division: Montana, Idaho, Wyoming, Colorado, New Mexico, Arizona, Utah, Nevada; Pacific Division: Washington, Oregon, California, Hawaii.

Chapter 3

1. Cott, *Grounding*, 85–114.

2. New Jersey was an exception until 1807. See Turner, "Women's Suffrage in New Jersey, 1790–1807."

3. Cott (*Grounding*, 99) makes this point precisely in presenting and analyzing the opinions of Mary Anderson, director of the U.S. Women's Bureau in 1924.

4. Cott, *Grounding*, 13–50.

5. Pisan, *The Treasure of the City of Ladies; or, The Book of the Three Virtues*. See also the collections by Spender, ed., *Feminist Theorists*, and *Women of Ideas*.

6. Giddings, *When and Where I Enter*.

7. Cott, *Grounding*; Giddings, *When and Where I Enter*.

8. The quotation about "special protections and privileges" is from a Wisconsin law, cited in Harrison, *On Account of Sex*, 30. The "Women's Bureau coalition" is discussed in Harrison, *On Account of Sex*, 8. See also Cott, *Grounding*, for a history of this conflict.

9. Harrison, *On Account of Sex*, 89–105.

10. I present only the full analysis for the three major types of family structure. Two women, Elizabeth Latimer and Linda Helms, who were born and grew up in the period between the world wars, grew up in shared-discipline families. In this type of family, both parents discipline the daughters, though the father may be perceived as the dominant head of the household. Neither of these women claimed to be "feminists" when I interviewed them. Two other women, Betty Mason and Bess Shumaker, born during this same period, grew up in mixed-switched families. In this type of family, the daughters describe first a male-centered family that becomes a female-centered family because of divorce or because a dead father is replaced by a disliked stepfather. These women, too, disavowed "feminism" when I interviewed them. Presumably for these latter two women, their initial relationships to adored fun-loving fathers imprinted them as male-identified women. This imprinting would have been reinforced by growing up during the historical period when "feminism" was in disrepute. For the other two women, presumably the historical period provided the necessary context for growing up as male-identified women. Future research should seek out additional instances of the "minor" family types I found as well as of the "major" family types and of any other possible types that did not emerge in my study.

11. There are exceptions, for example in Hirsch, *Poverty and Politicization*, and in Langton, *Political Socialization*. Langton (21–33) provides a useful review of studies of the effects of different aspects of family structure on political socialization.

12. Jennings and Niemi, *Political Character*, 153.

13. Ibid., 165–74, 324–26.

14. Ibid., 326.

15. Dinnerstein, *The Mermaid and the Minotaur*; Chodorow, *The Reproduction of Mothering*.

16. Harding, *Science Question*.

17. See a short and concise overview of Lacan's theory in McDermott, "Post-Lacanian French Feminist Theory."

18. Jennings and Niemi, *Political Character*, 334–35.

19. Jennings and Niemi, *Generations and Politics.*

20. My interview questions were: How many brothers and sisters do you have? Which are older and which are younger than you? Could you describe your relationships with them? How would you describe yourself, first as a child, and then as young woman? How would you describe your mother/your father when you were growing up? How would you describe your relationship with your mother/your father over the years, from as early as you can remember and on to now/her/his passing? Were there any other family members or family friends who influenced you in particular ways? Were there any teachers who influenced you in particular ways? Have there been any other memorable influences in your life growing up, for example, people you have worked with, events, situations, ideas, books? How so?

21. Friedan, *The Feminine Mystique*; Harrison, *On Account of Sex*, 6.

22. Friedan, *The Feminine Mystique*; Harrison, *On Account of Sex*, 3–6.

23. See for example Jones, "The Dynamics of Marriage and Motherhood," but note that the collection as a whole attempts to reflect the great diversity of women and women's situations; see as another example O'Reilly, "The Housewife's Moment of Truth."

24. See for example Ferguson, "Women's Liberation Has a Different Meaning for Blacks," or Ware, "The Black Family and Feminism."

Chapter 4

1. Shelby Lewis presents this standpoint in "A Liberationist Ideology."

2. See esp. Lorde's collection of essays and speeches developing the significance of difference, *Sister Outsider.*

3. See Bartky, "Toward a Phenomenology of Feminist Consciousness."

4. See Frye, *The Politics of Reality*, esp. 152–74.

5. Bartky, "Toward a Phenomenology," 27.

6. Opening doors seems to be an often-chosen example of gentlemanly behavior toward "ladies," but these "Ladies" are not the only ones who will connect femininity with gallantry in the form of opening doors. For a philosophical analysis of the phenomena of opening doors and gallantry, see Bell, "Gallantry."

7. Daly, *Gyn/Ecology*, esp. 313–424.

8. Friedan, *The Feminine Mystique.*

Chapter 5

1. See Smith, *Everyday World*, esp. 54–57.
2. Ibid., 49.
3. These questions appear at various places in the last section of the interview, which is the place where I address issues surrounding "women" and politics directly. Because of negative responses by some women to the earlier survey I was involved in conducting—"why all these questions about women?"—I purposefully put these questions in the last section. The questions, in order of appearance in the interview, interspersed among other questions, were: "How do you feel about the women's movement? Do you see it continuing? What do you see as its goals? What do you like, dislike about it? . . . What does feminism mean to you? Do you consider yourself a feminist?"
4. Hartmann, "The Unhappy Marriage of Marxism and Feminism."
5. Petchesky, "Dissolving the Hyphen."
6. See Jaggar, *Feminist Politics and Human Nature*, esp. chaps. 6 and 10.
7. hooks, *Feminist Theory*, 126–27.
8. Woolf, *Three Guineas*.
9. Cf. Eisenstein, *Feminism and Sexual Equality*, 246–54.

Chapter 6

1. Schlesinger, *Ambition and Politics*.
2. The same has been found in studies of the political socialization of elites, predominantly white males. Family influences are important, but the later in life a person becomes politicized, the less likely the family is to be the source of influence in that process. See for example Eulau, Buchanan, Ferguson, and Wahlke, "The Political Socialization of American State Legislators."
3. Cf. Jennings, "Another Look at the Life Cycle and Political Participation."
4. Cf. Susan Carroll, *Women as Candidates in American Politics*, 30–32. Carroll found that supportive husbands played a significant role in women's candidacies for public office.
5. Cf. McWilliams, "Contemporary Feminism, Consciousness-Raising, and Changing Views of the Political."
6. Cf. Allen, *Free Space*.

7. See for example Carroll, *Women as Candidates*; and Mandel, *In the Running*.

Chapter 7

1. Fowlkes, "Conceptions of the 'Political.'"
2. Ibid., 69.
3. See for example Fowlkes, Perkins, and Tolleson Rinehart, "Gender Roles and Party Roles," and Boneparth, "Women in Campaigns."
4. Schlesinger, "The Primary Goals of Political Parties."
5. Concerning women's and feminist interpretations of "power," see Flammang, "Feminist Theory," and Hartsock, *Money, Sex, and Power*, 210–30.
6. Cf. Valian, "Learning to Work."
7. Locke, *Some Thoughts Concerning Education*; Rousseau, *Emile*; Plato, *The Republic*.
8. Fliegelman, *Prodigals and Pilgrims*, 13.
9. Sapiro, *The Political Integration of Women*, 135.

Chapter 8

1. Pratt, "Identity," 12. See also Frye, *Politics of Reality*, esp. 110–27; Rich, "Disloyal to Civilization," and *Blood, Bread, and Poetry*; Lillian Smith, *Killers of the Dream*; Anne Braden, *The Wall Between*.
2. See esp. Rich, "Disloyal to Civilization."
3. On emerging issues as politics of identity and difference are put into practice, see for example Adams, "There's No Place Like Home"; Harriss, "New Alliances"; and Briskin, "Comment."

Bibliography

Abdulahad, Tania, Gwendolyn Rogers, Barbara Smith, and Jameelah Wa- heed. "Black Lesbian/Feminist Organizing: A Conversation." In Barbara Smith, ed., *Home Girls*.

Adams, Mary Louise. "There's No Place Like Home: On the Place of Identity in Feminist Politics." *Feminist Review* 31 (Spring 1989): 22–33.

Allen, Pamela. *Free Space: A Perspective on the Small Group in Women's Liberation*. New York: Times Change Press. 1970.

Bartky, Sandra Lee. "Toward a Phenomenology of Feminist Consciousness." In Mary Vetterling-Braggin, Frederick A. Elliston, and Jane English, eds., *Feminism and Philosophy*. Totowa, N.J.: Rowman and Littlefield, 1981.

Beck, Evelyn Torton. "The Politics of Jewish Invisibility." *NWSA Journal* 1 (Autumn 1988): 93–102.

Bell, Linda A. "Gallantry: What It Is and Why It Should Not Survive." *Southern Journal of Philosophy* 22 (1984): 165–73.

Boneparth, Ellen. "Women in Campaigns: From Lickin' and Stickin' to Strategy." *American Politics Quarterly* 5 (1977): 289–300.

Bourque, Susan, and Jean Grossholtz. "Politics an Unnatural Practice: Po- litical Science Looks at Female Participation." *Politics and Society* 4 (1974): 225–66.

Braden, Anne. *The Wall Between*. Knoxville: Univ. of Tennessee Press, 1992.

Briskin, Linda. "Comment: Identity Politics and the Hierarchy of Oppres- sion." *Feminist Review* 32 (Summer 1990): 102–8.

Brown, Steven R. "Intensive Analysis in Political Research." *Political Meth- odology* 1 (1974): 1–25.

Campbell, Angus, Philip E. Converse, Warren E. Miller, and Donald E. Stokes. *The American Voter*. New York: John Wiley, 1960.

Caraway, Nancie. *Segregated Sisterhood: Racism and the Politics of Ameri- can Feminism*. Knoxville: Univ. of Tennessee Press, 1991.

Carroll, Berenice A. "Review Essay: Political Science, Part I: American Politics and Political Behavior." *Signs* 5 (1979): 289–306.

Carroll, Susan. *Women as Candidates in American Politics*. Bloomington: Indiana Univ. Press, 1985.

Cassell, Joan. *A Group Called Women: Sisterhood & Symbolism in the Feminist Movement*. New York: David McKay, 1977.

Chodorow, Nancy. *The Reproduction of Mothering: Psychoanalysis and the Sociology of Gender*. Berkeley: Univ. of California Press, 1978.

Clausen, John A., ed. *Socialization and Society*. Boston: Little, Brown, 1968.

Combahee River Collective. "The Combahee River Collective Statement." In Barbara Smith, ed., *Home Girls*.

Connell, R. W. *The Child's Construction of Politics*. Carlton, Victoria: Melbourne Univ. Press, 1971.

Costantini, Edmond, and Kenneth H. Craik. "Women as Politicians: The Social Background, Personality, and Political Careers of Female Party Leaders." *Journal of Social Issues* 28 (1972): 217–36.

Cott, Nancy. *The Grounding of Modern Feminism*. New Haven: Yale Univ. Press, 1987.

Cottrell, Leonard S., Jr. "Interpersonal Interaction and the Development of the Self." In Goslin, ed., *Handbook of Socialization Theory and Research*.

Daly, Mary. *Gyn/Ecology: The Metaethics of Radical Feminism*. Boston: Beacon Press, 1978.

Davies, A. F. "Criteria for the Political Life History." *Historical Studies, Australia and New Zealand* 13 (1967): 76–85.

Dawson, Richard E., and Kenneth Prewitt. *Political Socialization*. Boston: Little, Brown, 1969.

Diamond, Irene. *Sex Roles in the State House*. New Haven: Yale Univ. Press, 1977.

Dinnerstein, Dorothy. *The Mermaid and the Minotaur: Sexual Arrangements and Human Malaise*. New York: Harper Colophon Books, 1977.

Dollard, John. *Criteria for the Life History*. New Haven: Yale Univ. Press, 1935.

Dworkin, Andrea. *Right-Wing Women*. New York: G. P. Putnam's Sons, 1983.

Easton, David, and Jack Dennis. *Children in the Political System*. New York: McGraw-Hill, 1969.

Eisenstein, Zillah R. *Feminism and Sexual Equality: Crisis in Liberal America*. New York: Monthly Review Press, 1984.

Eisenstein, Zillah R., ed. *Capitalist Patriarchy and the Case for Socialist Feminism*. New York: Monthly Review Press, 1979.

Elshtain, Jean Bethke. "Methodological Sophistication and Conceptual

Confusion: A Critique of Mainstream Political Science." In Sherman and Beck, eds., *The Prism of Sex.*

"The Essential Difference: Another Look at Essentialism." Special issue of *Difference: A Journal of Feminist Cultural Studies* 1 (Summer 1989).

Eulau, Heinz, William Buchanan, Leroy Ferguson, and John C. Wahlke. "The Political Socialization of American State Legislators." *Midwest Journal of Political Science* 3 (1959): 188–206.

Ferguson, Renee. "Women's Liberation Has a Different Meaning for Blacks." In Gerda Lerner, ed., *Black Women in White America: A Documentary History*. New York: Vintage Books, 1973.

Flammang, Janet. "Feminist Theory: The Question of Power." *Current Perspectives in Social Theory* 4 (1983): 37–83.

Flammang, Janet A., ed. *Political Women: Current Roles in State and Local Government*. Beverly Hills: Sage Publications, 1984

Fliegelman, Jay. *Prodigals and Pilgrims: The American Revolution against Patriarchal Authority, 1750–1800*. New York: Cambridge Univ. Press, 1982.

Fowlkes, Diane L. "Ambitious Political Woman: Countersocialization and Political Party Context." *Women & Politics* 4 (1984): 5–32.

———. "Conceptions of the 'Political': White Activists in Atlanta." In Flammang, ed., *Political Women.*

———. "Developing a Theory of Countersocialization: Gender, Race, and Politics in the Lives of Women Activists." *Micropolitics* 3 (1983): 181–225.

Fowlkes, Diane L., Jerry Perkins, and Sue Tolleson Rinehart. "Gender Roles and Party Roles." *American Political Science Review* 73 (1979): 772–80.

Freeman, Jo. *The Politics of Women's Liberation*. New York: David McKay, 1975.

Friedan, Betty. *The Feminine Mystique*. New York: W. W. Norton, 1963.

Frye, Marilyn. *The Politics of Reality: Essays in Feminist Theory*. Trumansburg, N.Y.: Crossing Press, 1983.

Fuss, Diana. *Essentially Speaking: Feminism, Nature & Difference*. New York: Routledge, 1989.

Giddings, Paula. *When and Where I Enter . . . The Impact of Black Women on Race and Sex in America*. New York: William Morrow, 1984.

Glaser, Barney G., and Anselm L. Strauss. *The Discovery of Grounded Theory: Strategies for Qualitative Research*. New York: Aldine, 1967.

Goslin, David A., ed. *Handbook of Socialization Theory and Research*. Chicago: Rand McNally, 1969.

Grant, Judith. "I Feel Therefore I Am: A Critique of Female Experience as the Basis for a Feminist Epistemology." *Women & Politics* 7, no. 3 (1987): 99–114.

Greenstein, Fred I. *Children and Politics*. Rev. ed. New Haven: Yale Univ. Press, 1969.

Harding, Sandra. *The Science Question in Feminism*. Ithaca: Cornell Univ. Press, 1986.

Harding, Sandra G., and Merrill B. Hintikka, eds. *Discovering Reality: Feminist Perspectives on Epistemology, Metaphysics, Methodology, and Philosophy of Science*. Dordrecht, Holland: D. Reidel Publishing, 1983.

Harrison, Cynthia. *On Account of Sex: The Politics of Women's Issues 1945– 1968*. Berkeley: Univ. of California Press, 1988.

Harriss, Kathryn. "New Alliances: Socialist-Feminism in the Eighties." *Feminist Review* 31 (Spring 1989): 34–54.

Hartmann, Heidi. "The Unhappy Marriage of Marxism and Feminism: Towards a More Progressive Union." In Sargent, ed., *Women and Revolution*.

Hartsock, Nancy C. M. "The Feminist Standpoint: Developing the Ground for a Specifically Feminist Historical Materialism." In Harding and Hintikka, eds., *Discovering Reality*.

———. *Money, Sex, and Power: Toward a Feminist Historical Materialism*. New York: Longman, 1983.

Herbst, P. G. *Behavioural Worlds: The Study of Single Cases*. London: Tavistock, 1970.

Hess, Robert D., and Judith V. Torney. *The Development of Political Attitudes in Children*. Chicago: Aldine, 1967.

Hirsch, Herbert. *Poverty and Politicization: Political Socialization in an American Sub-Culture*. New York: Free Press, 1971.

hooks, bell. "Feminist Scholarship: Ethical Issues." In *Talking Back: Thinking Feminist, Thinking Black*. Boston: South End Press, 1989.

———. *Feminist Theory: From Margin to Center*. Boston: South End Press, 1984.

Hull, Gloria T., Patricia Bell Scott, and Barbara Smith, eds. *All the Women Are White, All the Blacks Are Men, But Some of Us Are Brave: Black Women's Studies*. Old Westbury: Feminist Press, 1982.

Iglitzin, Lynne B. "The Making of the Apolitical Woman: Femininity and Sex-Stereotyping in Girls." In Jaquette, ed., *Women in Politics*.

Jaggar, Alison M. *Feminist Politics and Human Nature*. Totowa, N.J.: Rowman & Allanheld, 1983.

Jaquette, Jane, ed. *Women in Politics*. New York: John Wiley, 1974.

Jennings, M. Kent. "Another Look at the Life Cycle and Political Participation." *American Journal of Political Science* 23 (1979): 755–71.

Jennings, M. Kent, and Richard G. Niemi. *Generations and Politics: A Panel Study of Young Adults and Their Parents.* Princeton: Princeton Univ. Press, 1981.

———. *The Political Character of Adolescence.* Princeton: Princeton Univ. Press, 1974.

Jennings, M. Kent, and Norman Thomas. "Men and Women in Party Elites: Social Roles and Political Resources." *Midwest Journal of Political Science* 12 (1968): 469–92.

Johnson, Marilyn, and Susan Carroll. *Profile of Women Holding Public Office II.* New Brunswick, N.J.: Center for the American Woman and Politics, 1978.

Johnson, Marilyn, and Kathy Stanwick. *Profile of Women Holding Office.* New Brunswick, N.J.: Center for the American Woman and Politics, 1976.

Jones, Beverly. "The Dynamics of Marriage and Motherhood." In Robin Morgan, ed., *Sisterhood is Powerful.* New York: Vintage Books, 1970.

Keller, Evelyn Fox, and Christine R. Grontkowski. "The Mind's Eye." In Harding and Hintikka, eds., *Discovering Reality.*

Kelly, Rita Mae, and Mary Boutilier. *The Making of Political Women.* Chicago: Nelson Hall, 1978.

Kirkpatrick, Jeane J. *The New Presidential Elite: Men and Women in National Politics.* New York: Basic Books, 1976.

———. *Political Woman.* New York: Basic Books, 1974.

Klagsbrun, Francine, ed. *The First* Ms. *Reader.* New York: Warner Books, 1973.

Klatch, Rebecca E. *Women of the New Right.* Philadelphia: Temple Univ. Press, 1987.

Klein, Ethel. *Gender Politics: From Consciousness to Mass Politics.* Cambridge, Mass.: Harvard Univ. Press, 1984.

Lane, Robert E. *Political Life: Why People Get Involved in Politics.* Glencoe, Ill.: Free Press, 1959.

———. *Political Man.* New York: Free Press, 1972.

Langton, Kenneth P. *Political Socialization.* New York: Oxford Univ. Press, 1969.

Lasswell, Harold D. *Psychopathology and Politics.* New York: Viking, 1960.

Lee, Marcia Manning. "Why Few Women Hold Public Office: Democracy and Sexual Roles." *Political Science Quarterly* 91 (1976): 297–313.

Lewis, Shelby. "A Liberationist Ideology: The Intersection of Race, Sex, and Class." Paper presented at annual meeting of American Political Science Association, Chicago, Sept. 1–4, 1983.

Lipset, Seymour Martin. *Political Man.* Garden City, N.Y.: Doubleday, 1960.

Locke, John. *Some Thoughts Concerning Education*. In *The Educational Writings of John Locke: A Critical Edition*, ed. James L. Axtell. Cambridge: Cambridge Univ. Press, 1968.

Lorde, Audre. *Sister Outsider: Essays and Speeches by Audre Lorde*. Trumansburg, N.Y.: Crossing Press, 1984.

Lovenduski, Joni. "Toward the Emasculation of Political Science: The Impact of Feminism." In Dale Spender, ed., *Men's Studies Modified: The Impact of Feminism on the Academic Disciplines*. Oxford: Pergamon Press, 1981.

Lugones, Maria C., and Elizabeth V. Spelman. "Have We Got A Theory For You! Feminist Theory, Cultural Imperialism and the Demand for 'The Woman's Voice'." *Women's Studies International Forum* 6 (1983): 573–81.

Mandel, Ruth. *In the Running: Women as Political Candidates*. New York: Ticknor & Fields, 1981.

McDermott, Patrice. "Post-Lacanian French Feminist Theory: Luce Irigaray." *Women & Politics* 7 (1987): 47–64.

McWilliams, Nancy. "Contemporary Feminism, Consciousness-Raising, and Changing Views of the Political." In Jaquette, ed., *Women in Politics*.

Mead, George Herbert. *Mind, Self and Society*. Chicago: Univ. of Chicago Press, 1934.

Millett, Kate. *Sexual Politics*. Garden City, N.Y.: Doubleday, 1970.

Nelson, Barbara J. *American Women and Politics: A Selected Bibliography and Resource Guide*. New York: Garland, 1984.

Niemi, Richard G. "Political Socialization." In Jeanne N. Knutson, ed., *Handbook of Political Psychology*. San Francisco: Jossey-Bass, 1973.

O'Reilly, Jane. "The Housewife's Moment of Truth." In Klagsbrun, ed., *The First* Ms. *Reader*.

Petchesky, Rosalind. "Dissolving the Hyphen: A Report on Marxist-Feminist Groups 1–5." In Eisenstein, ed., *Capitalist Patriarchy*.

Pisan, Christine de. *The Treasure of the City of Ladies; or, The Book of the Three Virtues*. Trans. with an introduction by Sarah Lawson. New York: Penguin, 1985.

Plato. *The Republic*. Trans. Allan Bloom. New York: Basic Books, 1968.

Pratt, Minnie Bruce. "Identity: Skin Blood Heart." In Elly Bulkin, Minnie Bruce Pratt, and Barbara Smith, *Yours in Struggle: Three Feminist Perspectives on Anti-Semitism and Racism*. Brooklyn: Long Haul Press, 1984.

Reagon, Bernice Johnson. "Coalition Politics: Turning the Century." In Barbara Smith, ed., *Home Girls*.

Renshon, Stanley Allen. "Assumptive Frameworks in Political Socialization Theory." In Renshon, ed., *Handbook of Political Socialization*.

———. *Handbook of Political Socialization*. New York: Free Press, 1977.

Rich, Adrienne. *Blood, Bread, and Poetry: Selected Prose 1979–1985*. New York: W. W. Norton, 1986.

――――. "Disloyal to Civilization: Feminism, Racism, Gynephobia." In *On Lies, Secrets, and Silence: Selected Prose 1966–1978*. New York: W. W. Norton, 1979.

Rousseau, Jean-Jacques. *Emile, or On Education*. Trans. Allan Bloom. New York: Basic Books, 1979.

Rubin, Gayle. "The Traffic in Women: Notes on the 'Political Economy' of Sex." In Rayna R. Reiter, ed., *Toward an Anthropology of Women*. New York: Monthly Review Press, 1975.

Sapiro, Virginia. *The Political Integration of Women: Roles, Socialization, and Politics*. Urbana: Univ. of Illinois Press, 1983.

――――. "Women's Studies and Political Conflict." In Sherman and Beck, eds., *The Prism of Sex*.

Sargent, Lydia, ed. *Women and Revolution: A Discussion of the Unhappy Marriage of Marxism and Feminism*. Boston: South End Press, 1981.

Schlesinger, Joseph A. *Ambition and Politics: Political Careers in the United States*. Chicago: Rand McNally, 1966.

――――. "The Primary Goals of Political Parties: A Clarification of Positive Theory." *American Political Science Review* 69 (1975): 840–49.

Schutz, Alfred. "On Multiple Realities." In *Collected Papers* 1. 4th ed. The Hague: Nijhoff, 1973.

Shanley, Mary L., and Victoria Schuck. "In Search of Political Woman." *Social Science Quarterly* 55 (1974): 632–44.

Sheridan, Mary. "The Life History Method." In Mary Sheridan and Janet Salaff, eds., *Lives: Chinese Working Women*. Bloomington: Indiana Univ. Press, 1984.

Sherman, Julia A., and Evelyn Torton Beck, eds. *The Prism of Sex: Essays in the Sociology of Knowledge*. Madison: Univ. of Wisconsin Press, 1979.

Sigel, Roberta S., ed. *Learning About Politics*. New York: Random House, 1970.

Sigel, Roberta S., and Marilyn Brookes Hoskin. "Perspectives on Adult Political Socialization—Areas of Research." In Renshon, ed., *Handbook of Political Socialization*.

Smith, Barbara, ed. *Home Girls: A Black Feminist Anthology*. New York: Kitchen Table: Women of Color Press, 1983.

Smith, Lillian. *Killers of the Dream*. New York: W. W. Norton, 1949.

Smith, Dorothy E. *The Everyday World as Problematic: A Feminist Sociology*. Boston: Northeastern Univ. Press, 1987.

Spelman, Elizabeth V. *Inessential Woman: Problems of Exclusion in Feminist Thought.* Boston: Beacon Press, 1988.

Spender, Dale, ed. *Feminist Theorists: Three Centuries of Key Women Thinkers.* New York: Pantheon, 1983.

——. *Women of Ideas (And What Men Have Done to Them).* London: ARK Paperbacks, 1983.

Stoper, Emily. "Wife and Politician: Role Strain among Women in Public Office." In Marianne Githens and Jewel L. Prestage, eds., *A Portrait of Marginality: The Political Behavior of the American Woman.* New York: David McKay, 1977.

Tresemer, David. "Assumptions Made About Gender Roles." In Marcia Millman and Rosabeth Moss Kanter, eds., *Another Voice: Feminist Perspectives on Social Life and Social Science.* Garden City, N.Y.: Anchor Books, 1975.

Turner, Edward Raymond. "Women's Suffrage in New Jersey: 1790–1807." *Smith College Studies in History* 1 (1916): 165–87.

U.S. Department of Commerce, Bureau of the Census. *Historical Statistics of the United States, Colonial Times to 1970.* Part 1. Washington, D. C.: Government Printing Office, 1975.

Valian, Virginia. "Learning to Work." In Sara Ruddick and Pamela Daniels, eds., *Working It Out.* New York: Pantheon, 1977.

Wahlke, John C., Heinz Eulau, William Buchanan, and Leroy C. Ferguson. *The Legislative System: Explorations in Legislative Behavior.* New York: John Wiley, 1962.

Ware, Celestine. "The Black Family and Feminism: A Conversation with Eleanor Holmes Norton." In Klagsbrun, ed., *The First Ms. Reader.*

Weitzman, Lenore J. "Sex-role Socialization." In Jo Freeman, ed., *Women: A Feminist Perspective.* 2d ed. Palo Alto: Mayfield Publishing Company, 1979.

Wittig, Monique. "One Is Not Born a Woman." In Alison M. Jaggar and Paula S. Rothenberg, eds., *Feminist Frameworks: Alternative Accounts of the Relations Between Women and Men.* 2d ed. New York: McGraw-Hill, 1984.

Woolf, Virginia. *Three Guineas.* London: Hogarth Press, 1938.

Index

analytical methods: explication, 27–29; grounded theory, 26–27; theorizing in the everyday world, 150

antifeminism: analysis of, 130–34; relationship to "being a woman," 98–99, 142, 143–50; relationship to family structure and historical period of growing up, 32, 43, 66, 68, 75–86, 216. *See also* countersocialization, socialization

Bartky, Sandra Lee, 98–100, 109, 128

Black feminists: challenge to complex domination, 215; challenge to white women, 3; as mentors, 3; problems of organizing, 5. *See also* Combahee River Collective, complex domination

Black men, 4, 58

Black women, 2, 3, 10–11, 41, 56, 57, 58, 117, 121, 139, 228–30

capitalism, 186, 205, 208–9, 214, 218

centering white women: advantage, 1; as analytical device, 1, 29; problem, 1–2

Chodorow, Nancy, 60

"coalition politics," 8–10, 13, 24, 29, 227, 230–31

Combahee River Collective, 19, 20, 23, 99; "Statement" as source for complex domination, 3–7

communism, 186. *See also* politicization

complex domination: and countersocialization, 16–17; defined, 6; and feminist consciousness, 98–99; as framework for an inclusive oppositional feminist perspective, 3–11, 233 n.3; as framework for political morality play, 227–31; as inclusive "reality," 215; as location for "politics of identity," 219–20, 233 n.4; and "the political," 12–13, 43, 96; social construction of, 6–7; social location in, 22–24, 215; and standpoints of women, 22–24. *See also* "politics as usual," "politics of reality"

consciousness: Black, 18, 37, 58; class, 18; feminist, 18, 36–38, 40, 98–99, 128–30; grounded, 129, 148, 150; ideological, 129, 135, 138, 144, 146, 149–50, 187; political, as shaped by social location in complex domination, 96–97

consciousness-raising, 17–18, 96–99, 109, 155–56, 178–79, 182–83, 203, 215; as form of educating, 212–13;